TRADING WORDS

TRADING WORDS

Poetry

·

Typography

·

and

·

Illustrated Books

·

in the

·

Modern

·

Literary

·

Economy

·

CLAIRE HOERTZ BADARACCO

THE JOHNS HOPKINS UNIVERSITY PRESS

BALTIMORE AND LONDON

© The Johns Hopkins University Press
All rights reserved. Published 1995
Printed in the United States of America on acid-free paper
04 03 02 01 00 99 98 97 96 95 5 4 3 2 1

The Johns Hopkins University Press
2715 North Charles Street
Baltimore, Maryland 21218-4319
The Johns Hopkins Press, Ltd. London

ISBN 0-8018-4859-8

Library of Congress Cataloging-in-Publication Data
will be found at the end of this book.
A catalog record for this book is available from the British Library.

For my parents

CONTENTS

ILLUSTRATIONS

ACKNOWLEDGMENTS

I wish to thank all those whose generosity contributed to this book. The Graduate School of Marquette University, the Bibliographical Society of America, the British Academy, the Newberry Library, and the National Endowment for the Humanities funded this research, and I gratefully acknowledge their support. The Midwest Universities Research Consortium, through which the Marquette University Graduate School supports faculty research at the Newberry Library, has been an invaluable resource. The staff and materials in the John M. Wing Foundation Collection of the Newberry Library have been essential to this work. I am grateful to the Fellows Programs of the library, especially to the Newberry's British Academy fellowship. I am indebted to Diana Haskell, curator of Midwestern Manuscripts, for her observations, particularly those about Sherwood Anderson. To Paul Gehl, the custodian of the John M. Wing Foundation Collection on the History of Printing at the Library, I owe a special word of thanks for his delight in the history of printing and books, and for many fine conversations. James Wells, former custodian of the Wing Foundation Collection, read a late version of this manuscript; his response contributed to refinements in chapter 3.

I also am grateful to two emeritus professors, Harrison Hayford of the Department of English at Northwestern University and the Melville Edition, and Arthur Golden of the Department of English at the City University of New York and editor of Walt Whitman's *Blue Book*, for their responses to the first draft of the Four American Books Campaign material. I would like to acknowledge the important role in my early research played by the late Dr. Lola Szladits, among the first women admitted to membership in the Grolier Club, and curator of the Berg Collection of the New York Public Library, where I completed my doctoral thesis, an edition of the *Cuba Journal 1833–35* of Sophia Peabody Hawthorne.

At the Library of Congress, the Director of the Center for the Book, John Cole, took an interest five years ago in the chapter concerning R. R. Donnelley Corporation, and his initiative, commitment, and steadfast excitement resulted in *American Culture and the Marketplace*, a limited-edition, facsimile monograph published by the Library of Congress in 1992. The late Gaylord Donnelley also read the material with great attentiveness. Phyllis Onazawa also was helpful in accessing materials from company archives.

The Jesuits have supported this research in a number of ways. I would like to thank Rev. Thaddeus Burch, S. J., Dean of the Graduate School of Marquette, for extending support from the university's modest research budget at every point where it made a real difference. I am also appreciative of the support of the Jesuit Center for the Study of Communication and Culture in London, and to Brother William Biernatzki, S. J., for making those resources available. The Jesuits at Oxford University also made possible two uninterrupted days in the John Johnson Collection at the Bodleian, and I offer my thanks.

In England, James Mosley, director of the St. Bride's Library, was an important force in shaping this book. My conversations with Mr. Mosley about Beatrice Warde and the Monotype years contributed substantially to the thematic developments in the whole book, and the collections at St. Bride's are highly important to chapter 3. I am also grateful for Mr. Mosley's gracious introductions: to John Dreyfus and Nicolas Barker, who have written important scholarly works based on their knowledge of the Morison-Warde era; to David McKitterick of Trinity College Library, Cambridge; to John Trevitt of the Cambridge University Press; to David Saunders of the Monotype Corporation, and to Mrs. Hans Schmoller. My conversations with these individuals contributed to the connoisseurship of this study as well as to a feel for the British printing world of the Monotype era and the excitement of those times.

I am also grateful to Alicia Street, who knew Beatrice Warde, for a delightful afternoon of reminiscences and an unforgettably delicious tea, while we worked our way through several piles of manuscripts from the Warde estate and enjoyed several hours of equally rich conversation.

I have greatly enjoyed working with my editor at the Johns Hopkins University Press, Robert J. Brugger, whose experience, encouragement, and interest in the material made the book possible. I am also appreciative of the Business History Conference and the Economic and Business History Society where I presented my research and obtained feedback at several conferences, and to Glenn Porter of the Hagley Museum who assisted with moving the initial book proposal forward.

Finally, I would like to express my love and gratitude to my parents, Ben and Martha Jean Hoertz-Badaracco, who supported my interest in books, in business, and in history.

To my friends whose good company and friendship have endured for many years and despite the miles, I am also most grateful. I would like all these people to share in the credit for the merits of this book; I alone am responsible for any shortcomings.

TRADING WORDS

*

THE

·

IMAGINATION

·

IN

·

BUSINESS

*It amounted to something as radical as the American Revolution
in politics: it was the idea of self-government in the arts.*
—William Dean Howells, *A Hazard of New Fortunes*

Between 1900 and 1940 the marketplace transformed literary culture, the web of writing, printing, promoting, and reading that
made it possible for some people to make a living from words. Ordinary English and American readers in these years came to value all
printing for its ability to speak to them, whether it conveyed a commercial message or poetic image. It was a change that was revolutionary in its implications. According to popular image, the late-
nineteenth-century poet had worked alone in a garret and the solitary painter in a studio, and fine artists earlier had produced limited
editions of beautiful books for the aristocracy, clergy, or academy.[1]
Then, at about the beginning of the twentieth century, these proverbial aesthetes left the garret, studio, and private press for the factory
floor. Suddenly there were two classes of printing that mattered
above all—book composition and display advertising—and it was
imperative that both catch the public eye or rapidly become obso-

lete. Trading words in the mass-market literary economy, commercial printers, trade publishers, advertising writers, and designers were governed by their ideas about audience. Common readers developed what Sherwood Anderson called a "strange, childish faith" in words. In his eyes, advertising became the "central, the true faith."[2]

Publicists in this new economy acted as talebearers, working for publishers, advertising agents, poets, book clubs, printing plants, and equipment manufacturers. No product lacked a voice. The most prosaic of craftsmen, publicists relied on the reader's imagination just as did the novelist or poet. With plentiful stocks of well-designed ephemera, the publicity literature designed for the masses used to promote books, typefaces, inks, or paper, publicists created images of an ideal, universal reader who could be manipulated through a combination of psychology and aesthetic appeals. In their search for such an audience, publicists constructed an international language of business symbols, typefaces, and commercial icons. What began as a language of advertising eventually influenced prevailing ideas about culture and society.

Publicity posters and slogans worked rhetorically because they exaggerated human emotion. All literary products thus had "personality." Type fonts became "aggressive" or "reserved," thin or stocky, with feet or without. The terms *fiction* and *realism* distinguished serious literary efforts of imagination from those depicting historical events and the world of newspapers, but the distinction fell away as market considerations seemed to call for fresh hybrids: "Realistic fiction," for example, became a catchword among commercial artists as well as journalists. The term *hype* became a mix of fiction and realism, describing staged events, commodities, even philosophies or public beliefs.

The gullibility of Anderson's "childish believers" seasoned public events. In the early decades of the twentieth century, newspapers served as a platform for would-be heroes. The public display of all textual performances—whether commercial, political, or cause related—in beautiful typography or advertising images begged for and soon obtained a wide audience. Readers became participants in an economy based on the business imagination. Jules Verne pre-

The Imagination in Business

dicted in 1902 that before the century's end newspapers would monopolize the public imagination: "The DeMaupassants who will delight the world in years to come will do so in the newspapers of the day," he said in a newspaper interview. "The real psychology of life is in its news—'a kind of "truth"' gathered from the police-court story, the railway accident, from the every-day doings of the crowd."[3] Anderson wrote that the modern world was one in which "all the Napoleons are dead" and the bourgeois idealist "settled" for newspaper heroes.[4]

This study examines how theories of mass society first appeared as developments in the commercial sector; how artists, poets, writers, graphic designers, and illustrators contributed to the modern literary economy; how those in the publicity trades relied on an audience whose "childish faith" in words seemed nearly universal; and how the business imagination shaped certain ideas in twentieth-century culture. Integrating literary and business history within a cultural-studies perspective, this book examines telling campaigns as case studies in the emergence of the modern printing, publishing, and advertising industries. Further examples can be found in the Wing Foundation Collection on the History of Printing at the Newberry Library; the special collections of the Regenstein Library at the University of Chicago; the Library of Congress; the Houghton Library at Harvard University; St. Bride's Printing History Library, London; the Bodleian Library, Oxford University; and the special collections of the Cambridge University Library. *Trading Words* uses select materials from these repositories to ask how a popular market for words developed in the early twentieth century, on both sides of the Atlantic, and what commercial language achieved through its attempts to become popular.

THE ROLE OF INDUSTRY

The rotary press that was unveiled at the 1893 Columbian Exposition in Chicago considerably expanded production capabilities in the printing, publishing, and advertising trades and broadened marketing horizons for printed goods worldwide. The composing machine made possible larger type sizes and a greater variety of display styles for advertising. The reading public exercised critical judg-

ment at the point of sale, deciding to buy or not based on packaging
and appearances. Developments took place in three rough stages.

Between 1900 and 1913, when printing constituted the third-
largest worldwide industry, the nineteenth-century advertising solicitor gave way to a new breed of language merchant and print planner. The older solicitors, according to Sherwood Anderson, were
traveling salesmen in loud clothes, cheap jewelry, and a "grip on the
affections of dining room girls." Their advertising advice was "cock-
sure." Clean by contrast and well read in the "dailies" and "trades,"
the professionals who replaced them told people "the reasons why"
they advised as they did.[5] They distributed handsomely printed
broadsides, booklets, and leaflets whose design benefited from the
advice of maverick typographers.

Most of these printers had worked either for newspapers, where
they earned low wages, or for established family printing firms with
the latest in technology and professional training. After the turn of
the century, some printers of commercial paper went into business
for themselves. Along with writers, graphic designers, and advertising experts, they formed amalgamated full-service agencies—an ad-
vancement over earlier firms that specialized in placing newspaper
advertising. As independent design experts, they could manage the
production of printing as well as could any large firm and quote
advertising rates as well as any newspaper. From 1903 to 1913, according to N. W. Ayer's circulation records, more than two hundred
independent publicity shops opened in the United States. During
this time self-declared graphic-design experts in these publicity
agencies enjoyed an unprecedented, if short-lived, popularity.

The daily metropolitan newspaper association thought correctly
that such shops siphoned revenues away from their former employ-
ers. Long-established printing firms such as R. R. Donnelley &
Sons Company in Chicago reacted to the maverick experts' rise in
numbers and popularity by establishing in-house departments of industrial design and typography.

Between 1913 and 1923 publicity experts with college degrees aspired to join the industrial managerial elite. They rested their claim
for notice on the work of theorists like Walter Lippmann, Ivy Ledbetter Lee, and Edward Bernays, all of whom had made public

The Imagination in Business

opinion engineering academically respectable. Calling themselves "counselors," publicity agents sought the professional status of lawyers or even doctors. The very name "public opinion engineer" reflected the idea that the mass market was a vast machine that only experts could control. They believed they could do so by using printed messages as stimulae.

In the third phase, from about 1925 to 1940, printing corporations such as English Monotype or Donnelley & Sons created publicity materials that set high standards for production layout and display design. In Britain, Monotype as a brand dominated the printing and publishing world as did Linotype in the United States. Frederic Goudy, Paul Bennett, and others influential in American typographic design flourished at Linotype, while Beatrice Warde and Stanley Morison rose to prominence amid a welter of innovative typefaces and machinery at Monotype. Morison and Warde further publicized the wonders of Monotype products by educating printers in art schools and selling the public on modern design.

Donnelley & Sons—among the leading producers of catalogs, directories, brochures, and commercial ephemera in the United States between 1900 and 1920—wisely recognized the mass-market publishing sector of the printing industry as the trade's richest future growth area. Between 1924 and 1926, William Kittredge, director of Donnelley's typographic design department, hired the well-known artists and engravers Rockwell Kent, William Dwiggins, Edward Wilson, and Rudolph Ruzicka to illustrate four works that in Kittredge's view epitomized American literature. A five-year production effort went into the books, which were to be given away to mass-market publishers in order to attract their printing business. By means of the Four Books campaign, Kittredge sought to improve production-quality standards in the publishing industry and at the same time to shape American literary taste.

Meanwhile George Macy's Limited Editions Club and Burton Emmett and Elmer Adler's quarterly *Colophon* aspired to define biblio connoisseurship. Although both enterprises produced noteworthy and sometimes remarkable literary goods, Macy's club owed its profitability (as did *Colophon*'s subscription list) to direct-mail strategy. At first Macy had merely hoped to avoid the booksellers' cut of

The Imagination in Business

the list price. But directly approaching readers also carried broad implications for the realism and public fictions that made up the language of advertising.

THE PLACE OF THE ARTIST

The modern artist served the many rather than the few. Sinclair Lewis called writers "the principal entertainers of the day."[6] Poets wrote advertising copy, advice columns, or magazine fiction depending on readers' demand. Writers exploited myth and archetype to sell household products. Journalists reported facts or were paid by the column inch for supposedly critical opinion. Sculptors designed typefaces, bakers' labels, handbills, Bibles, or trade magazine covers, as the market required. At this time, William Dean Howells recognized the artists' response to the market rather than to the muse as a radical change in the history of literature.[7] As Harriet Monroe wrote, poets "paid their shoe bills" with commercial work in advertising, magazines, and newspapers.[8]

Public fascination with psychology, along with the radical aesthetics of revolutionary manifestos, raised expectations about theatricality in public language. Commercial writers, Anderson wrote in his trade column, routinely claimed that by "eating a certain kind of breakfast food we could next week paint a great picture, write a poem or lead an army to victory."[9] Full of dramatic promises, publicity writers necessarily relied on the imagination—their own and their readers'—while serious artists competed for the interest of common readers distracted by publicity.

The literary arts increasingly had to shout for attention in a market glittering with well-designed words, and adaptation soon followed. Hacking out advertising copy, serious writers learned promotional skills from those in the publicity trades. Monroe, for example, used marketing techniques to advance her own literary cause, and she foreshadowed the examples of Fitzgerald and Hemingway. Artists discovered how to market their reputations just as magazines and newspapers used a writer's fame to boost circulation. The modern artist emerged from the joining of journalism and literature, psychology and realism, art and commerce; he or she was an artistic engineer, a scholar-publicist, a poet-businessperson. Ander-

The Imagination in Business

son called this new hybrid someone who combined a "picturesque past and an aesthetic present [and] who could strike everything that is imaginative and romantic in the newspaper soul" of the common reader.[10]

THE NATURE OF THE READER

Debate over the place of the individual consumer in the burgeoning mass market preoccupied commercial artists, serious literary writers, and intellectuals alike in the early twentieth century. William James in *The Will to Believe* (1899) posed the difficult question of whether greatness lay in people of extraordinary achievement because they themselves were great or because of the fact that others considered them so—because society effectively made them great. Among developments in the emerging publicity trades, at least two followed James's work (even if they were not noticeably influenced by it). Promoting their blend of theatricality and hope, advertising experts adopted the view not only that it was the opinion of others that defined one, but also that public reputation acquired through the media was itself virtuous. The publicist Ivy Ledbetter Lee's tautological motto "Great men were good men" captured a common belief among mass-communications professionals for most of the twentieth century. Meanwhile, at the turn of the century, social realists, artistic revolutionaries, and exuberant graphic designers joined forces in an attempt to lure the public away from its infatuation with the conventional ideal of greatness and instead to see the heroic proportions of the common or ordinary life. In this way, it was believed, well-designed printed goods, celebrating the ordinary, could articulate the beautiful and the good. If done expertly enough, printed material could elevate one aesthetically, intellectually, or spiritually. Such products were seen as having a potential impact on an entire population, raising standards of public taste and/or standardizing culture. As Phineas T. Barnum might well have observed, most people are fascinated by things larger and smaller than themselves.[11]

Barnum's observation would jibe with the ideas of Darwin and Freud, who used human evolution and mass psychology to explain the habit of public belief in doubtful tales. Advertising appeals

The Imagination in Business

worked on mass publics because people in crowds craved the certainties about the value of the individual expressed through myth, fiction, and even promotional biographies of political or literary figures.

In the early 1920s the relationship between the individual and the crowd became an intellectual hotspot, and out of the literature of social science naturally emerged theories about the relationship between mass production and mass-market consumption. How did the individual and national style go together? What was the function of public belief in defining cultural values? At this time, the social anthropologist Margaret Mead, the political-social commentator Walter Lippmann, and the founders of *Public Opinion Quarterly* at Columbia and Princeton Universities made public-opinion management a scholarly inquiry. In Lippmann's *Public Opinion* (1922) the term "pseudo-event" defined a perpetual discrepancy between an individual's mental image of an event and the event itself. Reconciling that discrepancy, according to Lippmann, took place through public mythology. Public fiction consisted of manufactured events, images, stereotypes, or impressions of the way society functioned. "Our popular taste," Lippmann wrote, "is to have the drama originate in a setting realistic enough to make identification plausible and to have it terminate in a setting romantic enough to be desirable, but not so romantic as to be inconceivable."[12] Describing the political psychology of the common reader, in his *Phantom Public* (1927), Lippmann said that "when the private man has lived through his romantic age in politics and is no longer moved by the stale echoes of its hot cries, when he is sober and unimpressed, his own part in public affairs appears to him a pretentious thing, second rate, and inconsequential."[13]

Margaret Mead's classic "Public Opinion Mechanisms in Primitive Societies," written from Bali and published in the first issue of *Public Opinion Quarterly* (1937), laid out typologies fundamental to public-opinion formation in three different tribes. Meade believed she had confirmed the premise that individuals reacted to authority, ideology, and politics according to how they perceived the opinions of the rest of the tribe. (She qualified her analysis by observing that simple societies do not necessarily correlate with complex ones.) Later in 1937 Bernays wrote in an issue of *Public Opin-*

ion Quarterly that publicity campaigns for American industrial giants had "awakened the public to the onslaught of competing industries—coal versus oil, steel versus lumber, vegetable versus animal fat."[14]

Biographies of "barnumizers" (William Dean Howells's phrase) are footnotes to a larger cultural story. The business imagination that drove the marketing of words, language products, and printed goods in the early twentieth century transformed the common readers' intellectual landscape and the artists' grasp of the ordinary. The following case studies from the history of printing, publishing, and advertising suggest how trading words moved the business imagination from a period of romanticism into modernism and how producers engineered this aesthetic movement via their ideas about how the audience would respond to what was new.

The Imagination in Business

*

UTOPIAN

·

TYPOGRAPHY

·

AND THE

·

PUBLIC EYE

·

1890–1915

We are forcing our Michael Angelos to carve in snow.
—John Ruskin, *The Political Economy of Art*

Commercial letters acquired a philosophical dimension in the early decades of the twentieth century. Aesthetic movements questioned the influence that commodities exerted over consumers' thinking about the nature of style. Ideologues worried that mass production might diminish individualism. The aesthetic revolutionary feared that bourgeois taste—dulled further by the consumption of bland, indistinguishable goods—could result in a "national mind." In the modern literary economy, standardization and mass consumption presented financial opportunity, but also a threat to the values of artistic individualism, classical ideas about heroism, and storytelling itself.

PHILOSOPHY AND COMMERCIAL VALUE

The theoretical questions raised by artistic revolutionary movements between 1890 and 1915 served the commercial purposes of

professionals in the printing, publishing, and advertising industries. The publicist and the revolutionary philosopher, the novelist
and journalist, the poet and commercial artist all had to compete for
readers. Each sector and every genre had to balance images and text.
Well-designed images in advertisements and on posters captured
the public eye. Publishers defined editions of classic texts through illustration.

Two approaches, one utopian, the other utilitarian, distinguished
commercial letters from classical literary genres. The first emerged
from the aesthetic theories of artistic revolutionary movements
between 1890 and 1915 in England, Russia, Italy, and Germany.
Through social ideals and ideologies proposed by William Morris
in England, El Lissitzky in Russia, Filippo Tommaso Marinetti in
Italy, and Jan Tschichold in Germany—all leaders of aesthetic
movements—the printing industry developed design principles for
book and advertising typography. To exercise revolutionary design
ideas, each movement demonstrated through innovative product development how to integrate aesthetic principles in manufacturing
for the decorative arts. Through better design, idealists hoped to elevate the taste of the masses, reform the social order, and integrate artists in industry.

The constructivist, dadaist, futurist, and expressionist movements used print products, typography, illustrated books, advertising posters, leaflets, and broadsides to disseminate their ideas about
modern design in the public square. For artistic revolutionaries or
skilled tradesmen in family firms, commercial designs conveyed corporate, cultural, or national identity. Employing kiosks, newspapers, cinema, lecture tours, and leaflet drops, the groups disseminated manifestos about the political and social relevance of their
typographic principles in metropolitan newspapers, then started
their own publications.

Book publishers, commercial printers, and advertising agents recognized that readers determined the market value of printed goods.
An intangible quotient called "public appeal" applied equally to
clever propaganda and to products with strong sales potential. The
common readers trusted in the style of material goods to retain their
investment value.[1] In the preface to Virginia Woolf's 1925 collection

Utopian Typography and the Public Eye, 1890–1915

of newspaper articles entitled *The Common Reader*, she invoked Dr. Samuel Johnson to verify the "worth" of writing for those in rooms "too humble to be called libraries." In his *Life of Thomas Gray*, Johnson "defined" and "dignified" the aims of "a pursuit which devours a great deal of time, and is yet apt to leave behind it nothing very substantial." He wrote of the ordinary person with no critical training in literature who reads at home for pleasure: "I rejoice to concur with the common reader; for by the common sense of readers, uncorrupted by literary prejudices, after all the refinements of subtilty and the dogmatism of learning, must be finally decided all claim to poetical honours."[2]

The philosophies of John Ruskin and William Morris offered tradesmen a rationale for linking ideas about style and commercial value. Other aesthetic movements developed principles that industry found useful: the Wiener Werkstätte in Vienna (1900–10); the German expressionists (1907–27) and the Bauhaus (1919–33); the Dutch de Stijl movement (1907–20); Russian futurism, suprematism, and constructivism (1912–18); Italian futurism, the rayonnists and fascists who identified with its violence and misogyny (1909–25); Italian dadaists (1910–20) and English dadaists and vorticists (1914–18) in London. Led by the British writer Wyndham Lewis and the American expatriate Ezra Pound, vorticism represented the last of the "isms," the one with the most bombast and least public appeal. Pound also disseminated a revisionist interpretation of imagism from his London editorial office before disowning the group to join Lewis, then Marinetti's fascists.[3] Among those individuals prominent in the twentieth-century Anglo-American printing trades—Stanley Morison, Beatrice Warde, William Kittredge, George Macy, Elmer Adler, Burton Emmett—the intense interest of revolutionary groups translated into a deep concern about the industrial standards for book production, typography for newspapers and advertising, and the aesthetic value added to any printing enterprise by employing versatile illustrators. The sheer volume of innovation from the manufacturing side of the trade in typefaces, books, magazines, and publicity ephemera between 1900 and 1940 must have stimulated as much debate among readers about what modern-

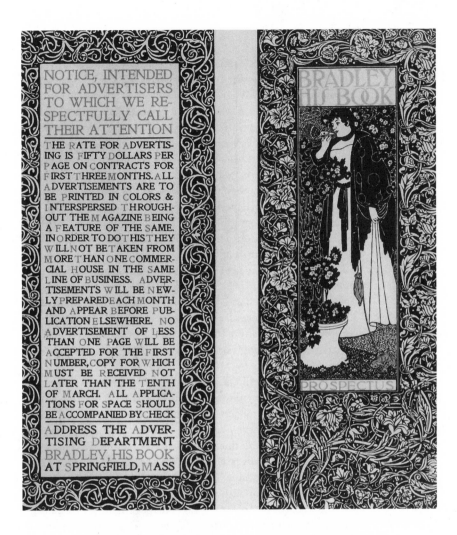

Will H. Bradley, Wayside Press *prospectus inserted in* Bradley, His Book
*for May 1896, a publicity periodical offered free to advertise the Wayside
printing style, using literature. The volume also printed a Harriet
Monroe poem to demonstrate the Kelmscott borders popularized
in America by Bradley and the private-press movement.*
Courtesy of the John M. Wing Foundation, Newberry Library.

ism meant for the public as aesthetic groups had stirred controversy about the politics of aesthetics among would-be revolutionaries.

Convinced that readers would improve their minds if they saw well-designed displays in advertising and industrial signs, manufacturers of commercial printed materials designed to promote books and typefaces treated ephemera as if they had permanent aesthetic importance.[4] Each avant-garde group reformulated themes about balancing word with image and the idea of printing as a transmitter of social value with the vision of a better, future utopian state. The Bauhaus, for example, experimented with the "typophoto" (type superimposed on a photograph); the cubists used collage; and the Russian futurists constructed a universal language of pure sound without syntax called Zaum. The futurists also developed the cine-book, to be seen as well as read in a series of still-life photographs depicting consecutive movements. Constructivists developed the Proun, a design experiment with layout where type fonts were meant to evoke sound rather than sense. In visual and typographical terms, however, it may be that many of these artistic statements looked no more serious to the public eye than advertisements for beverages, food, or household soap.

The Bauhaus, de Stijl, futurist, and constructivist movements assumed that the reader enjoyed a rapport with the artist through layout, design, and an arrangement of image and text on a page. Everything counted: the quality of paper; its weave, color, and weight; the opacity of inks; the thickness of ascenders and descenders in type fonts; and the spare or elaborate use of printers' devices such as flowers, bars, lines, and dots. Trade advertisements made similar assertions about the relationship between the reader and the artist, or about the visual impact of the message on a page or on a poster. Revolutionaries wanted to be free from the need to entertain readers. Dadaism, for example, represented an individual artistic ego separated from the audience. Although dadaism and surrealism engulfed readers with the consequences of mass psychology, neither "ism" regarded the imagination as powerful enough to defeat its negative effects. Although Dada and surrealism offered readers an easy acceptance of the subconscious, both contained market applications for painters and typographers.[5] One might conclude, as Edmund

Utopian Typography and the Public Eye, 1890–1915

Wilson had, that surrealism demonstrated the "antiliteral."[6] By that he meant a devaluation of narrative and text as a principle of composition.

Rejecting social evolution as an explanation for the course of history, the leading spokesman for Russian futurism, El Lissitzky, also rejected any cause-and-effect relationship between reader and artist, among aesthetic movements, or between art and industry.[7] Although one art epoch "may not directly precipitate another," as Lissitzky argued, ideas transmitted through the exchange of printed goods between 1900 and 1940 did precipitate industrial and social change. Individuals working in the commercial literary trades in the early twentieth century assumed an active role in shaping the history of their own industry. The leaders defined through design principles the aesthetic relevance of classical models and genres. Printers, publishers, illustrators, and writers were as serious about their commercial productions as any artist or revolutionary. Individuals in the trade borrowed philosophical explanations as readily as they adapted their leading competitors' design principles.[8] The cumulative force of the avant-garde artistic revolutionaries between 1900 and 1940 precipitated an unparalleled period of innovation in print-product design that led to improved industrial standards nationwide in everything from railroad schedules to newspapers.

Revolutionary manifestos had proclaimed the importance of print in creating a public culture of aesthetic and political significance. The Italian futurist Marinetti, for example, used the daily newspaper *Le Figaro* to publish his first manifesto, then founded his own paper, *Lacerba*. He also used kiosks, trumpet blasts from high places, and leaflet drops. He preferred bombast as a style in his public lectures, because eccentricity attracted larger headlines. In Vienna, the Wiener Werkstätte published its magazines *Der Sturm* and *Die Aktion* to high critical praise. In Berlin, the Bauhaus published its journal under its own name, along with other booklets. In London, Wyndham Lewis published his magazine *Blast*.

Design principles in the early mass-communication industry developed toward an absence of decoration. Industrial design principles reinterpreted classical form for the modern world: new forms held implications for the meaning and uses of the old. The printing

Utopian Typography and the Public Eye, 1890–1915

historian and type designer Stanley Morison believed that film and collage threatened to replace the alphabet, though he thought that the change was "justified" historically.[9] Two aesthetic rationales justified the debate among printers and typographers about "modern" style and form in printed goods. Those who favored the plain, unadorned line claimed that theirs was the more innovative or modern approach. Those who favored the arabesque or more decorative style, called imitative by critics and monarchist by detractors, clung to a more sentimental style. In a 1937 article in the printing journal *Signature*, a printer named Donald Piper compared the dichotomy between the useful and the avant-garde to a tension between the symmetry of the crystal, in which everyone could glean some meaning, and the asymmetry of the potato, which is "casual," "bulbous," and difficult to think of as beautiful.[10] A different interpretive power inhered in each shape. From the "potato" or natural side of the argument, he explained, came an excess of emotion in typographic design—the exclamation point, a baroque effect created by overuse of devices, serif faces, and elaborate fonts more nostalgic than legible. From the symmetry of crystal, he suggested, typography could mimic the multifaceted human personality in all its moods. The latter brought printing closer to literature than to the aesthetic principles inherent in more "natural" handcrafts.

The print publicist Beatrice Warde, known to contemporaries as "B.W.," once remarked that every society made a philosophical statement in any given age about its expectations for women by "noticing what modification fashion" made "in their figures." Similarly, fashions in typography spoke about social expectations for public culture by modifying classical and natural letter forms. As Piper had observed, the arabesque or leaf patterns that had decorated the capitals and columns of Greek and Roman sculpture attempted to modify the natural to distinguish it from the sacred. The Moorish arabesque, Piper suggested, came from "the intense visual worship" by artists "forbidden to depict the divine." Idealism about the power of aesthetics to form public culture strengthened the potential for business and commercial designs to acquire the status of symbol in the public mind. B.W. and other leaders of the movement for good design in Anglo-American commercial printing during the 1920s and

1930s asserted that they had intended "to debunk the commonly held concept" that an artist took on commercial work "because he was really a creative failure."[11]

Printed goods exerted an aesthetic influence over mass culture, whether in advertising poster styles, display typography for public spaces, newspapers, or the visual characteristics of books. The traditional critic had argued that art ought to remain far removed from business, industry, and the political economy. Nevertheless, among tradesmen as well as critics, aesthetic concerns and economic realities became inextricably mixed; the commercial artist struggled to provide beautiful products that the common reader would find valuable in a highly competitive marketplace. The idea that revolutionary print products could determine the politics of the day led commercial firms to assert themselves as standard-bearers in an industry or in a national culture.

John Ruskin worried about what he called modern "Michael Angelos" forced to pour their best talents into commercial ephemera.[12] He also asked about how business might identify those with "special genius," and how a company could preserve and disseminate such work "to the best national advantage."[13] Producing durable goods in an era of mass production raised the specter of a "standardization" of styles, along with improved product durability, as though mass-produced designs would result in a dangerous cultural homogeneity. For Ruskin, two questions pertained: how to produce enough of a product, and whether that sufficiency would be good for society.[14] He also suggested in "On the Nature of the Gothic," in *Stones of Venice*, that a good art economist should ask whether the durability of the product diminished its value, or whether some products should be disposable. The consequences of these questions influenced the observer, the reader, and in turn, the whole society.[15] Although Ruskin's division of workers into "great men, lesser men, and little men" —depending on whether they "wielded a shuttle, hammer, or throttle"—seemed elitist to those in the printing trades, they otherwise approved of his philosophy.[16]

William Morris had reacted against "the visual depravity of the Industrial Revolution," in what later became known as the modern movement in arts and crafts. He believed "once again, as in happier

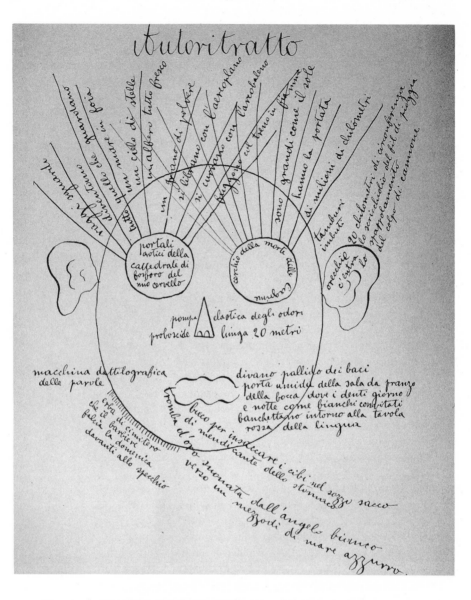

"Tutoritratto," F. T. Marinetti's futurist manifesto concerning the role of image in human communication, from Rarefazioni E Parole in Liberta, Milan, 1915.
Courtesy of Northwestern University, Special Collections.

medieval days, the personality and ability of both artist and craftsman could be reunited." Morris's attitude opened a door for others
who worked in printing houses, publishing companies, and advertising agencies to apply his design ideas in mass production. In the
1870s, the Morris family design firm produced wallpaper, tapes-
tries, furniture, and books. Although Morris divided artistic products into intellectual or higher art, produced by "gentlemen," and
lower or decorative art, produced by "trade and craftsmen," his designs addressed the needs of consumers.[17] In an 1877 manifesto addressed to the "Working Men of England" and in many articles and
speeches, Morris outlined his vision of an ideal twentieth-century society.[18] Favoring the look of hand-set letters printed on hand-laid paper, Morris's style was imitated throughout the advertising trades in
England and the United States. A commercial pseudo-Kelmscott
style emerged after Morris's death.[19]

PRINCIPLES OF THE NEW TYPOGRAPHY

Aesthetic design impressed industrial stylists in the post–arts-and-
crafts era. Kelmscott influenced the Bauhaus educational experiment and helped define the New Typography. Unlike William Morris's family-firm experiment, the Bauhaus reflected the thinking of a
philosophical school, and "many individuals' philosophies unified
in a single" corporate culture.[20] Walter Gropius, Le Corbusier, and
Ludwig Mies van der Rohe studied under Peter Behrens, the design
consultant and publicist for the group called the "turbine factory" in
1908 in Vienna, who directed the Advanced School for Architecture
in 1922. Gropius founded the Bauhaus in April 1919 and published
its journal based on the principle that "no distinction should be
made between the artist and craftsman" because "every artist must
command a range of crafts," and he urged an end to the distinction
between higher and lower decorative objects and printed goods.
Gropius envisioned a bridge between art and industry to "rise" like
the "crystal symbol of a new faith."[21]

Gropius observed that "ideas about culture" could be developed
by artists only as fast as the society "which they seek to serve" could
understand them and "put them to some practical purpose."[22] The
idea of "functionalism"—an attempt to integrate form and func-

tion, intellectual and decorative art—in printed products developed as an outgrowth of the Bauhaus. The Bauhaus ideal united all artistic disciplines—sculpture, painting, and the crafts—without categorical distinction.[23]

Although no typographical workshop had existed previously, Gropius and Laszlo Moholy-Nagy had experimented with type forms and layout. In 1925, Gropius placed twenty-four-year-old Herbert Bayer in charge of typography, and over a three-year period he established himself as the pioneer of modern visual communication—especially in the areas of letter forms, photography, and display design.[24] He organized typographic elements by function and created contrasts by alternating point sizes and color, emphasized single words, "pulling them out of horizontal alignment," and used running bands of color to look like slogans.[25]

Bayer emphasized psychological factors in advertising typography. In an article in the journal *bauhaus*, published in Dessau in 1928, he enlarged upon Moholy-Nagy's aesthetic by developing a "physiology of the eye." He questioned the impact of new typographical design on the mind, as well as on the public eye. He objected that advertising tended to be based solely on intuition rather than on the "laws of psychology and physiology."[26] Bayer argued that the publicity arts ought to be constructed on a broader theoretical base, with typography an integral factor in designing effective delivery of messages.

Whereas Bayer was influential as a teacher, it was Moholy-Nagy who articulated the Bauhaus aesthetic for the group. He wrote that "typography must be clear communication in its most vivid form. Clarity must be especially stressed, for clarity is the essence of modern printing."[27] He argued against squeezing letters "into an arbitrary shape, like a square." He hoped to create a new language, combining elasticity, variety and a fresh approach to applied materials."[28] Moholy-Nagy's historical interpretation of the poster, "an intermediary" between the content of a message and the recipient, also put forth theories later advanced by Bayer as a teacher.[29] Moholy-Nagy argued that legibility and clarity "must never suffer" because of "preconceived aesthetic ideas."[30]

Utopian Typography and the Public Eye, 1890–1915

Jan Tschichold, also a member of the Bauhaus group, related the aesthetic and psychological theories of Moholy-Nagy and Bayer to the concerns of the ordinary printer "in terms they could understand." He called these theories a philosophy of functionalism.[31] Tschichold codified the Bauhaus aesthetic and psychological principles concerning integrated design patterns of posters, catalogs, advertisements, and books in his 1925 manifesto "Elementare Typographie" and his first book, *Die Neue Typographie* (Berlin, 1928). The New Typography movement attracted young printers working in Germany, the Soviet Union, Holland, Czechoslovakia, Switzerland, Hungary, and Britain.[32] Tschichold's principles emphasized legibility, clarity, social utility, and durability in a style some thought eccentric in its eclectic plain style and willingness to experiment. According to Tschichold, all elements of print, including lines, bars, and photographs, belonged to the typographic arts. He thought that type design should not be used to express national identity. Rather, Tschichold's ideal was that of a stylistic simplicity so universal it could become an international language. He distinguished his new typography from the old by asserting the social relationship between printed goods and popular ideas among readers.[33] For years, the idea that print ought to be restful to the eye had determined how typesetters worked and what typefaces they used. The New Typography rejected such categorical limits and professed to be "antitraditional" rather than "nontraditional."[34]

While some printers called the Dada movement "sheer idiocy," Tschichold declared dadaist propaganda the first documentary evidence showing the new attitude toward modern language. All graphic-design principles, according to the young Tschichold, followed from the common reader's reaction to printed goods, including the arrangement and size of type, and its legibility at a distance.[35] He credited the dadaists with innovative ideas about spatial arrangement of type through Marinetti's Italian futurism and his privately printed broadside "Words in Freedom" (Milan, 1919). In his *New Life in Print*, Tschichold summarized not only his principles but also their effect within the Bauhaus group. He defined design as the "legible ordering" of type and text, and he concluded that "it is a matter of values, of fitness in structural contrasts and relationships."[36] When he began working for Penguin, his mature opinions, compared with his youthful experiments in typography, seemed more conservative.

REVOLUTION, INDIVIDUALISM, AND ECCENTRISM

The link between Tschichold and Lissitzky may account for the perception of "eccentricity" that some British printers attributed to the unadorned lines of the new typography.[37] Between 1910 and 1940, Lissitzky concentrated on overturning conventional design ideas in all types of visual communication, including posters, books, and exhibits. He recounted that in 1913 Kasimir Malevich exhibited a black square painted on a white canvas and thus revolutionized viewers' concept of art. Malevich's painting *Eight Red Rectangles* (1914) constituted the "first canvas without reference to real objects" under the influence of French cubism.[38] Art historians describe him as having resolved "the conflict between the two camps" of Russian painters—the suprematists, led by Malevich (1878–1935), and the constructivists, led by Vladimir Tatlin (1885–1953).[39]

Malevich claimed that his style belonged to the revolution, because "objects are not real," and reality "resides only in ideal forms."[40] He argued that art could unite the world if the public identified it less with a spirit of nationalism. Language free of indigenous associations could seek a level of global standardization, Malevich claimed.[41] As he moved to transcend the decorative arts entirely and "annihilate" painting, Malevich threw out all ideal forms.

Lissitzky, however, wanted to develop designs for a variety of decorative-arts fields, and he offered a redefinition of the aesthetic object. Incorporating the work of Malevich and the principles of the suprematists, Lissitzky invented a new form he called the Proun, a three-dimensional painting. Through it, he offered, the salon painter who retreated from the world would become an anachronism. Declaring "art and its bosses to be outside the law," he urged the artist to go into the factory, onto the assembly line, and integrate artistic ideals with pragmatic production considerations.[42] He believed it better to print a poster than to paint one because the former

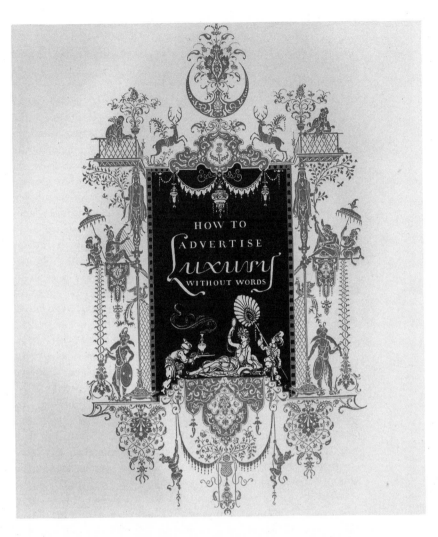

"How to Advertise Luxury without Words," colophon page for a free publicity brochure advertising a limited-edition catalogue raisonné *of T. M. Cleland's achievements in commercial art; printed by the Pynson Press of New York. The advertisement, designed by Cleland in 1929, represents his "restoration" style, an attempt to recreate an earlier historical period in printing. Rockwell Kent supplied a frontispiece portrait for the book.*

Courtesy of the John M. Wing Foundation, Ransom Papers, Newberry Library.

could be read by the masses, and every artwork should be a "spur to action" toward forming a classless society.[43]

The Russian futurists' revolutionary principles—first articulated in "The Insult to Universal Taste," printed on rough packing paper —and their slogan—"Throw Pushkin, Dostoyevsky, Tolstoy from the steamship of contemporaneity"—criticized their own indigenous traditional expectations about artistic form.[44] They mocked the nineteenth-century ideal of Morris's book beautiful and ridiculed the meticulous lines of fine printing and the ornate illustrations of the Kelmscott-style page. The Russian futurists mocked the modernist aesthete's attachment to classicism. With his collaborators, Lissitzky designed the "bioscopic cine-book," which could be read and viewed at the same time. His montage-book *Komsomolya* (1928) required a screenplay, director, scenographer, photographer, and cameraman. The typographic principles of Russian futurism included a reliance on optics instead of phonetics, gestures instead of dialogue, communication of ideas through single letters instead of words.[45] Lissitzky wrote, "The rich visual language of the book was composed and woven into the text, coloured accents scattered about the columns, complicated schemes of type-fonts of various cut and size—and, finally, various decorative elements from the printer's moulds."[46]

While his comrades searched for a "truly Russian" futurism, Lissitzky advanced the concept of a global language that would transcend borders. The Russian futurists published more than fifty avant-garde books and periodicals between 1912 and 1916 in Moscow and St. Petersburg. A number of dissident groups including the Ego-futurists, Acmeists, Union of Youth, Hylaeans, and later the Rayists in 1910 quarreled about the "nature of their opposition to the past" while engaged in publishing activities.[47] "Zaum," a language invented by the Russian futurists, transcended conventional words and international boundaries, moving toward Lissitzky's ideal of a universal artistic language for the masses.[48] In *Our Book*, Lissitszky developed the ideogram, symbolic language that could serve as an international vernacular. The book of the future, he wrote, would be "a-national," "simultaneous," which meant striking a balance between sound as it functioned within time and words as representatives of space.[49] Lissitzky explained the "dominance" of illustrated weekly magazines as a part of a "transition period" to a focus on the audience: "It is the great masses, the semi-literate masses, who have become the audience. The Revolution in our country accomplished an enormous educational and propagandistic task. . . . The book is becoming the most monumental work of art: no longer is it something caressed only by the delicate hands of a few bibliophiles; on the contrary, it is already being grasped by hundreds of thousands of poor people."[50]

The advertising prospectus, brochure, and inexpensive novel served the ideologue easily as a means to reach the modern public. According to Lissitzky's *Typographical Facts*, published in 1925, the billboard, not the letterpress, represented "the future" of photogravure printing and other photomechanical processes. In the layout of modern advertising and poetry Lissitzky saw a style of public thought and speech "more faithful" to the masses than syntax or grammar.[51] The poet Victor Khlebnikov, a Russian futurist, sought a universal language of decorative arts, typography, and book design.[52] The artist Rodchenko elevated mass printing of book covers and ordinary brochures, candy wrappers, newspaper advertisements, labels, and film leaders to the rank of "geniuine graphic art," according to proponents.[53]

Marinetti boasted that he had started Russian futurism. When he visited Moscow and St. Petersburg in January 1914, he observed that the 1912 Russian manifesto "A Slap in the Face of Public Taste," written by Vladimir Mayakovsky, resembled his own of 1909.[54] Critics observed that Italian and English futurism looked superficial compared to the Russian experiments with form.[55]

In 1913 Marinetti published another manifesto for the Italian futurist group, "Imagination without Strings—Words in Freedom," apparently borrowing his ideas about the destruction of syntax from the Russians as they had borrowed the idea of the manifesto itself from his 1909 statement in *Le Figaro*. His "wireless imagination" was Marinetti's way of explaining why he "freed" images and words by printing them in a disjointed fashion.[56] Marinetti's manifesto declared the death of free verse. He replaced it with "words in freedom," the "loosening of syntax and punctuation," so that analogies

Utopian Typography and the Public Eye, 1890–1915

Cover page, Certificate Bond Paper Co. four-page brochure advertising
William Addison Dwiggins's letterhead designs, ca. 1930.
Courtesy of the John M. Wing Foundation, Ransom Papers, Newberry Library.

and images would be "unhampered" by meaning. Marinetti declared that the easy relationship between the poet and audience made possible a "rapport" as if "between two old friends," who make themselves understood with half a word, a gesture, a glance. So the poet's imagination must weave together distant things with no connecting strings, by means of "essential free words."[57]

In *Spitting on the Altar of Art with a Capital 'A,'* Marinetti asserted that the traditional reverence for high art constituted a "clericalism of the creative spirit." He called the aestheticism of the beautiful page, hand-set typefaces, decorated capitals, and rubricated letters "passé." He also condemned as precious the sensibility of poets who searched for the elegant adjective, the rare word. Marinetti preferred the "torpedo-like" effect of disconnected words. He wrote, "My revolution is aimed at the so-called typographical harmony of the page; we will use three or four colours . . . or even twenty different typefaces if necessary."[58]

In March 1915, Marinetti made his first public appearance onstage with Benito Mussolini. Mussolini, who had been an editor of *Avanti*, the leading Socialist daily, until he became editor of *Popolo d'Italia*, the Fascist daily, in November 1914, adopted the publicity techniques of Marinetti for his political goals. As "the impressario of propagandistic manifestos," Marinetti received widespread coverage from the press between 1913 and 1914, the year he made ten visits to London. His impact on the British journalist Harry Nevinson and the poets Wyndham Lewis and Ezra Pound led them to develop vorticism, a term coined by Nevinson from Marinetti's ideas.[59] In "Manifesto Against English Art" (1913), which Nevinson published with Marinetti in the *Times, Observer,* and *Daily Mail,* they attacked English middle-class tastes.[60] In *Blast,* the group's magazine, Lewis published the group's manifesto, "Long Live the Vortex!" denouncing futurists as romantics. He separated the vorticists from Marinetti's fascination with technology, calling his bombast a "hullo-bulloo" about "motor cars and knives and forks."[61] With vorticism, Lewis argued, the importance of the individual had been rescued from the glorification of the masses.[62]

Although the vorticists were English, they impressed the British reader less than any of the other aesthetic movements. As a matter of political principle, Lewis and Pound isolated themselves from the middle-class audience, thus undermining their own purposes. Lewis regarded the public with philosophic dissatisfaction and the "business interests that control us" as sinister. Pound's animosity toward the crowd, detailed in his poetry, led him on a futile search for an artistic autocracy. The common reader, along with critics and artists, simply found the vorticists tiresome, although the newspapers were the last to admit they were bored.[63]

The commercial printing industry borrowed design ideas rather than ideology from revolutionary movements. Americans continued to embrace the private-press movement as an expression of native individualism rather than as a socialist experiment or avantgarde ideal, according to B.W., "long after the idea had been upstaged" in Britain by the cubo-futurists, constructivists, and other innovators in the printing renaissance.[64]

By mid-century, the British printer and scholar Stanley Morison declared all the ideological debate that had gone into designing commercial printing between 1900 and 1940 sheer nonsense. He wrote that history rather than ideology should provide the basis for artistic form. Although novelty, according to Morison, had been responsible for much of the revolutionaries' allure, the movements had resulted in aesthetic eccentricities. He believed that dropping capital letters, or using all capitals, eliminating or substituting punctuation for letters was eccentric.

The utopian printer worked less for an audience than for his fellow revolutionaries, as Morison and others observed. As a result their ideas were widely diffused without actually gaining public acceptance. Much of the "bad" work, in his backward glance, embodied "self-consciousness and naïveté."[65] History could provide the classical models for a philosophy of design, but the printer relied on the imagination of the reader to make it contemporary. When Morison demonstrated how typographical experiments—even eccentric ones—had been attempted during the eighteenth century, the impact among commercial graphic designers stimulated manufacturers and producers to take design risks.

The marketing of modernism as a way of seeing words and trading impressions of images for sound, and even for sense, evolved into a kind of aesthetic brinkmanship that hovered between the beautiful and the useful. Between a utopian vision of the future with an imaginary audience or a romantic vision of the past with a nostalgic one lay the vast reality of the mass-market public, whose appetite for printing, while largely ephemeral, seemed voracious. "Modernity cannot stand still," Morison wrote. "I am no more in favor of giving full rein to all the tendencies of either the 'modern' element in the design and organization of advertising, or in the 'revivalist' element that brings back early nineteenth century fonts or conventions."[66] What Beatrice Warde called the "invisibility" of modern typography struck the middle ground, where the audience could see into print rather than take away from print a lesson or a preconceived, didactic vision. Words contained meaning and held images as their essence. Aesthetic revolutionaries showed how public belief could be mustered in a new way from the masses, or engineered for mass appeal or emotional affect. Commercial artists seemed to have had little regard for the individual. Rather, they designed public fictions made up of letters in persuasive messages. Because of the activities of artistic revolutionaries, the vernacular of publicity achieved a balance in the 1920s and 1930s between those who wanted modernism to be full of promise about how things ought to be and those who equated the past with the glories of individualism that had gone before.[67] Even among commercial printers dubious about the market value of such designs, the precedent for accepting the social consequences of mass persuasion through publicly traded letters established the aesthetic debate as part of the modern literary economy.

Utopian Typography and the Public Eye, 1890–1915

ADVERTISING

·

POETRY

·

AS

·

A VISUAL ART

·

1912–1922

Advertise. Advertise. What a strange childish faith!
—Sherwood Anderson, *Perhaps Women*

For the common reader to find poetic images interesting in the poster age, the literary arts needed to be as visually provocative and typographically alluring as a good bicycle advertisement by the American printer Will Bradley.[1] Although T. S. Eliot wrote that literary judgments about the artistic merits of language ought not to be made according to geography, a sense of place governed how readers responded to poetry as a modern visual art.[2] Harriet Monroe in Chicago, Amy Lowell in Boston, and Ezra Pound in London collaborated and competed as poets in a so-called pseudomovement they dubbed "imagism." In 1912, when imagism began, poetry competed with advertising in a democracy of printed goods. Imagism offered a competitive vernacular of commodities. Similar visually to the language of advertising, it was a poetry of objects, of ideas embodied by "things," as the physician-poet William Carlos Williams wrote.[3] Imagist poems were short, well suited to a magazine page or a broadside.

IMAGISM AS A PSEUDOMOVEMENT

A response to the printing renaissance, imagism began at a time when readers were surrounded by catalogs, posters, and all manner of finely printed commercial ephemera including luxurious advertisements for the so-called ordinary housewife.[4] As art historians described Kelmscott, the arts-and-crafts movement revived printing when it was "at low ebb." Similarly, according to literary historians, imagism revived a "drooping" poetic art that "languished" in what Monroe called a "desperate fix" and "needed some type of marketing handle."[5] Alice Corbin Henderson, an editor of Harriet Monroe's *Poetry* magazine, wrote that "imagism is essentially a graphic art . . . like the finest etching print or wood-cut."[6]

Imagism and the new typography shared an aesthetic of public letters based on "revolutionary" principles. Both asserted that language had to *function* on a page. Image and text employed what Ezra Pound called a "hard-edged light," in an economy of space, an austere, spare consistency of form, stripped of ornament, designed to make the page as beautiful to the eye as to the ear.[7] Both imagism and typographic arts treated compositional technique as sacred. "Art is not like theology," as an advertising type specimen for the American Type Founders Company declared in 1905. "You do not have to represent the world. . . . think of technique when you rise and when you go to bed."[8] Although they claimed direct descent from the French symbolistes, imagists were more interested in craft than in the symbolic power of words.

Harriet Monroe and Amy Lowell hoped to penetrate the mass market for poetry the way Cyrus Curtis's *Saturday Evening Post* had the short story. Ezra Pound, Harriet Monroe, and Amy Lowell each claimed to have been the driving genius behind the movement. All three employed marketing techniques to sell modernism in general, imagism in particular, and their individual literary reputations in the bargain. Each artist defined imagism somewhat differently.

Advertising Poetry as a Visual Art, 1912–1922

Using publicity skills adapted from maverick graphic-design "experts," imagists differentiated themselves by virtue of how they saw language rather than how they saw the world. The romantic poet idealized the emotions; the imagist poet invested every object with emotion. The imagists wanted to distance themselves from other literary trades. Monroe wrote that "prose is still too much under the domination of magazine editors to have broken away and started anything very new. Our prose writers are still inferior to . . . England. Our poets . . . inferior to none living today."[9]

Beginning with Monroe's first issue of *Poetry* magazine in 1912, imagists used periodicals, lectures, advertising, and anthologies to create the impression that imagism had many followers. As Pound's biographer Hugh Kenner implied, imagism constituted a pseudo-movement.[10] Only a few belonged, and they lacked "enough stuff for a volume." Literary historians concluded that "imagism was many things for many people."[11] Although realistic in their use of objects, the imagists were nevertheless romanticizing when they imagined that they would gain an economic foothold in the commercial mass-market through poetry.

In a burgeoning ephemeral literary economy, Monroe sold imagism as democratic poetry—*new, improved*, and *modern*. *Poetry* magazine played an important role in establishing and disseminating the ideas inherent in the group's identity. Monroe's salesmanship for the magazine and for poetry as a visual art was "revolutionary," to borrow Howells's phrase.[12]

Monroe, Lowell, and Pound argued that writers needed to command an audience, although they disagreed about an artist's relationship to the crowd. The economic realities of the mass market demanded what Monroe termed "a reciprocal relationship between the writer and audience." The rapport between poet and audience was based on the artist's ability to evoke an emotional response from an indifferent reader.[13] Monroe wrote that scientific explanations about the reactions and relations of matter made it "increasingly clear that nothing can stand alone, genius least of all."[14] In the twentieth century, the "science of the crowd" made public opinion more important than critical opinion in shaping the way readers responded to literature.

Advertising Poetry as a Visual Art, 1912–1922

Monroe's success as a propagandist has been obscured by the literary prominence that Ezra Pound achieved before 1918 as *Poetry* magazine's chief advertiser.[15] Even among her admirers, few considered Monroe to be a great poet. To her closest associates, she had less literary sophistication than she did a modern attitude toward language. More of a journalist and publicist than poet, Monroe embraced marketing the cause of poetry with the zeal of a social reformer.[16]

While imagist doctrines set boundaries "too narrow for the poets of the future," as Monroe wrote, the imagists' philosophy was to try to improve the public perception of poetry.[17] Monroe embraced imagism in 1912 because in it she saw an artistic form that could have broad public appeal. Long after the idea had become an aesthetic doctrine, Williams accused Monroe of misrepresenting imagism.[18] Pound admitted to his friend Glenn Hughes that imagism served mostly as a label to launch Hilda Doolittle ("H.D.") and Richard Aldington before they had matured as poets.[19]

Monroe liked to say she had invented imagism, although she occasionally had to remind some people of that claim; even her close friend Vachel Lindsay found it a "surprise" in 1915.[20] Monroe claimed that the imagist movement began with the 1912 publication of Richard Aldington's poem "Choricos" in the first issue of *Poetry*. Later, however, when the *Atlantic Monthly* published her own "Hotel," she said that hers had been the first imagist poem, preceding by four years anyone else's use of the term in print.[21] After *Poetry*'s 1912 issue appeared, coining the term and announcing imagist principles, a half dozen literary entrepreneurs wanted to be known for defining the movement. Ezra Pound and Amy Lowell published works by these poets in their imagist anthologies.

Lowell concluded that the movement had begun when Pound discovered H.D.'s poem published in January 1913. After Pound gathered a number of poems illustrating the imagist point of view, he published *Des Imagistes* in London in April 1914. Amy Lowell's three subsequent imagist anthologies published in successive years by Houghton Mifflin followed the design of Pound's 1914 volume published by Albert and Charles Boni in this country. As literary historians later assessed the situation, the 1912 group's involvement in

Advertising Poetry as a Visual Art, 1912–1922

propaganda and publication, led by Monroe and Pound, distinguished it both from the 1909 group led by T. E. Hulme and the 1914–17 group championed by Amy Lowell.[22]

The anthologies were Lowell's strategy for reinforcing the identity of the group as a school of "young experimentalists." In each anthology she would publish different works every year by the same poets, an equal number of British and Americans. According to Lowell's preface to the 1916 anthology, imagist principles "united" the writers, although as she had pointed out in the 1915 preface, they "were not a clique."[23] Pound's anthology of 1914 had included ten poems by Richard Aldington, seven by H.D., five by F. S. Flint, six by Pound, and one each by Lowell, William Carlos Williams, and others.[24]

After her 1916 anthology had been published, Lowell tried to assume leadership of the group. Leaving London for Boston in September 1914, she brought manuscripts for all three anthologies and plans for the annual to help position the movement with publishers in England and America.[25] T. S. Eliot charged that Lowell had "politicized" art by her role as "Director of Propaganda" for the imagists, something that struck him as "most unfortunate." This led Eliot to conclude that "literature must be judged by language not by place."[26] The chief limitations of imagism, from a critical standpoint, might be seen as having resulted from the group's search for a definitive national style.

Although Lowell protested that she wanted to "do away with" the stylistic limits imposed by culture or national place, or what she called the "politics of poetry," she often provoked rivalries, cultivating differences between publishers and her fellow poets. Subsequent critical assessment concluded that Pound saw imagism as a publicity tool for his friends, and that poets F. S. Flint and Robert Frost "never took its ideals seriously." Detractors charged that imagism was a "hog butcher" school of poetry.[27]

Monroe and Lowell clung to the imagist label for years, long after anyone else thought it important. The two women, well-traveled, unmarried, middle-class writers, defended Poetry as high Art (they always used the capital letters *P* and *A*) with the intensity of mothers defending their offspring. Monroe's appearance was deceptive: a thin spinster in wire-rimmed spectacles who wore her hair in a bun, she edited, published, promoted, and distributed her magazine, *Poetry*, worldwide between 1912 and 1922, the decade when most advertising trade magazines began and failed.

Monroe's ability to build a literary market is even more impressive when compared to the fate of most house organs published by specialists in the advertising field during the same period. As Frank Luther Mott's mid-twentieth-century census of American journalism established, the house organ was a significant force in shaping the early modern mass-communications industry: two hundred went through a boom-and-bust cycle between 1903 and 1913.[28] The small magazines bore the marks of trade turbulence: they contained clip art, a constant change of masthead, and employed established as well as itinerant writers, poets, solicitors and barker-style agents. By the turn of the century, Chicago had dubbed itself the world center for the production of business literature of all grades, from house-organ cheap to fine.[29] The proliferation and demise of the advertising agency house organs represents a typical life span among the magazine experiments of the second decade of the twentieth century.[30]

Because of the proliferation of ephemeral printing from the advertising industry, common readers saw good and bad poetry on printers' type-specimen sheets, railroad broadsides, and soap jingles. Ersatz poetry appeared in metropolitan newspapers, women's magazines, and house organs. Whether on a page or on a poster, all verse looked somewhat alike to the common reader. Serious poets lamented the passing of the nineteenth century, when readers knew the difference between real and ersatz poetry.[31]

Monroe wanted to make poetry popular in a brawny world. *Poetry* resembled many of the organs of the 1903–13 period that appeared on Printer's Row on Cass Street in downtown Chicago near her editorial offices, but she boldly announced that hers was different. In her magazine, she declared, the public would find poetry democratic. They might also find their heroes in poetry again, she hoped, rather than in the newspaper. She used Whitman's democratic sentiment, "To have great poets there must be great audiences too," as her slogan, printing it on the masthead, letterhead, and brochures.[32]

Unillustrated, quarto, in a plain style, the magazine did not boast. In Monroe's editorial manifesto, "The Motive of the Magazine," printed in the first number, she wrote that "in the huge democracy of our age no interest is too slight to have an organ."[33] She spent much of the summer of 1911 in the Chicago Public Library poring over the "despised page-end magazine fillers" looking for talent. One poet, the young advertising copywriter Sherwood Anderson, in the nearby Long and Critchfield agency, published his first verse in Monroe's magazine.[34]

Anderson predicted in 1905 that the hunger for novelty precipitated by the boom in the commercial language trades would so permeate the American reader's appetite for news that it would change expectations about the quality of publicity. In his "Rot or Reason" column, written between 1903 and 1905 for his agency's house organ, *Agricultural Advertising*, Anderson predicted that for a whole new generation of "efficient public" readers, imagination and realism would "mesh imperceptibly."[35] Readers would be unable to distinguish newsworthy events such as wars and elections from artificial ones based on messages about sales.

Advertising held a measure of popular fascination that must have diminished poetry and fiction by comparison. The promise inherent in the language of publicity offered an exaggerated view of the "photographic reproductions of life."[36] Literary realism would be undermined, Anderson wrote, by the need to meet the demands of a larger reality, the mass-market consumer of modern language products. He acknowledged writing for that "huge, self-satisfied American audience made up of all kinds of people with little prejudices, hates and fears that must not be offended."[37] His advertising world, one in which all "the Napoleons are dead," seldom offended or inspired anyone. Occasionally, one genius emerged, a pilot like Lindbergh, a hero who was "all action and few words." Anderson asked his readers, "Was he not all poetry once? . . . for a day and a night, out there alone over the Atlantic—the American eagle come to life—flown off the American dollar for the time."[38]

Advertising Poetry as a Visual Art, 1912–1922

For Anderson, the "only real gentleman" in the modern literary economy was someone who could make news and manage the resulting public reputation. The twentieth-century aristocrat, a "Good Fellow" and "Sales Master," possessed an ability to live up to a newspaper image and not be undone.[39] President Theodore Roosevelt was Anderson's aristocrat. The president could sell political ideas, national policies, or his own image on horseback.

Monroe tried to make news and manage her reputation by positioning poetry as a visual art made available to the masses through her magazine. *Poetry*'s success had less to do with literary quality than with Monroe's effective marketing and publicity techniques. In correspondence between 1910 and 1915, Monroe expressed her admiration for the work of two fine printers Ralph Fletcher Seymour and Eric Gill. Seymour, who had produced engravings for an edition of William Blake's poetry, also produced her advertising from his print shop in the Fine Arts Building on Michigan Avenue.[40] Eric Gill, a British printer, designed the magazine cover.[41] Given the volatility of trade journalism at the time, Monroe's success is as impressive as her magazine's longevity; it has been published continuously since 1912.[42]

Critics later credited Ezra Pound's "flair for publicity" with putting imagism "on the cultural map."[43] However, it was Monroe's talent for marketing as much as Pound's flair that sustained the enterprise. Nevertheless, when Pound brought the earliest issues of *Poetry* magazine to the London publisher Elkin Mathews—who wrote to Monroe that "Pound's name is of course much better known here than yours and it would help the magazine here if his name was bracketed with yours on the cover . . . as contributing editor or something of that sort."[44] Monroe named Pound foreign editor of *Poetry*. She did so despite her readers' criticism of him as brash, rude, and not an especially good poet.

Although Monroe and Lowell were shrewd publicists, Pound had the louder voice. Monroe seemed to think that Pound represented a real movement, one she had initiated but for which she never received credit. Lowell, more combative and confident than Monroe, recognized that the source of imagism had been in the Midwest, although she continued to resent the fact. Nine years after imagism began, Lowell wrote that the Chicago group was "a narrow and militant sect decrying everything which is not themselves." She thought *Poetry* had "strangely little effect, considering; Harriet Monroe's reviews mean nothing to anyone," although she did think that her own in the *New York Times* and *New York Post* "are beginning to have a strong effect."[45]

Lowell considered briefly Pound's invitation to relocate to London as editor of his *Poetry Review*—an invitation that included, on her part, an initial investment of $5,000. If she accepted, he told her, he planned to continue to run the magazine "in his own way."[46] When Pound had left the midwestern group to affiliate himself with the British one, he denounced the American imagists; and although he borrowed Monroe's ideas, he excluded her from his imagist clique. He joined Wyndham Lewis's vorticists and their short-lived organ, *Blast* (1914). Lowell thought that the magazine was beneath Pound's talent. She wrote to Monroe, "'Blast' will give you a good idea of what Ezra has been obliged to descend to in order to keep his name before the public, and he admitted in a speech at an Imagist dinner, that it was nothing but advertising. . . . Advertising is all very well, but one must have some goods to deliver, and the goods must be up to the advertising of them."[47]

Rejecting Pound's offer to relocate to London, she resolved to publish American imagist annuals to compete with his British quarterly. Lowell wrote, "It seemed to me that to re-publish the 'Imagiste Anthology' with the same group of people, year after year, for a period of five years, would enable us, by constant iteration, to make some impression upon the reading public."[48] Houghton Mifflin published *A Few Imagists* in 1915, 1916, and 1917. Through the anthologies, Lowell expanded the market for her own books; she published ten books of poetry over the next ten years, distributed in London and in the United States. At this time, she explained to Pound, "I find myself completely isolated over here, and although the magazines are very good and print me, there is nothing that really sympathizes with me or my objects. I feel that to gain the recognition that I deserve, it will be necessary to create a public."[49]

The publication of books created the impression of a permanent

Advertising Poetry as a Visual Art, 1912–1922

group in a way that a magazine did not, however well distributed it might have been. Pound's 1914 anthology, *Des Imagistes*, published in London, established the group's identity abroad; and Lowell's 1915 anthology, published in Boston by Houghton Mifflin, bolstered the imagists' claim to be an American movement. Lowell used Pound's imagists to promote her own books; Monroe used Pound to sell magazines; and Pound used *Poetry* to promote what he called "his ideas" about imagism.

This arrangement worked only up to a point, however. After leaving the Chicago group, Pound tended to be more guarded about new ideas, and his poetry became increasingly more private.[50] For Pound, "the crowd" was not an imagistic abstraction but a grubby reality of the modern mass-market economy. Monroe, on the other hand, saw public appeal as inevitable—part of the modern business of literature. People did not buy poetry, she observed; they bought the poet's reputation. Pound, however, rebelled against the way that Monroe and Lowell used their audience.

MONROE'S MARKETING TECHNIQUES

Monroe's life experience contributed to her instinctive feel for the "science of the crowd." The money she had earned as a girl for one poem, a ceremonial "Ode" written for the 1893 Chicago World's Fair, raised her expectations about her ability to make a living as a poet. The ode brought $1,000 from the fair committee, which was headed by Cyrus McCormick, a family friend. She also won $5,000 from a successful lawsuit waged with the aid of her lawyer-father against the New York *World* for its copyright violation, when it printed her "Ode" the night before opening ceremonies.[51] With the $6,000, Monroe traveled to Europe and the Orient. When she returned to Chicago, however, she discovered that poets seldom earned more than $75 for publishing a poem in the popular magazines. Indeed, editors at *Atlantic*, *Collier's*, and the *Ladies Home Journal* would not even offer that much, rejecting her work in favor of more sentimental verse and shorter poetry as being more the fashion.[52]

After she returned to Chicago, Monroe's earned income grew slowly, from $573 in 1900 to $1,636 in 1910.[53] Over the next twenty years, even after her magazine became well known, she could not find a book publisher who would print a volume of her verse. "No poet can pay his shoe bills," she stormed in 1910. All the while, she noted how all around her—in Chicago, New York, and Boston —cheap magazines flourished, and on billboards, handbills, house organs, in trade journals and popular magazines bad verse proliferated from the Eastern Seaboard to the Hawaiian territories.[54] Monroe ended up paying her shoe bills by writing art criticism in the Sunday *Chicago Tribune*. The fall from her beginning as an ingenue whose first work was recited by a chorus of 500 fueled her drive to improve the lot of poets she knew who also barely scraped by.[55]

Public opinion belonged to the "new and improved" spirit of the modern age, she believed, and the concept of the common reader, inherently a "democratic" one, proved vital for artists' prosperity. Innovations, whether in poetry or typography, must be introduced to the public, Monroe thought, and tried by the readers as experts. She wrote that "in a democracy, publicity is the only remedy for evils. . . . The author makes the public her confidant."[56] Much as Monroe looked down on the "common" quality of the commercial literature produced in the magazine age—believing her enterprise to be a cut above—she adapted publicity techniques suited to mass markets to advance her "fine" literary cause.[57]

Monroe hoped to "arouse a sense of responsibility in the public" by direct appeals to their civic-mindedness. In a *Chicago Tribune* article entitled "How Will Twenty-first Century Critics Rank Artists of the Present Day?" Monroe asserted her readiness to appeal to the future and to the globe for the cause of poetry. She called isolationism "old world," defunct. She believed that setting a national standard for aesthetic style underestimated the power of the emerging universal audience by relying too much on the romantic notion of geographical identity. China, she reported, could be found "just across the river." Monroe wrote that "modern art is a huge democracy, an arena of the many, not the few." Her use of the public and marketing techniques were the key to her success. Understanding public opinion "is instructive," she wrote in "The Poets' Bread and Butter"; "In art as in politics . . . watch the workings of the public mind."[58]

Advertising Poetry as a Visual Art, 1912–1922

Long & Critchfield Agency of Chicago advertisement for its takeover of the Frank B. White Co. of New York, printed in the agency's monthly publicity magazine Agricultural Advertising, *September 1903. The issue also carried Sherwood Anderson's advice column (1903–5) "Rot or Reason."*
Courtesy of Newberry Library, Special Collections.

Monroe's marketing strategy developed from three principles: she used an effective system of media relations, marketed printed language as a performance, and tied the success of her publishing venture to marketing the city of Chicago. In what became standard language on all her publicity appeals, she wrote that poetry had a natural audience that needed only to be discovered: "We believe that there is a public for poetry, but that it is scattered and unorganized. Poetry has no organ to speak for it, and its public does not know where to find it."[59]

As a regular columnist for the *Tribune*, she kept her own name before the public.[60] She also maintained a national press list, corresponded with literary-page editors, and sent circulars and flyers designed to attract them as advertisers. She appealed to their subscribers, soliciting contributions from the mass of undiscovered poets who were "out there" already working in printing, advertising, and publicity trades. In 1912, Monroe retained Henry Moneike, who ran a New York clipping service, the First Established and Most Complete Newspaper Cutting Bureau in the World, to monitor the magazine's reputation and inform her of its progress. To monitor European reaction to her magazine, as early as 1914, she retained a service in France, Le Courrier de la Presse, "ce qui est publie dans les Journaux et Publications de toute nature et en fournit les extraits sur tous sujets et personnalités."[61]

Monroe treated verse as a public work, not unlike a symphony, a fountain, or a piece of sculpture. She established a board of guarantors as if her magazine were a civic enterprise. Amy Lowell agreed to serve as one of her guarantors, as did a number of Chicago's industrial elite. In an open letter to the city carried in the *Daily News*, Monroe pointed out that Chicago's Art Institute, built on public land, spent $100,000 annually in public taxes. The Chicago Symphony also owned a valuable building, she continued, obtained through public subscription. *Poetry* magazine aspired to provide a comparable public exhibition space for poets. The other cultural institutions also enjoyed a pension fund and donations from individuals. Her magazine, by comparison, spent only 2½ percent of what the Art Institute spent to "give painters and sculptors a chance to be seen in their own place."[62]

Advertising Poetry as a Visual Art, 1912–1922

A decade before state legislatures in the Midwest established poet laureates, Monroe saw marketing potential in creating a regional identity through the voice of native artists who celebrated their sense of place.[63] She established early her magazine's importance for enhancing the reputation of Chicago as a leader in the American industrial-arts movement. She repeated the point often, and the newspaper establishment embraced it. The *New York Times* "guessed" "that next to none [of our readers] know that the best magazine of poetry in the English language is not published in London (where dwells Mr. Masefield), nor in Dublin (where every Sinn Feiner is a poet), nor yet in New York, but in Chicago, Ill.—loop, levee, stockyards and all."[64] The Chicago *Daily News* reprinted the excerpt. An undated solicitation letter sent to the Association of Commerce requested financial support because *Poetry* was "the most important aesthetic advertisement the city ever had." Monroe's letter asked that "public-spirited citizens" contribute $2,000 each to enlarge the magazine's endowment. Monroe wrote, "We are doing the same kind of work for the city which is done by the Art Institute, the Orchestral Association, the Chicago Grand Opera Co., the two endowed theatres."[65]

When the Depression threatened *Poetry*'s survival, she continued claiming "to be the chief" publication to put Chicago and the Midwest on the American literary map, developing a new movement "so rich, so vital, as to be a veritable renaissance."[66] In her 1917 renewal appeal, she asserted a "certain claim" to support from Chicago, because the publication "represented a mid-country idealism" that Chicago "cannot afford to let die."[67] In her 1919 campaign for funds, Monroe's press release puffed *Poetry* as a "public institution" that "boosts" Chicago.[68]

Guarantors endowed Monroe's publication as if it were a public institution. She also sold subscriptions (at $1.50 per year or 15 cents per copy) and accepted advertising ($15 for a full page, $8 for a half page, $5 for a quarter page) although that was "strictly limited to productions of an artistic and educational nature."[69] In one of her direct-mail pieces, billed a "Card to Chicagoans," Monroe described her publication as "an endowed Chicago enterprise, the unique example of a magazine devoted . . . to the development of

Advertising Poetry as a Visual Art, 1912–1922

public appreciation of poetry as a fine art," although "the city of New York supplied 40% more subscribers than its own Chicago." In another broadside, she claimed the periodical had achieved a "significant place in the literary life of the country," promising advertisers "results" if they placed advertisements in *Poetry* because the publication appealed to a "highly specialized public."[70]

Although Monroe's marketing success became one of her achievements, she never forgot that it was born of necessity. In order to survive the modern mass-marketplace, a writer had to be rooted in economic reality, not aesthetic theories. Monroe had hoped the magazine would be able to pay writers more than the standard $10 a poem. Alice Corbin Henderson, one of the magazine's editors, counted anyone "who would buy" the magazine her "public." Others, such as the "considerable public for which no account is taken in the yearly summaries of *Publishers Weekly*," served as a source for "new images" but were not part of the audience base.[71] Henry Fuller, a member of Monroe's advisory committee, pictured a typology of publics "engaged in consolidating the framework of a new American art and even in establishing the tradition that a solid national art requires." Only through images that meant something to the public would their magazine succeed. He wrote that tradition made "Certain groups of images unite" to make a "frame through which" the public saw both the artist and the world.[72] The public and the crowd were what Fuller's editorial called "living realities."

Poetry editors adapted the magazine's content to their sense of the crowd; they published poetry containing images of "plain people." Based on very elementary feedback, they researched the audience as a constituent of the magazine.[73] Although imagism became passé by mid-1914, as Pound's biographer Hugh Kenner wrote, "the term came to mean little more than a way of designating short vers libre poems in English," the doctrine of a language of things "remained vital."[74]

Different attitudes among Monroe, Lowell, and Pound toward the public and the artists' need for an audience caused problems for the group. Monroe was aware of the importance of garnering public interest in her enterprise. By contrast Pound's antipathy for readers, whom he saw as intruding on his brilliant, solitary songs, controlled the metaphors in his poetry published in *Poetry* magazine. In "Contemporania," Pound is separated from readers by a screen of noise (usually critical voices) that emphasizes his alienation. In "The Garden," Pound refers to Kensington Gardens, but he broods about being in a self-cultivated Golgotha, where the "rabble," "the filthy, sturdy, unkillable infants of the very poor . . . inherit the earth." The woman who walks by is an aloof if "emotionally anemic" muse, a proverbial madonna or magdalen at the foot of the cross, her garments drifting "like loose silk." Her presence in the scene is both aimless and ambiguous. She is "blown" by forces that are natural, head-on into what is real. The "wall" is the crowd crying for Barabbas, the voices in a public chorus of stupidity. They reach for the common when they are offered the divine. Given all his bluster against the existence of the crowd, Pound becomes demure: when confronted by the physical reality of the woman, he is too discreet for conversation. He is afraid to touch her, although she longs to be touched by the real emotion in his verse. The poet plays it safe; he hides in an objectivity afforded by images rather than in the ambiguity of emotions.

In "Ortus," the dominant theme is asserted by an individual who clings to his personal identity against the crowd's pressure to conform.[75] In "Dance Figure" (at the Marriage at Cana), the poet singles out one woman "not found at the well-head/Among the women with pitchers," whom he addresses as unlike everyone else: "There is none like thee among the dancers." In the lone woman the poet sees a projection of his private self. In him there lives the heart of a poet who is also a snob. In "Commission," the poet charges his songs to "go out and defy opinion."[76] Pound's last poem in the series, "In a Station at the Metro," became synonymous with the movement. The image in the poem captures the poet as an ordinary passerby, emerging from the underground railway station. The emotional instant captured by the image is neither the lure of the crowd nor its beauty, but the poet's passionate desire to be saved from the mob.

For Monroe, on the other hand, the audience represented neither a literary abstraction nor a reason for emotion, but a writer's economic salvation. She saw the image of the mass market as a metaphor for the modern relationship between poetry and what she called its "natural" audience. The image of the crowd pitted individualism against the power of the mass market. Readers, caught somewhere in between, were presented with their own insignificance. The image also advanced the social evolutionists' argument about human proportion and perspective. Late-nineteenth-century Americans flocked to see Tom Thumb in P. T. Barnum's "great moral show," while in the 1890s William James and others in articles for the *American Mercury* debated why people sought out "those greater and smaller than themselves."[77] In Monroe's editorial "The Fight for the Crowd" (1915), she described her vision of the audience as a parable of the marketplace, writing about "the myriads of 'new readers' stretching from sea to sea—the huge easy-going American public following trampled roads, gulping down pre-digested foods, seeking comfortable goals," always suspicious of "torches." Against the vast indistinguishable mass market, Monroe continued, "the crowd rebels against the universal theme of art—the littleness of man—or rather, the abysmal contrast between his littleness and his greatness." Modernism placed readers squarely in the midst of realism, according to Monroe, as "humanity facing the infinite with inadequate and unattainable dreams."[78]

The relationship between an individual and the "magnitude of things" once defined the heroic. Commercial modernism, however, diminished the relative importance of things. Monroe expressed, at the end of her life, a continuing fascination with the "blasting unreality" of the age. She wrote, "The mystery is not the greatness of life, but the littleness. That we, so grandly born, so mightily endowed, should grasp with blind eyes and bound limbs in the dust and mire of petty desires and grievances, until we can hardly see the blue of the sky or the glory of the seasons, until we can hardly clasp our neighbor's hand or hear his voice—this is the inexplicable mystery."[79]

Monroe's responsiveness to her readers' reality drove her early editorial philosophy. The public reacted to her democratic experiment as if there had been a flood, as she described it, "as if the dam burst, the floodgates opened."[80] People contributed poems who had never

composed a poem before or even read poetry. What Monroe classi-
fied as either a "boost" or "slam" came from typists, clerks, shop
owners, factory workers, a permanent-wave developer, people who
had never finished school, as well as great poets.[81] By 1919, nearly
twenty-five hundred poems from four to five hundred people arrived in the office each month. As one reader urged in a letter to the
editor, "Poetry must be advertised by its friends . . . you are trying
to discover and develop the Public for Poetry. . . . Music stepped
down from her throne, and through ragtime and vaudeville created
her wide Public. Poetry in some way must do likewise if she would
be heard by the masses."[82]

Monroe replied, scribbling in pencil across the top of one cover
letter, "Don't give up your job," before handing the note over to her
assistant editor to respond in a rejection letter.[83] Another individual
wrote, "My dear Sir," wanting to contribute a piece about Lindbergh, addressed to Monroe, "the main stanzas are supplemented
by songs appropriate and sung by the New Jersey aviator. Your own
big popular city received a stanza that will interest and amuse, if not
edify you."[84] Monroe gave personal attention to every letter that
arrived in her office from the mass of "new readers." She marked
each letter a "boost" or "knock." On some she noted "ans. longhand
HM." On others she stamped the date received and indicated that
her assistant should respond to the canceling subscribers.[85]

Most of the negative mail, some of it vicious, targeted the imagists, particularly Ezra Pound. Disappointed poets whose verse had
been rejected often canceled subscriptions. Others objected because they thought the magazine favored Chicagoans over others.
Some complained that the magazine's "open door policy for unknown writers," promised when the magazine began, constituted
false advertising. One reader from St. Louis charged that the editor
wished to "establish a cult Monroe, the apotheosis of which shall be
one Pound, but not sterling."[86] The reader complained, "You yearn
for the esoteric writhings of the 'new school,' twisted and broken-
backed tho' they be, and for the self-centered fantasies of that cote-
rie of insufferable snobs calling themselves the 'Imagistes.' . . .
This may be good form in Chicago; but meanwhile if the Amalgam-

Advertising Poetry as a Visual Art, 1912–1922

ated Society of Literary Prigs should at any time be lacking a President, I should have no hesitation in recommending for that office the present editor of *Poetry!*"[87]

Another attacked, writing, "Guts, that's the stuff, favorite word of modernist poets. . . . Imagists speak only of things seen or heard—or smelt. . . . You are many things, Spring, in many places, but in the quarters of the poor you are always Imagistic."[88] One reader charged that Monroe was "Titania to Pound's Bottom."[89] Another St. Louis woman vacationing in Denver took the time to write and commend the "improvement" in the June 1913 issue by "the elimination of Pound's insulting . . . attacks upon Americans—He being featured in all previous numbers."[90] To another reader who had reported having "thrown the magazine in the fire" because of Pound, Monroe responded with a news clip, apparently a favorable review. The angry ex-subscriber retorted that Monroe had missed the point: "It says very plainly that although Ezra Pound thinks he is a poet, 'Tis doubtful."[91] Monroe handled each piece of correspondence herself, patiently responding to every reader's letter. Her response was invariably an apology for their distress, and cancelation as requested, with a refund of the remainder of their subscription fee.

All the Chicago daily newspapers carried stories about the rivalry between the *Dial*, a staid magazine "which attempted to transplant New England culture in the Midwest," and *Poetry*'s attempt to uncover new forms of indigenous literature. The *Dial* blasted *Poetry* as embodying the "hog-butcher" school of verse, indelibly linking the Midwest and imagism in the public mind. Such commentary proved useful to Monroe. She distributed quotes from 1913 newspaper commentaries as if they were testimonials, printing both "boosts and slams" on handbills and advertising flyers, sending press releases containing all attacks by the *Dial* to the local and national press. The Chicago *Record Herald*, among others, thought the competition significant enough to warrant an editorial on the "predestined foes" in one of their yearly "set-to's."[92]

Monroe used readers' negative response to Pound as part of a plan to reach an indifferent public. In her view, a writer's public persona represented a publicity advantage, rather than a danger to litera-

Advertising Poetry as a Visual Art, 1912–1922

ture. Yet not all writers would have agreed with her. Pound's Italian writer-friend Emanuel Carnevali, for example, feared public scrutiny. He thought market forces could corrupt a writer's imagination.[93] Carnevali wrote to Monroe, calling it dangerous for writers to "believe themselves the megaphone . . . talking the world's language," using "all the filthy symbols . . . along the ash-can guarded streets of the mob."[94] The mob of readers in the newspaper world would force writers to descend to the level of the audience in order to get their attention, he believed. Carnevali worried about the writer being controlled by a sense of what the common reader wanted rather than what the writer needed to express in a thought, idea, or opinion. "I do not understand and never will understand what you, my friends, mean by new expressions, new images, originality. That which I enjoy, the image, pays me. . . . I am not for show, I never felt the need of exhibiting myself. . . . The image and my joy for the image is a circle and there is no break for anybody to get in. I want to be what the world misses."[95] The discrepancy between an author's real and imagined self raised questions for Carnevali about whether the text could be said to belong to the audience or to the writer, and to what extent consumers of art possessed or controlled the artist.

Vachel Lindsay, who thought that aspirations about poetic immortality were as false as the hope for newspaper notoriety, was destroyed by the public reader, just as Carnevali feared. Eventually Lindsay exhausted his "enforced public self"; as he became more popular, his audience seemed to diminish him.[96] Monroe claimed that Lindsay was her most famous "discovery"—"perhaps the most gifted and original poet we ever printed." With his "Gospel of Beauty" poetry leaflets in hand, Lindsay walked, distributed his poems, and recited his verse to anyone who would listen, for months at a time. In 1906 he walked from Florida to Kentucky, in 1908 from New York to Ohio, and in 1912 from Illinois to New Mexico. Between June 1907 and February 1909, he published five articles in *Outlook*, publicizing the walks as much as he could.

Monroe discovered him in May 1912, when she read his article "Rules of the Road." An idealist, Lindsay wrote about his vision of the Middle West as the American heartland, the democratic ideal.

Advertising Poetry as a Visual Art, 1912–1922

Lindsay's public appeal, according to literary historians, catered to the masculine taste for roughing it, for "striking out for the open road, for tramping and writing about it."[97] Similarly, works by Carl Sandburg, Robert Frost, and Jack London struck a chord with the American public. According to essayist Robert Sayre, Lindsay romanticized the wide-open spaces of the heartland as Richard Dana, Herman Melville, and Francis Parkman romanticized the sea. On each of his walks, Lindsay would distribute his "Gospel of Beauty" broadsides, which were part drawing and part calligraphy, and recite four or five of his poems. It turned out that he was "unable to escape his own uniqueness as a performer, and the hungry twentieth century publicity machinery" made up of his "yesterdays." He claimed his audience kept him from writing anything new, and he longed to be known for his pre-Monroe self, complaining to Monroe, "not by my speaking tours, but by what I did before October 1912, even before *Poetry* magazine began, and before those tours began."[98] He thought America "longed for great rather than good poets." Every would-be bard needed a "diploma" granted by magazines, "and the tyrannical majority of Americans disliked all poetry because they fidgeted, and learned to dislike poetry in school."[99] Critics called Lindsay a reciting freak. Writing to Monroe, Lindsay grieved for his own artistic death before he committed suicide, lamenting "I went [on a poetry tour to England] aping or recording . . . shouting . . . the Vachel of ten years ago, for one gets in rhyme only a self that is long dead. . . . I care not what the apparent praise or reward. I am a dead man in my own eyes." Around the same time he confessed to her that he "would give almost anything to escape forever the reciting and chanting Vachel. My whole heart is set on escaping my old self."[100]

Although Lindsay celebrated the image of troubadour poets in his work, several of the imagist group thought he "didn't quite fit" their identity. Lowell disagreed in a letter to Monroe, saying that she thought "plenty of room" existed for him. Lowell found room for his theories and the imagists' "running along" "side by side" where they could admire one another.[101] For his part, Lindsay thought poets looked "babyish huddled together." He declared himself "unafraid to face the wide open corn fields (and the public)

Advertising Poetry as a Visual Art, 1912–1922

alone."[102] His contemporaries thought him an itinerant, a solicitor for poetry advertising a spiritual circus he mistook for an opera. Something about the man refused to grow up. He wrote to Monroe, "It is my profound conviction that Poetry . . . is the best and worthiest and most permanent child of that World's Fair. . . . When I think of the Chicago World's Fair I think of something that must be re-created permanently."[103]

In a letter to Lowell, Lindsay referred to himself as a secular Mary Baker Eddy. He compared his *Golden Book of Springfield* to a civic version of her *Science and Health*. He insisted his book worked "for the healing of cities" rather than individuals. Although Lowell admired the way he managed his public lecture tours, she stopped short of praising his poetry. However, she "puffed" his talents to Houghton Mifflin, asking the publishers to consider the merits of his verse. She urged them, without success, to consider how "Boston is not like the West. They do not care much for lectures here. . . . I cannot help feeling in spite of your generosity that you are a bit hurt at my not including you. . . . It was not because of lack of merit, it was simply that your work did not fit into the scheme of my book."[104]

LOWELL'S MARKETING TECHNIQUES

Of the three leading imagists, only Lowell succeeded in publishing a half dozen books before 1925, while those she called her "confreres" struggled to interest publishers in a single volume. While Lindsay's reputation grew from his walks and publicity, Pound and Monroe stood "with their backs to the wall." They "struck out blindly with clenched fists in an impulse to fight" against publishers, whom Pound called a "mass of dolts." Along with most of the other imagists, Pound railed against that "whole list of American publishers and editors" of the magazine era who would not buy what writers offered because their "public would not buy it."[105] Though Macmillan and Houghton Mifflin published her verse, Lowell had to carry the full expense of publishing and advertising, giving her time gratis as copywriter and publicity editor. At the same time, she served as a guarantor of *Poetry*, which paid her $200 per year. More often than not, she advertised her books in *Poetry*, the *Egoist*, or other small literary publications, and in mass-market magazines. Bolstered by this success, she appointed herself manager of the group.

Claiming leadership of the imagists in America, Lowell told her editors at Houghton Mifflin that she "would take upon herself" the responsibility to answer "any questions" from the press or public about "Imagism in general" or about the three group anthologies she published between 1915 and 1917. In addition to promoting Lindsay's poetry to her publishers, Lowell acted as agent for others who wanted to publish with Houghton Mifflin, including Richard Aldington. In asserting herself as manager of the group's identity, she and Pound argued about a 1914 advertisement for her Macmillan book.[106]

Pound had waged, according to his biographer Hugh Kenner, a "brief but deliberate campaign for Imagism in the fall of 1912." Pound planned his *Des Imagistes* anthology of 1914 for two years, but his involvement with the group declined after he published his manifesto "A Few Don'ts by an Imagiste," in the first issue of *Poetry*. Kenner concluded that Pound "grew tired" of the uphill campaign long before March 1913. For his part, Pound did not discuss imagism again until a fracas with Lowell in 1914 over a Macmillan advertisement for her book of verse. Pound's correspondence reveals that he felt threatened by her leadership, even though he had already left the group.[107] The trouble between Lowell and Pound took place when he read an advertisement for Lowell's volume *Sword Blades and Poppy Seeds* with W. B. Yeats and Ford Madox Hueffer dubbed "imagists," and Lowell herself billed as its "foremost member." Lowell suspected she had gone too far with this claim; she wrote to Monroe admitting, "I am very much afraid Ezra may try his best to injure me owing to his fury at that unfortunate advertisement. It would therefore be a great kindness to me if you could review my book somewhat at length as all his friends in England see 'Poetry' and a few nice words will do a great deal towards allaying the impression he is trying to give."[108]

After seeing the advertisement, Pound fired off a one-line, sarcastic volley on a postcard to Lowell congratulating her on the appearance of her volume of poetry and inquiring why she had not also had her publisher include in the advertisement the name of the deceased nineteenth-century British novelist Thomas Hardy.[109] Lowell shot back that Pound had lived too long outside the United States and had forgotten how American advertising worked, that name-dropping proved a constant, provided the names possessed worldwide recognition. She insisted that she had "tried to stop it in time," and she charged Pound with having designated her an "imagist" against her will when he included one of her poems in his 1914 anthology. "As to my being put down as an Imagiste, you yourself are responsible for that. . . . You will remember that I wrote you last winter and told you that if yours was to be an Imagiste Anthology I did not think I belonged to it. . . . The next thing I knew was that I saw my name in the advance advertisement which appeared in the *New York Times*. Having been given the name of Imagiste I shall certainly not repudiate it."[110]

Pound wanted to sue Macmillan for libel. He wrote to Lowell that he had coined the term *Imagiste* and that the publisher had violated his exclusive right to its use. Lowell pointed out that he held no patent and that even in the "world of cement and soap," he would need a patent to assert his copyright legally. If Pound decided to sue Macmillan, Lowell warned, the publishers knew how to turn negative publicity to their advantage and use his lawsuit as an advertisement. As for the use of *Imagist* in the title of Lowell's anthology, Pound allowed grudgingly that he would give his "sanction" as long as her preface included an explanation. The statement, he instructed her, should contain some word about how he had dissociated himself from the American group, and how the imagists had split over aesthetic principles. After the quarrel over the advertisement, Pound pulled away entirely from the group. Lowell kept the rest of the poets intact. She drafted the preface according to Pound's prescription, writing to her publishers, "Here is the altered preface. You will see that I have changed it very slightly, merely leaving out all reference to Mr. Pound and suggesting a schism in the ranks has induced us to publish under a different title from that of the volume of last year. I think this is the best arrangement, and, if Ezra chooses to come out and row us in the public prints, we will row back through the same medium."[111]

Advertising Poetry as a Visual Art, 1912–1922

THE LINKS BOOK. (BROOKS BROTHERS, NEW YORK)

THE PROBLEM: Golf was just growing into popular favor. What sort of a book would a gentleman golfer appreciate, keep and refer to?

The Problem

THE SOLUTION: The Links Book was tiny (2 x 3½ inches), 96 pages, so thin as to go easily into a card case, bound in limp cloth, stamped with gold. It contained the Laws of Golf, a list of all the Golf Clubs in this country, and information as to trains and facilities for getting to every Golf Links within 100 miles of New York. It bore none of the earmarks of advertising. It was a useful manual.

The Solution

DON'T FORGET
ON GOING AWAY
GOING TO EUROPE
THE PACKING OF YOUR LUGGAGE
APTITUDES
THE CARE OF THE WARD-ROBE

SCHOOL CATALOGUE
CAB FARES AND DISTANCES
SOCIAL FIXTURES
MOTOR BOOK
AUTOMOBILE BOOKLET
GENERAL CATALOGUE
PARTIAL LIST
CHRISTMAS SELECTIONS

Other Work for Brooks Brothers

"DON'T FORGET (Brooks Bros., N. Y.) is a satisfactory and altogether charmingly made book."
BROOKLYN CITIZEN

"Don't Forget" received similar notices in 40 other newspapers throughout the United States.

"THE firm of Brooks Brothers, Broadway and Twenty-second Street, has never used space in newspapers, but depends upon small booklets containing information that will be useful to the class of people who buy furnishings. These little booklets are sent out with the monthly statements, usually, except where designed to go to a special class, as was a recent pocket volume entitled 'The Motor Book,' which gave tables of distances, routes, automobile laws and similar information."

"APTITUDES, with its dainty cover and deft little preface, will undoubtedly appeal to all who receive it."
PRINTERS' INK, N. Y.

"WE are very highly pleased with our 'Automobile Booklet' which has been the recipient of much favorable comment. It seems to us the best of all the excellent productions which we have had from you during the past seven years.
"We are glad to learn that, as you go deeper, the vein of 'Cheltenham Press Originality' seems—instead of becoming exhausted—to grow even richer."
With best wishes for continued success

Yours very truly,
BROOKS BROTHERS,
Walter Brooks, Director

(Letter to Brooks Bros.)

Wilmington, Del.

"ANY firm who will go to the care and trouble of getting out such a neat little thing as the 'Links Book' should receive at least thanks. It seems just right for a vest pocket."
WILLIAM C. SPEAKMAN

Press Comment and Letters

Send for A Representative

Agency report, 1897–1907, New York. "The First 10 Years of the Cheltenham Press: Being An Account of Various Problems in Printing and in Advertising and of their Solution." The American "Cheltenham" typeface dominated the advertising scene between 1890 and 1920, until it was displaced by more modern "sans" style faces for publicity purposes. Courtesy of the John M. Wing Foundation, Newberry Library.

Whatever the state of their relations, Lowell clearly wanted to salvage what Pound had accomplished by linking his name to the imagists' reputation as a group. Lowell's preface to the 1915 American anthology implied that there existed a direct link between her work and Pound's 1914 British volume. Explaining to readers that his departure from the group had been over aesthetic principles, as he had dictated, she wrote, "Differences of taste and judgment . . . have arisen among the contributors . . . forcing them along different paths . . . much of the misunderstanding of the former volume was due to the fact that we did not explain ourselves . . . we have thought it wise to tell the public what our aims are, and why we banded together between one set of covers."[112]

Afterward Pound relented, writing that he "did not mind" her use of the name *imagist* although he thought her anthology would have been better titled *Vers Libre* because it would be read largely by people "who have not taken the trouble to find out what I mean" by imagism. He thought Lowell ought to quit calling herself an imagist.[113] She suggested that the group be governed by a committee. Pound fumed.

The fact that Lowell paid for her own advertising and took such an assertive role in promoting her own literary reputation in the press must not have been very widely known. In fact, it would have been regarded as something of a compromise had it been known. In any event, Pound tried to manipulate Lowell during their quarrel, writing, "You have attributed to me malicious remarks that I have never made. I have heard that you pay for your advertising, but I have never said so to anyone."[114]

Reader interest in the three anthologies, although far from robust, was not entirely indifferent. According to the publisher's records, the 1915 volume sold 1,301 copies the first year out, the 1916 volume sold nearly 1,300 within the year, and by 1919, Houghton Mifflin had sold out of the 1917 issue. When Houghton reprinted 270 copies of the 1917 anthology in 1919, Lowell "ordered" the publisher to let the imagist anthologies "go out of print." She reasoned that the anthologies "had done their work very well": poets by now had interested publishers in producing one of their own books. She explained that poets naturally wanted the public to buy their books instead of the anthologies, so they could receive more royalties.[115] Lowell's own volumes continued to sell at an average rate of four hundred per year, a steady if not brilliant showing, attributable to her unflagging efforts to publicize the works.[116] Although she admitted that she remained doubtful about the direct impact of advertising on a book's sales, she did admit that advertising had an "enormous" indirect impact.

Lowell faulted Houghton Mifflin for catering to the popular novel and sacrificing those authors she thought more serious. Because the publisher's senior management believed that biography and history appealed to readers more than poetry, they did not include Lowell's books in their promotional trade shows. Nor did the company usually list her work among the popular trade titles, such as *Captain Blood*, by Rafael Sabatini, *Stella Dallas*, by Olive Higgins Prouty, or *Babbitt*, by Sinclair Lewis. Only Lowell's *Critical Fable*, an anonymously published work in which she invested nearly $4,000, made the company's trade list, and she had to pay the publisher to be included in its advertisement. Criticizing the weakness of Houghton Mifflin's general list, she wrote that "I cannot help feeling (and you will pardon my saying so), but I do think your firm has injured its prestige somewhat by publishing so great a number of cheap novels, and by letting so many of the better class of modern authors slip through their fingers."[117]

Claiming to be the "best-known poet" on the Houghton list, she set out to "obviate by advertising" the publisher's "failure" to include poets on its house list. She attempted to force booksellers to purchase titles outright rather than from publishers' representatives.[118] She explained, "Your theory that your salesmen are a great factor in the selling of poetry is . . . entirely wrong. Poetry must be treated quite differently from the way one would treat fiction. The advertising of poetry must reach the public directly, not indirectly through the bookseller, hence the stress which I feel sure should be laid upon advertisements in papers and magazines."[119]

Lowell also became dissatisfied with Houghton's "unfortunate" habit of reprinting a work without renumbering the edition. Leaving out the reprint number left the public with the "faulty impression" that the book did not sell quickly. According to Lowell, the public thought the publisher "still had copies of the first edition on hand." The perception of a surplus discouraged sales. To give readers the impression of high public demand, she wanted Houghton to try Macmillan's practice of publishing a limited edition, followed by short consecutive runs of several more limited editions, noting the number of the reprint on the title page.[120]

Lowell involved herself in every aspect of the publishing process including jacket design, typeface, point-of-sale display considerations, binding, and cutting. Addressing the matter of booksellers' displays with the publisher, she wrote, "People pick up a book from the counter, run through it, and when they find the pages uncut, their interest is not sufficient to carry them along. . . . they [Doubleday Page] have chopped off its eyelids and its hands. The space between the running title and the top of the page should be the same as in my other books, and the margins at the outside and inside should also be the same."[121]

Lowell took sole responsibility for the editorial process, poring over every comma and letter in the proofs. She chided the publisher's failing: "Flint and Mrs. Aldington are very particular about not having anything capitalized just because it is the beginning of a line. They have both written me about this with some feeling, so that if the ends of the lines are capitalized, they will just have to be changed back again, that is all. I remember that your printer had an awful time getting it into his head last year, so would you jog his memory again?"[122]

Lowell informed the publisher from the beginning that in her they had not only a poet, but also an advertiser. She spoke by telephone or corresponded with her publisher once or twice a day—in slow periods, weekly. She wrote, edited, and rewrote her own advertising copy. On various occasions, she denounced her publisher's "sentimental" advertising as "amateurish." Although she acknowledged it might "affect" readers, she thought the use of the phrase "attractive volume" sounded "cheap and department store-y."[123] She wrote, "The title of the book was not large enough to make an impression on people's minds. . . . I would suggest that we either begin with your colophon, and right under it, 'A New Book by Amy

Advertising Poetry as a Visual Art, 1912–1922

Lowell,' in slightly smaller print than that in which it now appears, enabling it to go right across the page; and then put [the titles] in the same type . . . followed underneath by the two quotations. . . . I think we want to get the name of the book into people's minds now in this third advertisement very strongly."[124]

Houghton Mifflin covered manufacturing costs, including shipment of the printed sheets, to be folded and bound in London, but Lowell paid a flat fee to reimburse the publisher for the publishing costs. They asked her for prompt payment, writing, "Since the account represents expenditures of our own now some months old, and it will be some months in the future before we begin to receive our cash returns from the book stores for the copies of the book sold to them, we should be glad, if entirely convenient, to have your check for this balance."[125]

Lowell covered promotion expenses, including the costs of free books distributed to critics, author's corrections, and the costs of replacing broken or battered type in second editions (about $40 to $70 per edition). She recommended that the publisher advise its printers to be cautious and "be sure and keep down the various leads which are sticking up all over." According to her initial contract with Houghton Mifflin, the publisher agreed to provide "group advertising free of charge" in five of Lowell's volumes and in the house's "New Poetry Series." Apparently, Lowell misunderstood her contract. She remained solely responsible financially for advertising the edition.[126]

Although Houghton gradually assumed partial costs after 1920, Lowell continued to cover the promotional expenses for her own books and for the imagist anthologies. The cost of placing advertising in magazines ranged from $75 to $230 per insertion, depending on circulation, although many small magazines simply charged what the traffic would bear. The *Poetry Review*, for example, with a circulation of three hundred, charged a higher rate than the *New Republic*, which had a circulation of five to ten thousand.[127] The publisher limited advertising expenses to $200 on an initial sale of 2,500 copies, the standard run for one of Lowell's works, although some titles sold substantially fewer copies. If the volume sold an additional 1,000 copies beyond the 2,500, then the company would

Advertising Poetry as a Visual Art, 1912–1922

spend an additional $100 on advertising. The author herself covered any promotion expenses beyond this amount.

Between 1915 and 1925, advertising rates skyrocketed. In 1915, *Poetry* charged $10 for a half-page advertisement. For forty lines of advertising copy, newspaper charges seemed affordable: the *Boston Transcript* charged $18; the *New York Times Book Review*, $28; and the *Chicago Evening Post*, $16. Within two years, newspapers doubled their charges: the *Boston Transcript* charged $27; the *New York Times Book Review*, $42; the *Chicago Evening Post*, $20; and the *Chicago News*, $41. Lowell reported paying $302.27 for advertising costs in 1917 for the imagist anthology, including composite or illustrated advertisements in the *Atlantic* and *Outlook* magazines (at $10 each), the *Nation* ($5), the *New York Tribune* ($4), and the *New York Evening Post* ($5). By 1925, prices had increased dramatically: for a full-page advertisement, the *Dial* charged $75, the *Bookman* $100, and *Harper's* $200; for a quarter page the *International Book Review* charged $115.[128] Lowell explained her rationale to the publishers as follows: "The *Atlantic* with its half-million readers, cannot, by any stretch of the imagination, be considered a 'highbrow' medium . . . we are advertising primarily for the person who would perhaps not read 'Legends' himself, but who might consider it as a gift to some person who is suspected of having an interest in poetry."[129]

By spring 1925, with advertising costs inflated and the price per volume for books relatively low, Houghton reported spending $3,181.70 to promote Lowell's two-volume critical biography of John Keats.[130] To get around the rates, publishers printed testimonials by critics and distributed them in brochures. Houghton printed fifteen thousand brochures at a cost of $540 for Lowell's *Legends* and offered to print additional ones at a reduced rate of $500 per ten thousand. This figure included order forms, envelopes, and the like, excluding postage. In 1920, Lowell's books sold for $1.75 per volume for current releases, a special of $2.00 for four earlier editions, and $3.50 for two volumes of her prose criticism.[131] The following year she ran a promotion for *Legends*. The publisher agreed to spend approximately $200 on advertising, more if sales were good. Lowell agreed to cover any additional costs, including printing the brochures. Houghton Mifflin's itemized expenses for *Legends* indicated the firm would pay more than $300 for advertising, a sum "considerably larger than the sales so far would normally justify." Lowell's advertising expenses came to an additional $600. She paid $250 to the publisher for including her book in the house list and $80 for "miscellaneous items," including announcements sent to booksellers.[132]

In order to promote the imagists in 1917, Houghton assigned the company's in-house advertising expert, a Mr. Linscott, who worked as a broker. Declaring himself "supremely interested in the Imagist movement," he advised Lowell to cut advertising costs, by using an "explanatory reading note" as the best style for advertising poetry. Linscott wrote to Monroe that "the reading public . . . is indifferent, or slightly prejudiced against Imagist poetry, and . . . will . . . simply ignore the usual advertisement. . . . a brief exposition of Imagism that will perhaps awaken the curiosity of a few of that strata of poetry buyers whose interest makes the difference between a sale of 500 and a sale of 10,000."[133] After the first four hundred copies of the imagist anthology for 1917 sold by early summer, Linscott advised Lowell to hold off advertising until fall, "when people returned from their summer houses" in the country and "library lamps are being lit again."[134] He offered other ideas, including rhymed trade letters he proposed to send directly to the booksellers. Lowell, however, feared this might lower her reputation rather than advance sales. With uncharacteristic understatement, she advised against it, explaining, "I think perhaps his technique is not quite up to that in the book, and I think it will probably hurt sales more to send out trade letters in rhyme than it would to send out trade letters in plain prose."[135]

By the end of the summer of 1916, the publisher's advertising broker managed to place notices in the *Dial*, the *New Republic*, *Seven Arts*, and the *North American Review*, getting a discount below the "card rate" that resulted in some saving. Linscott favored the printing and distribution of booklets and brochures. The company distributed more than ten thousand booklets in one year.[136] He advised Lowell, "Requests for the circulars are coming in very rapidly from booksellers and we have just had to go to press with an additional printing of 11,500 of which Putnam N.Y. will take 5,000 and the Bookshop for Boys and Girls in Boston 1500."[137] Lowell told him she thought writing about herself "a perfectly artificial thing to do." To use a phrase less than superlative about oneself she thought "a disgrace." She asked, "How much of one's own point-of-view can the public stand without reacting?"[138] Linscott replied, encouraging Lowell's idea of a publicity tour, including a stop at Wanamaker's in Philadelphia and their special display of her books for one week as "probably pretty good advertising."[139]

Lowell assumed the risk, but the rights to her works remained with the publisher, reverting to her only after a set time. The publisher received a 20 percent royalty on books she owned, more on those they owned. Houghton Mifflin received 15 percent of the net price from Blackwell's on English sales, although the American Macmillan had not claimed any royalties on her English sales, she explained.[140]

In the process of handling her own book promotion, Lowell became involved in commissioning favorable reviews from critics in newspapers to use as testimonials. Her motivation for controlling the critical reception of her work was financial. Pound had charged Lowell with being unladylike in her marketing prowess, a "hip-poetess." She solicited literary critics to write favorable reviews of her books, to be published in leading publications, including the *Smart Set*, the *Little Review*, the *New Republic*, the *Poetry Journal*, the *Poetry Review*, *Poetry*, the *Egoist*, and *Blast*. She routinely used excerpts from these reviews as testimonials in her newspaper advertisements, booklets, circulars, or handbills. She wrote to her publisher that "we will have a sham interview in which somebody will seem to have noticed the announcement in 'Who's Who.' . . . We will have a nice big interview with a picture, and the individual can talk to me about it, and by that process we will start something. I cannot write the interview myself for the simple reason that I have not the interviewer's touch. I think we shall have to let Mr. Linscott or somebody do it . . . see if you think it is a good method."[141]

She paid the critic Royal Snow $50 out-of-pocket for a favorable notice after advising Houghton that it "would be better if the idea seemed to originate" with the publisher rather than with the author. Linscott agreed. Lowell may have been impatient with her publisher, but she wrote directly to Snow inviting his comment and even suggesting what he ought to say. Cajoling him, she suggested that the review could provide an opportunity to promote his critical ideas on the Oriental influence in modern literature. She directed him to tie these ideas to her own Orientalism, and to the imagists' love of naturalism and the haiku. Snow's critical review provided the copy for popular promotional brochures distributed by Houghton Mifflin.[142]

With another critic she tried to manipulate the content of the review without guaranteeing acceptance. Lowell suggested that Houghton Mifflin would "be most likely to use" reviews that included sentiments declaring "no American writer in either poetry or prose" could match her "brilliant color effects," or the unmistakable, "weirdly beautiful work" in her volume of poetry, *Legends*.[143] She reported to her editor at Houghton Mifflin that Mark Van Doren in the *Nation*, Padraic Colum in *Freeman*, and Malcolm Cowley in the *Dial* had written favorable reviews of *Legends* in 1921. These reviews apparently surprised Lowell; they probably were unsolicited. After other unsolicited favorable reviews by D. H. Lawrence, Stephen Vincent Benét, and John Livingston Lowes, a professor, the author herself orchestrated with Houghton how to lay out and print excerpts to be reprinted in her advertisements. She wrote that "D. H. Lawrence should be in pretty big type . . . and 'Legends' very strong and big. . . . whatever you do, do not sacrifice Lawrence's remarks."[144] Rebuking the publishers over a misquotation of Lawrence's review, she wrote, "Did you notice that they misquoted Lawrence in the 'Times' advertisement? In the sentence '[It isn't a myth of the sun, it is something else] All the better that we can't say offhand what,' they left out the 't' and made it read, 'All the better that we can say offhand what,' which was perfectly awful. Please see that this does not happen again."[145]

Lowell spent additional time and money on promotional tours, speaking before literary and civic clubs, for as little as a $5 fee. Once she embarked on a campaign covering a three-state area, with ten lectures in six weeks. Following each lecture, she would sell (and proba-

Advertising Poetry as a Visual Art, 1912–1922

bly sign) copies of her books, which the publisher would ship to each location in advance. In 1922, she broadcast a twenty-minute radio presentation of her poetry, using the newspapers to get "quite a little" advance publicity for the shows, as she reported to the publisher.[146]

Lowell left Houghton Mifflin for Macmillan in 1914, dissatisfied with how they treated her work. By 1918, however, she had returned to Houghton. Then she tried to play one publisher off against the other to negotiate better contract terms, although it appears that they actually played her against her own best interests. On a number of occasions, she seems to have misunderstood her contract terms. Two years after publishing her first book with Houghton Mifflin in 1912, *Dome of Many-Coloured Glass*, Lowell notified the publisher that the plates had reverted to her as author, according to their contract. She had intended to hand the plates over to Macmillan, which would publish a second edition. Her second volume of poetry, already in press with Macmillan, would carry advertisements for the second edition of her first volume, because she believed that public demand would be stimulated by the appearance of new editions of her work.[147] In switching back to Houghton Mifflin from Macmillan, Lowell reported she lost 10 cents a volume as a result of her misunderstanding the contract terms.

On those early books, *Dome* and the *Imagist Anthologies*, which Lowell wholly owned, according to her contracts, the publisher recovered 20 percent royalties. At a $2 average selling price, Houghton Mifflin would recover 40 cents, Lowell 80 cents. In her view, this compared unfavorably to the terms at Macmillan, where she would have recovered 25 percent on the net price after the bookseller's commission of 40 percent had been taken out. When Lowell asked Macmillan to lower its commission to a 20 percent royalty and the publisher refused, she returned to Houghton. In the contract they signed in 1917, the publisher set a 20 percent royalty based on the net; Lowell thought she had agreed to 20 percent of the gross, a blunder that resulted in "a heavy loss" of ten cents per volume. Once under contract again with Houghton, Lowell begged the publisher for more equitable terms. She complained, "Where I do all the pay-

Advertising Poetry as a Visual Art, 1912–1922

ing out you wish 20% for yourself," noting that Houghton could claim 15 percent on the books that it owned. The publisher stood firm on the original arrangement of a 20 percent royalty on the books Lowell owned and on an even royalty split on those the firm owned.

Costs for publishing Lowell's verse rose steadily over the 1915-to-1925 decade. The house justified its demands on the grounds that "more time is given to your books . . . than to any other books on the same volume of sale."6[148] In 1922, Lowell tried to renegotiate her contract. She used the expenses of her advertising and promotional tours to justify her claim for a greater royalty. She wanted to own all her books outright. She argued that "my method sells more books than yours does," and she wanted some compensation or financial recognition for the active marketing role she played in promoting her own books.[149]

The publisher wanted her to put up one-fourth or one-fifth of the estimated total cost of publishing the book "to cover expenses," with the understanding that the balance would be due on the completion of the work. Houghton suggested that Lowell pay $1,000 down with the balance due. In order for the publisher to realize a profit, her editor explained, "we would . . . defer the payment for the press work, paper and binding, as well as the advertisement until the date of the first copyright accounting . . . we do not charge you a fraction of a cent more for the press work, paper and binding of the books than we should charge ourselves for the same work . . . never be more than the 20% of the list price."[150] Lowell recommended that the publisher raise the price of her books. She reasoned that if her books sold for $10, she would get $4.50 instead of $4. If the publisher reduced its commission from 20 to 15 percent, after twenty-five hundred copies, she would recover her investment.

After more than a decade of publishing books with Houghton Mifflin, Lowell reported that she could barely make ends meet. Nevertheless, she admitted that although she "wanted money," she "wanted fame more."[151] She worried that as the publisher increased the price of her books, "nobody would buy them." Although her advertising costs remained steady, if the publisher raised the price per volume, she would incur more debt. Asking the publisher to settle for a lower profit margin, she requested a larger royalty: "At the old

Advertising Poetry as a Visual Art, 1912–1922

rate, I found that I had to sell six editions to make any book begin to pay. . . . I shall never be able to make the books pay for themselves . . . it is impossible, you can see it yourself."[152]

The pressure to meet advertising expenses on slim royalties motivated Lowell to become a popularizer of her own works. From producing the *Imagist Anthologies*, she moved on to anthologizing poets' critical opinions, and then into textbooks. She thought being familiar to schoolchildren was one avenue to becoming a household word. In a volume of opinions by artists about modernism, *Tendencies in American Poetry*, Lowell enlisted poets to comment about trends and directions in order to "define" the movement. The six British and American poets she invited to comment, whose work had been published in the anthologies, represented "only a fraction" of the whole of the imagists, Lowell insisted. She wrote to Houghton, "My things are a little over the heads of the public, and I think anything that tends to make me a household word will help the books in the end."[153]

By promoting imagism as popular poetry, Monroe, Pound, and Lowell helped create a literary culture in which common readers accepted modernism as a bridge between the ordinary and the aesthetic. Imagists accepted the ordinary life as poetic in various degrees. Monroe and Lowell accepted their material universe and the limitations of art by commercial life; Pound fought the plausible and mundane, struggling abroad to shield himself against whatever was grubby or prosaic. By creating an increasingly dense fabric of meaning, he expressed more than resentment for his audience. He created a poetic language so ideogrammatic that few could follow him, even if they had cared. Finally, one might suggest, even Pound lost track of what he meant; for the last ten years of his life, he ceased to speak at all. Pound may have abandoned the romance of the studio, but he could hardly be said to have accepted the role of the poet in the marketplace as a competitor with other modern language trades. Nor could he come to terms with a literary economy in which the reader rather than the critic was a stakeholder. Monroe, Pound, and Lowell were realists, tied to their sense that the value of the common was the link between readers and literary modernism. Romanti-

Advertising Poetry as a Visual Art, 1912–1922

cizing the uncommon, the idea of an artist as the essence of individualism, proved his undoing. Rooted in the material objects and grounded in public appeal common to advertising, imagism laid the philosophical groundwork for readers to take seriously the fictions of public culture—those that created believable images.

Advertising Poetry as a Visual Art, 1912–1922

★

RECUTTING

·

MONOTYPE'S

·

ENGLISH

·

FACES

·

1922–1932

The mental eye focuses through type and not on it.
—Beatrice Warde, "Printing Should Be Invisible"

The monopoly that Monotype's English family of faces enjoyed in the global market for commercial and book printing for several generations during the interwar years was the result of its marketing and publicity operations as much as its innovative designs. Between 1922 and 1932, Monotype's innovations succeeded in modernizing typeface classics for use in commercial and book printing.[1] Between 1926 and 1969 the American-born Beatrice Warde was Monotype's publicist. She worked with the printing historian and typographic designer Stanley Morison, and together they were responsible for British advances in linking typefaces with a national identity campaign for a corporate entity. She observed that the integration of manufacturing and product design, or what she called "print planning," would become "more important than the self-expression of any single artist or the wonders of new machinery."[2] The Monotype name, originally associated with the machine compositor "designed

as a type, lead and rule caster," gained a global reputation during the
1920s not only as a brand, but also as the modern way to manage
print by publicizing its uses.[3]

THE COMPANY'S CHIEF PUBLICISTS

Although Monotype in Britain and Linotype in the United States became competitors almost immediately, the two companies began as
one firm.[4] While the Americans at Linotype in Philadelphia devoted
themselves to improving machinery invented by the founder, Tolbert Lanston, the British considered the machine compositor he dis-
played at the 1893 Columbian Exposition obsolete by 1898.[5] Re-
vamping existing machinery to suit its innovative typeface
specifications, Monotype enlarged its worldwide market for new
typefaces in non-English languages throughout the globe.

The American company did not lack design talent. As art director for Lanston, Frederic Goudy did create a diverse product range,
but a number of talented designers and publicists gave the British
a competitive advantage. The English Monotype brand name appeared on typefaces, typecasting, and typesetting systems developed in nearly every world language. Between 1903 and 1913, Monotype boasted that twenty-seven governments used its products. A
slight size modification in type sizes meant that the Philadelphia
branch could not exploit the British talent for type design to develop
its own domestic markets.

Beatrice Warde, or "B.W." as she was known by her colleagues
and friends in the trade, observed that the company histories of English Monotype and American Linotype illustrated how Britain and
the United States differed in their thinking about the printing industry.[6] Whereas the British tended to regard printers as craftsmen, she
wrote, the United States public considered printers to be working
class, with little interest in the arts. She observed that what the British referred to respectfully as a "printing house," the Americans referred to as a "plant."[7] From the viewpoint of an expatriate, she
wrote that the British considered printers craftsmen who belonged
to an "aristocracy of skill" that put them above the "scramblers" in
the rough and tumble of market competition.[8] She concluded that
the British may have made too much of the printer as a craftsman,

Recutting Monotype's English Faces, 1922–1932

Eric Gill, baker's label, London, ca. 1925.
Courtesy of the John Johnson Collection, Bodleian Library, Oxford University.

but the American public erred by making too much of the printer as a technician. In the American printer Daniel Berkeley Updike's view, Americans "resented experts" at the same time that they liked to "secretly" believe themselves experts."[9] New technologies meant, of course, new applications and new opportunities for mavericks calling themselves experts. From one side, printers felt themselves pressured by the maverick designers in the advertising sector; from another side, they felt the pressure of increasing professionalism within the trade itself.

In order to compete successfully with maverick experts housed in the new-style amalgamated publicity agencies that became popular after the turn of the century, printers needed a language in which to tell customers about which styles they should use and what effects they might expect from employing certain displays or specific types of ephemera as part of an integrated publicity campaign. The question of the relative effectiveness of styles and various vehicles for public persuasion remained for many an unimaginable horizon. The concept of human potential dominated the language of the business world as it did that of social critics. In the post–arts-and-crafts typographic era, the artist became a systematizer, one who integrated human potential for responsiveness to design with form and function.[10] Print planners like Beatrice Warde tried to integrate design and production on the factory floor, balancing word and image in innovative typography where public letters functioned as a symbol that potentially could address the collective psyche of the common reader.[11] At the same time, modern management experts developed theories about the effective functioning of human beings in work environments as if they, too, could be controlled for maximum efficiency like the new machinery. Human-motion studies, crowd psychology, and public-opinion engineering achieved a quasi-scientific dimension. Similarly, printing experts developed theories that approached print planning as if the public would react en masse in a predictable fashion, and they were eager to experiment by introducing innovative designs to the commercial world.[12]

Beatrice Warde often lectured about printing in art schools and apprenticeship programs. On one occasion she explained that the public "uses" print by looking at it. When talking about the "design of" a piece of printed matter, she went on, saying that printers should think about how the reader would see it, and about "how it 'works' at the moment when it is delivering its message to the sort of reader to whom it is addressed." She concluded that "just as the manager knows how to plan, organise and co-ordinate men and machines with his eye on 'delivering the job,' so the designer has to know how to plan with his eye on "delivering the message."[13]

British printing houses and American plants responded to the newly recognized importance of the advertising expert in graphic arts by creating positions within firms for "art directors" who wore more than one hat. To compete with printers, advertising agents learned the technology of the new improvements in printing. Warde conceded that "it must be admitted that the advertiser is nowadays somebody to be recognized in the printing world."[14] As a print publicist, for example, B.W. functioned in the Monotype corporation as a commercial message designer; distribution and dissemination manager; and as a writer, scholar, and editor of numerous articles in trade journals and in house organs, newsletters, and the like whose purpose it was to promote the brand through the product. Her contemporaries in the trade seemed to agree that she wore all these hats with equal verve.

B.W.'s first job in the trade was working for Henry Lewis Bullen, a self-described "veteran publicist in matters typographical," in the library of the American Type Founders Company (ATF) in 1921.[15] A pioneer in print publicity, Bullen waged one of the first successful marketing strategies for a typeface family, an 1897 campaign for a "slow-selling, cumbersome book face" called Old Style no. 1 in America and Old Face in England.[16] Bullen renamed the face Caslon Old Style, and he demonstrated that it could be used both for advertising and book composition. Having repositioned it, he pronounced Caslon Old Style "a best seller of the first class."[17]

Bullen regarded press agents and publicists for printers with healthy suspicion, even though he counted himself among them. He declared that a "new field has unfolded itself to the advertising managers of the composing machines."[18] Like neophytes in true missionary spirit, he condescended, most print publicists seemed unaware that the innovations in printing had been going on for centu-

Recutting Monotype's English Faces, 1922–1932

≡≡≡≡If you look after
truth and goodness . . .

BEAUTY
LOOKS AFTER
HERSELF

so in these collected papers

ERIC GILL

discusses the truth and goodness
of a number of different things, such as Industrialism,
Clothes, Modern Architecture, Philosophies of Art, the carving of stone,
Lettering, and Repository Art. Published by Sheed & Ward at 7s 6d.

ON SALE HERE≡≡≡

"Beauty Looks . . ." Eric Gill broadside for bookseller's window
advertising Gill's book (London 1933), probably printed by
Hague & Gill, Pigotts, High Wycombe. Black and blue
Gill Sans lettering on yellow paper (11¹/₂" by 15¹/₂").
Courtesy of the John M. Wing Collection, Ransom Papers, Newberry Library.

ries.[19] In Bullen's view, a grasp of printing history was a printer's asset, made more valuable because such knowledge was uncommon. He believed that press agents who were responsible for managing reputations of individual graphic artists ranked lower than those who managed a brand. He acknowledged that publicity in the modern printing industry would be "a necessary evil caused by the increasing competition from advertising," particularly from those posing as experts, who knew little if anything about printing history.[20] Further, as he observed, the dominance of one style over another undermined the printing industry's growing professionalism.

Even as a Barnard College undergraduate, B.W. had demonstrated an instinct for publicity. She wrote to her mother that she spent her "first earnings" on a self-portrait postcard, in which she posed in bib overalls with a straw hat. She was a young, impressionable devotee of poetry, calligraphy, and modern dance when she went to work for Bullen in 1921 within days after her graduation from Barnard. When Bullen hired her at ATF, she was a young woman in need of a career: she lacked the talent though not the training for a career in poetry and did not want to work in the shadow of her mother, a well-known New York *Herald Tribune* journalist. The same year, B.W. married the type designer Frederic Warde and, although their marriage lasted only five years, the Wardes shared a lifelong commitment to the printing industry. When the marriage ended in 1926, B.W. said she regretted that she "was no Mrs. to my Mr. Warde."[21] She adopted a pseudonym, Paul Beaujon, for her trade articles because "there was one Warde already" in the printing business and "nobody at that time had any idea that a woman could possibly know anything about printing."[22] One might well argue that B.W.'s greatest triumph professionally was in creating for herself and in selling others on an image of printing as a "class" trade in which a woman with some sense of style and élan could be in business. Still, the printing trades in Britain, where she spent her career, as well as in the United States, remained a man's world.[23]

B.W. felt fortunate to work as the ATF assistant librarian for Bullen, who allowed her adequate leisure to browse among the fourteen thousand volumes in the company's technical library on printing.[24] She admired James Thorpe's book *Printing for Business*, say-

Recutting Monotype's English Faces, 1922–1932

ing it was the first "important" volume about commercial printing styles she remembered reading.[25] While absorbing a great deal from reading, she discovered that the ATF position provided a "foot in the door" in other ways. Bullen suggested to her that anyone who unraveled the mystery surrounding the history of the ATF Garamond face (a design he suspected had been attributed incorrectly to a sixteenth-century printer) would "make a great reputation." So she directed her first scholarship accordingly. When she solved the Garamond mystery on a visit to the British Museum by discovering a page (by Jean Jannon of Sedan, France) containing the Garamond face, her career as a printing historian was launched. As she later retold the story, she had been in London at the time, preparing an article for the *Fleuron* magazine. Taking an overnight train to Paris, she consulted the full text in the Mazarine Library and rewrote her article, which was already in press. The result made a significant impact on the printing trade: the German audience of the *Fleuron* demanded a translation,[26] and the Monotype corporation offered Paul Beaujon an opportunity to work as editor of the company magazine, the *Recorder*. When B.W. accepted the offer and turned up in London on the company doorstep "to the petrifaction of the Monotype executives," who had been expecting a man, she enjoyed their surprised faces.[27]

More a gifted verbal communicator than a historian, she preferred the publicist's role and, once established in business, seldom took up the scholar's pen. In taking commercial printing seriously, however, she observed how the split between "the 'art' people and the 'business' people and the 'technical' people" seemed to cause real problems for the industry.[28] Throughout her successful forty-year career as a publicist for Monotype, she attempted to bring together the artistic and business elements of the trade. She cautioned that forces of market competition should motivate printers to learn more about both business and art, lest they run the risk of reducing printing to a service, where they offered advice about styles rather than manufacturing expertise.[29]

According to trade historians, English Monotype initially had produced an undistinguished set of seven typefaces before Stanley Morison and Beatrice Warde developed the company's family of faces in the 1920s. One face, called Imprint—designed by Gerard Meynell, J. H. Mason and Edward Johnston in 1912—launched a new trade journal of the same name. Despite a good trade reputation, however, the innovation failed to stir the public, as it too closely resembled the dense, gray pages many readers associated with book composition.[30]

The success of English Monotype's family of faces came about through the combined inventive genius of several people, and the publicity talents of Beatrice Warde. Among those influential in the growth of an innovative company, Morison had worked on book design at the Pelican Press, and he brought that style to Monotype. Founded by Gerard Meynell, Pelican became associated with the use of flowers and printer's devices. Pelican's contribution to the industry was not in its decorative use of typographic elements, though; it was in a new style of publicity.

Together, Morison and Meynell developed a new way of marketing Pelican books. Between 1911 and 1916, they established a close collaboration between the Monotype Corporation and the Pelican Press. Morison later wrote that Monotype produced the faces, but Pelican had "shown the way they could be used." Meynell described the *Fleuron* style of advertising Morison had devised as a "special type of publicity" linking historical and aesthetic "dissertations" with "self-praise."[31] Apparently Meynell had learned the blend of history and hyperbole from Oliver Simon, who edited the short-lived but distinguished *Fleuron*, which Stanley Morison took over in the early 1920s. When Morison joined Monotype in 1922, he developed the Pelican and *Fleuron* advertising styles—a "combination of instruction, demonstration and promotion" based solidly in historical interpretations of classical forms repackaged for the modern reader.[32]

When Morison and B.W. began to collaborate they expanded his plan to develop a family of faces for Monotype, tying the dissemination of well-designed printing to the idea of educating printers about the history of the classical faces many routinely employed. In publications distributed by the company, they wrote about printing history as part of an integrated educational campaign designed to make the common reader aware of the background of typesetting. Mono-

Recutting Monotype's English Faces, 1922–1932

type specialized, according to the advertising copy drafted by Morison, in historical recuttings and modernizing classical typefaces. Issuing its first example, Series 1, in 1900, the company subsequently released others: Modern 1 and Modern 7 were nineteenth-century faces recut in 1900 and again in 1902; 1900 Old Style was a refashioned 1858 face; a Plantin recut in 1913 originated with Claude Garamond in 1530; in 1915 a Caslon was a refashioning of an early eighteenth-century face (ca. 1734); Scotch Roman, recut in 1906 and then again in 1920, originated in 1812; and Bodoni, the well-known eighteenth-century face, also acquired a modern look.[33] Every printed word competed in the mass market according to its own distinctive "personality" and styling in language goods and commodities, including a modern feel for history.

Durability, the notion that certain products could be used repeatedly until they wore out, once served as a goal for manufacturers of type. Yet durable type fonts became less desirable than persuading an existing buyer to "scrap and replace" broken type when manufacturers discovered how to stimulate the market for nondurable goods by emphasizing style. Obsolete faces and broken type could be melted down and recast into more modern style.[34] In fact, there were print publicists who made a case for some print designs becoming obsolete.

B.W. called the idea of increasing sales by a forceful campaign of propaganda the "gospel of effectiveness" in print. Through promotional campaigns, she promised she could "stimulate a 100 percent increase in orders in a very short time."[35] Marketing a variety of typefaces with different personalities and styles struck some type designers as gratuitous. Designers such as William Addison Dwiggins or Eric Gill, for example, considered themselves more artists than tradesmen.[36]

By creating a new language to explain why printers should scrap obsolete or old-fashioned typefaces and replace them with newer ones, publicists created an ongoing need to communicate about the latest styles and products and how to use Monotype's innovative products. B.W. declared in an advertisement that "the printer, approaching his customer with the message SCRAP OBSOLETE PRINTING AND REPLACE WITH EFFECTIVE TYPOGRAPHY is as likely as not to be

McKnight Kauffer advertisement, ca. 1930.
Courtesy of the John Johnson Collection, the Bodleian, Oxford University.

met by a typographic enthusiast who will ask the most searching questions. If such a printer is not genuinely expert in these matters, his well-meaning efforts will be ignored and he will be told to confine himself to following the layout with rigid obedience, using the specified materials, and exercising his own private judgment in exactly one matter, namely the price to be paid!"[37]

Warde and her contemporaries, Morison and Eric Gill at Monotype and Hans Schmoller at Penguin, among many others, embraced the functionalist values of Jan Tschichold's New Typography of the Bauhaus, which emphasized utility and legibility. Under Tschichold's definition of functionalism, each letter acquired a social and political dimension in the context of the function of the whole page and the printed document. A celebration of the modern engineer, functionalism expressed a high regard for the social value of all printing, even ephemera. Tschichold maintained that printed texts of all types, whether they delivered commercial messages, reported news, or related fictional or historical narratives, had an inescapable social function. Letters that carried such aesthetic portent should be realistic. Photographic images belonged in Tschichold's typographic universe, too, as did all printed symbols: signs, lines, and bars. By readability, Tschichold meant legibility. Through their daily encounters with routine commercial printing, common readers would become so accustomed to seeing fine printing in public places that they would begin to demand the same from all printed goods, even from books. The term *readability* meant more than simply being able to make out the words on a page; it admitted that the effect of letter-face style and page composition, as well as the content of the language, included a psychological dimension.

THEORIES AND PRINCIPLES OF PRINT STYLE

Sir Cyril Burt conducted studies on the psychological impact of typographic style. Although the invalidity of his data later discredited him, B.W. thought his conclusions held a resonance for the marketing initiatives at Monotype. Burt wrote that legibility equaled ease of reading, and the accuracy and speed of reading letters, which he measured by eye movements. A child psychologist, he belonged to an investigating committee of the British education establishment

formed in 1912 to study the impact of schoolbooks on children's eye-
sight. The study concluded that for children under twelve, an old-
style serifed typeface seemed best, but for older readers, a ten- or
eleven-point-size modern face with two-point leading appeared to
be more readable. Burt's responsibilities included a series of experiments in the classroom and laboratory. The results, published in
1917, contained a "tabulated set of standards showing the size of
type and style suited to pupils of different ages," and this formed a
basis for later investigation. Weighing a range of influential factors,
Burt declared "serifed letters more legible than unserifed" for reading purposes and the sans serif better for short numbers than for
long. "Above all, psychologists have so often pointed out, the serifs
are not merely decorative. They correct the effect of irradiation ('visual spread'); and in any passage of consecutive print, they contribute towards 'the horizontal movement of the eye' (or rather of the
attention), and help in combining separate letters into distinctive
word-wholes."[38]

Measures of readability tested such factors as leading, interlinear
spacing, and margin size; old versus modern letter form; serifed
with ascenders and descenders, tails, and nibs, versus sans serif; the
undecorated and unadorned stroke; whether the thickness or boldness of the letters aided legibility or contributed to eyestrain, or
whether the space between the thick verticals or thin curves and
slanting strokes confused or wearied the eye.[39]

Burt tried to learn what particular qualities made different kinds
of typefaces attractive to different kinds of publics and concluded
that typography held strong implications for psychosomatic study:
"The introspective data obtained during our experiments on typographical preferences disclose a highly complex motivation—the
customary reading and the cultural interests of the reader playing an
unexpectedly important role. . . . the same motivational types as
. . . the appreciation of colours, pictures, and musical chords."[40]
By testing accuracy and speed of reading, eye movements, blinking,
and eyestrain, Burt found that effectiveness in typeface design resulted from an integration and interaction among several factors,
and assessments made on just one characteristic in isolation could be
highly misleading.

Recutting Monotype's English Faces, 1922–1932

Golden Cockerel Press prospectus, 1933, Waltham, Saint Lawrence, Berkshire,
England (Robert and Moira Gibbings, proprietors). Generally regarded as
the epitome of the finest in private-press craftsmanship, the eight-page
brochure solicited reader subscriptions of books in preparation.
Courtesy of the John M. Wing Foundation, Ransom Papers, Newberry Library.

According to Burt's theories, it seemed as if readers' "half-unconscious" aesthetic preferences could be divided into camps, between those who liked the calligraphic old style of script and those who liked the modern square letter forms with architectural origins. Burt observed that although printers, sculptors, architects, painters, and engravers had for generations applied their skills to type design, the need for modern advertisers to take into account the psychological impact of typography on common readers raised his inquiry from a purely academic level to a practical, even utilitarian one for the marketing department at Monotype.[41] In any event, Beatrice Warde saw great potential for the rationale of mass-market display type in Burt's theories.

Both Burt and Tschichold had the reader's comfort in mind. So, too, did the print publicists. The design ideal that used the medial axis (as in the traditional title pages of books) created what Tschichold called a "restful" visual experience for the individual reader in the privacy of a personal library. Tschichold's New Typography advocated principles of "designed unrest" that used "every manner of plane relationship and every direction of line" to create harmony and a visual economy according to the "swift tempo of modern business" that the common reader would find familiar, in public spaces, on billboards and commercial packages.[42] Tschichold called these ideas more "anti-traditional" than "nontraditional." He intended that printers and designers use every traditional as well as nontraditional face available, and every process of the new technology.[43] The modern look, he argued, resulted from an impression made by machines that could equal the aesthetic finesse of the artist. He also believed that machine-set pages were superior to hand-set type composition, and that machine-made paper represented an improvement over handmade paper, photographs over drawings, and photo process blocks over woodcuts.

According to Tschichold, the printer ought to embrace the "whole domain of printing." His principles of legibility contrasted advertising and book typography from the producer's as well as the readers' standpoint. New Typography advocated the geometric and harmonious ordering of surface and text and used all new technologies, including the conjunction of illustration and text in the typo-

Recutting Monotype's English Faces, 1922–1932

photo. The typophoto or collage, which mixed images and words in an integrated design representing a "breakdown of inhibitions," or the pure demonstration of psyche. The superimposition of photography over typography is a style also found in cubist paintings, imagist poetry, and the surrealist book. Color used to "heighten" or "tone down" the effects of type, not to beautify but to enhance the psychophysical properties of the printed product, he thought equally important. Tschichold concluded that "beautiful" typography could never be "new" if it sacrificed purpose to form: that is, if the form of the product exuded novelty or eccentricity for the sake of sheer artistic expression instead of its function or the common utility of its design.[44]

Although subsequently there was a debate over the extent of Tschichold's immediate influence, the scholar Ruari McLean concluded that the functionalist principle "had an immediate effect and was widely discussed: every compositor in the country learned the name Tschichold." B.W.'s colleague John Tarr, who directed the Monotype Corporation's training program during the 1920s, thought differently. According to Tarr, so few people knew about or understood Tschichold's ideas that his principles had less impact on Anglo-American typography generally than on post-Bauhaus Germany. Rather than the plain, readable face that he had intended to advocate, Tschichold's name became "synonymous with eccentric" typography.[45]

Further, Tarr's somewhat chauvinistic assertion that Monotype's innovations between 1929 and 1931 had restored "common sense" and "revolutionized" British job printing raises some doubts about his objectivity.[46] The Monotype Corporation's introduction of the Sans by Eric Gill and Times New Roman by Stanley Morison illustrates the company's convictions about the look of the new typography if not its adherence to every principle. Monotype's innovative designs and promotions suggest that the company did have an impact on the public eye. Although Tschichold's principles may not have been as influential as McLean implied, Morison and others at Monotype embraced his functionalism not only in principle, but also in the practice of its ideals. An industrial style contributed to

Recutting Monotype's English Faces, 1922–1932

McKnight Kauffer's illustration for "Marina," a two-page poem by T. S. Eliot, printed by the Curwen Press, London, 1930, bound in blue boards and signed by Eliot. A limited edition of 400 was printed. (No. 29 of the Ariel Poems*).*
Courtesy of the John M. Wing Collection, Newberry Library.

the public's sense of collective social reality, an ideal world in which the role of the common reader figured largely.

Morison's 1930 manifesto first published in his *Britannica* essay and later revised for the publication of the seventh volume of the *Fleuron*, as "First Principles of Typography," rephrased the assertions originated by Tschichold: Utility and permanence constitute the central value of typography. Type could be said to possess social utility, to the extent that it was readable. Although a certain flair might be allowed the publicist or propaganda writer, type should be without artistic pretense. Morison wrote in his statement of principles that "typography may be defined as the craft of . . . controlling the type so as to aid to the maximum the reader's comprehension of the text. . . . any disposition of printing material which . . . has the effect of coming between the author and reader is wrong." He argued that "dullness and monotony" were preferable to "typographical eccentricity or pleasantry." Although printing for commerce would be compelled to become innovative in order to remain "fresh," according to Morison, he declared that the typography of books had to "obey convention," "not only be good in itself—but good for a common purpose."[47] Morison urged printers not to relax their "zeal for the reader's comfort" or to sacrifice the public interest in their efforts to be called artists. Good public design in modern printing, Morison argued, would have to be rooted in historical form and display its modernity so subtly that "only very few recognise its novelty."[48] The commercial sans serif, admirable in its plainness, did not command the high regard generally bestowed on more literary-style typefaces.

Beatrice Warde's functionalist principles differed from Morison's only in her appreciation of the greater impact of image and sound on readers, and in her acceptance that these dimensions of public language would define them in the marketplace. She outlined her own typographical principles in her numerous articles in trade journals and her speeches, later collected in *The Crystal Goblet*. Her principles reiterated those of Morison and Tschichold on the value of utility, permanence, and readability. Although not original, she captured the popularity of these ideas as the trade accepted them at the time. She wrote that

Recutting Monotype's English Faces, 1922–1932

midway in the fifteenth century came the printing-press and the whole notion of the "Edition," or mass-producing identical copies corrected in advance. Now within our lifetime has appeared a new kind of scroll, not yet recognized as such or thought of [as] a "real book" by anyone. It is a tightly-wound reel of celluloid film printed with innumerable pictures, and we may recognize in it, for good or evil, the first fully-mechanized book. . . . It does do much that the conventional book does, in the way of communicating ideas, but it almost wholly eliminates that need to co-operate by a conscious effort of will which characterizes "reading," i.e., decoding arbitrary symbols such as the letters of the alphabet. Reading is a kind of performance, involving skill and familiarity. The present and future generation of book readers will be accustomed from childhood to being "read to out loud"—by the radio and by that cinema machine which mechanically does the "performing" (nearly the equivalent of reading) as its wheels turn.[49]

For the successful publicist, the best typography functioned as "invisibly" as a window between the reader outside the text and the landscape of language created by the message, news, fiction, or history that constituted text.

Comparing the printed page to a stained-glass window, B.W. observed that intricate patterns might provide a rich, superb, even baroque texture. Yet printing needed to be "looked through" rather than "looked at."[50] The complexity of modern life demanded clarity and translucence in public printing, she believed, although too often modern typography appeared to be more like the window in which "the glass is broken into relatively small leaded panes," distorting meaning and message delivery by an "arbitrariness" or "excess of color."[51] In her view, anything that interfered with the readers' "mental picture" of the text constituted poor planning. She wrote that "the running headline that keeps shouting at us, the line that looks like one long word, the capitals jammed together with hairspaces—these mean subconscious squinting and loss of mental focus."[52] Through her adaptation of the principles of Tschichold and Morison, Warde effectively marketed Monotype's innovations. She rephrased their principles as a publicist and delivered the message that typefaces worked for the good of the common reader, not just in the interest of the corporation.

Recutting Monotype's English Faces, 1922–1932

According to functionalism, printing should be a public service. Gratuitous decoration undermined the first principle of typographic organization, and the impulse to decorate should be resisted. Morison cautioned printers about the "safeguards" they might put up against "charges of monotony" that would lead them into twisting "the text into a triangle," or to "squeeze it into a box, torture it into the shape of an hour-glass or diamond," tricks of the late "revival of printing."[53] The balance between functionalism and beauty in commercial printing had been achieved by others, much earlier, of course, including Frank Pick and Edward Johnston, but it was in solving the tension between utility and legibility that Monotype found its niche.

In a volatile, rapidly expanding market driven by advertising, technology outdistanced developments in type design and marketing as well as in book typography. Book composition often required more than eight thousand punches of special types, including decorative ornaments. Newspaper typography, although less complex, presented similar challenges for readability and durability. The increased interest among readers in beautiful advertising led the *Times* and the *Manchester Guardian* to run special issues in 1912 and again in 1922 that served as models of newspaper readability, even down to 4-point type used for the classifieds.

A staunch defender of printing as a profession, B.W. advocated improvements in industrial education. She promoted Monotype's innovative products as one means to broader social goals. She argued that the printing trade should improve its social status as a public educator on the grounds that all classes of printed goods contributed to the general welfare by improving public taste. She purchased advertising space for Monotype products in national trade and popular periodicals to advance the cause of better printing. She entered into the debate on standardization just as Monotype's faces dominated the market for display type, using the common reader as a litmus test.[54] She wrote that "public interest is what maintains the level of design and production within the given style. The artist works to please himself, but the manufacturer who must compete on price sets his standards by what the public can stand."[55]

Recutting Monotype's English Faces, 1922–1932

THE MONOTYPE PROGRAM

The promotional techniques Meynell and Morison had perfected at Pelican helped Monotype launch "a programme" of typeface innovations based on historical models. Morison first presented his plan of producing a family of typographical designs, which involved substantial expenditures, to Monotype manager Harold Malcolm Duncan in 1922. He submitted a plan to develop and produce what he called "an extensive range" of typefaces for the firm's machinery. This program required support from prominent publishers before Monotype's management would agree that the plan seemed financially feasible, and the Cambridge University Press under Walter Lewis served as Morison's ally.[56] When Duncan promised to move forward with the plan, Morison accepted a position as typographical consultant and advisor to the company. Monotype's program of developing recognizable English typefaces modeled on historical letters in hand-set movable types progressed slowly, according to company reports: "Bread-and-butter Albions, Clarendons, Grotesques, Old Faces and Moderns" followed "Series 1," issued in 1900.[57]

As a result of Monotype's development of innovative product lines, British book publishers could cater to distinct periods of type taste, whether called "modern" or "old." Monotype issued a number of book faces for the Continent: Russian (Series 17) in 1907, Irish (Series 24) in 1903, German Fraktur (Series 28) in 1904, Greek (Series 90) in 1910, and Typewriter (Series 82) in 1911.

The publisher of Aubrey Beardsley's illustrated *Morte d'Arthur* (ca. 1893–94), J. M. Dent, designed a heavy Venetian fifteenth-century-style typeface in 1911 called Roman, which trade critics thought overwrought.[58] Although Beardsley's popular art-nouveau style leaned even further toward calligraphy than had William Morris's naturalism, Monotype responded with trade-oriented designs, satisfied that the public would demand spare, clean, unadorned faces.[59] Monotype's design of 1912 by J. H. Mason and Gerard T. Meynell, named for Meynell's short-lived but highly respected magazine, *Imprint*, attracted attention from printers and print buyers, not only to the Monotype brand but also to the idea of modern style

Recutting Monotype's English Faces, 1922–1932

Beatrice Warde as a Barnard College undergraduate, ca. 1920.
The future publicist had the self-portrait picture postcard made
"with her first earnings," she wrote to her mother.
Courtesy of Cambridge University Library.

in type design. B.W.'s publicity brochures touted Imprint as the "first original" book typeface to be designed specifically for mechanical composition that still kept the Kelmscott look of the hand press.[60]

As Monotype developed a program of recutting traditional letter forms to look modern, B.W. drew on the precedent set by Morison, Meynell, and Simon, but she developed her own distinctive style and reputation for a blend of scholarship, history, and publicity hype. The young, style-conscious publicist could look to Paris, Leipzig, Rome, and Moscow to learn about modernism in print styling from the avant-garde artistic revolutionaries. The American printing world seemed frumpy by comparison. As Morison pointed out, although the modern reader looked to art to "redeem" industrialism, earlier generations had tried to "crush" it.[61] Clearly Beatrice Warde liked to think she was making history if not redeeming it. She wrote about her own days at Monotype, that "the story [is one] of immense and irrevocable change which not only benefitted an industry [but] which made the printed word of the twentieth century look different and look better. That printer . . . publisher, designer or advertiser is fortunate . . . who can look back over the whole epoch of change and say: 'At this and that point, I played my part in the drama.' "[62]

Accepting the position as editor of the *Recorder* following Stanley Morison, B.W. developed Monotype's publicity plan for the program of a family of faces initiated by Morison in 1922. She managed the printing of traditional broadsides and specimen sheets, which she usually edited, wrote, and designed. Morison later concluded that these publications served as the progressive front for "the beginning of the new educational kind of publicity . . . an unprecedented step" which played an important role in the success of two print campaigns for London and North Eastern Rail and the London *Times*, respectively, both mounted by B.W. for Monotype.[63] She also "took over responsibility for the whole upper level of publicity and propaganda" for the company, mixing her historical research with an intuitive flair for hype.[64] Although popular biographers like to speculate that Warde and Morison were more than professional colleagues, Morison was a strict Catholic, whose manner people described as

Recutting Monotype's English Faces, 1922–1932

"Jesuitical." He had grounds for an annulment but did not seek one. Warde converted to Catholicism twenty years later, influenced by Eric Gill and by Morison. In any event, Warde and Morison remained lifelong friends, married to the same trade.

The *Recorder* editorship position offered Warde an ideal situation. The monthly giveaway house magazine provided a laboratory where she could play with her own ideas about typographic design and layout, debate the stylistic advantages of aesthetic avant-garde principles, and still reach a pragmatic audience.[65] Still in publication today, the *Recorder* remains the house organ of Monotype.

As editor, B.W. changed both the style and substance of the *Recorder*. Under Morison, the cover design had been a staid black-and-white filigree with ornamental borders designed by T. M. Cleland. The new editor's sense of style favored the bold, masculine, and imperious red-and-black flamboyance of the coat of arms of Cardinal Richelieu. She also developed the editorial content in more journalistic and critical directions, often using historical articles. B.W. changed the style of the Monotype house organ into one congenial to the trade but also with broader public appeal. Veiled advertisements for Monotype products appeared along with well-written critical and historical pieces. Although she advertised the *Recorder* in standard printing-trade journals and other nationally circulated industrial publications, "primarily as a means of creating a demand for more and better printing," the Monotype magazine did not carry advertising. Circulation figures are unavailable, but the *Recorder* masthead boasted that it appealed to all "users and prospective users" of the Monotype brand.[66] The publication probably enjoyed widespread British circulation with some distribution to the United States. B.W. issued special numbers of the *Recorder* to promote new products, exhibitions, and achievements as well as monthly newsletters of some typographic merit.

Beatrice Warde's best-known publication is a broadside. Indeed, she commented that she believed it would be "the thing to last" of all her writing. Reaching for an inspirational piece that printers would hang in their offices, and that would be patterned after the style of the popular calendars designed by advertising typographers, she drafted a manifesto-style specimen sheet that became so popular it was translated into some twenty-five languages, distributed world-wide, and adapted for propaganda purposes during the war.[67]

> This is a Printing Office
> Crossroad of Civilization
> Refuge of all the arts
> against the ravages of time
> Armoury of fearless truth
> against whispering rumour
> Incessant trumpet of trade
> From this place words may fly abroad
> Not to perish on waves of sound
> Not to vary with the writer's hand
> But fixed in time having been verified in proof.
> Friend, you stand on sacred ground
> This is a Printing Office.[68]

"Sacred ground" for Warde meant that printers ought to construct their present social status out of the fabric of their history and tradition, through typefaces and layouts relevant to the concept of a "working Democracy, which starts with Universal Literacy."[69]

Among the new technologies that extended its democratic reach, Monotype's Super Caster had a range of 251 characters with over-hanging strokes. With the powerful new machinery, Monotype cut Oriental and other exotic faces and concentrated on expanding its global market. Super Caster technology made possible the development of an interrelated group of no fewer than twenty-four varieties of designs comprising 235 fonts or sizes, "constituting a range unique in the trade."[70] With the Super Caster, display types could be blown up to seventy-two points, with variations of light, bold, and extrabold, condensed and extracondensed, and cameo and shadow. The larger sizes of Garamond, Baskerville, Cochin, Poliphilus, Lutetia, Fournier, and the new faces introduced exclusively for display purposes, including book jackets, the Albertus and Matura, sold well. The company developed an inventory of faces including Devengari, Tamil, Bengali, Gujerathi, and a variety of different Cyrillic, Arabic, Greek, and Hebrew fonts. As world markets

Recutting Monotype's English Faces, 1922–1932

for new typefaces developed in all languages, Monotype marketed the machinery to cast an unprecedented range and variety of type designs. The ideal of integrating type and print product design acquired a new legitimacy.[71]

GILL SANS

With its advanced Super Caster machinery, introduced in January 1929, Monotype launched two of the century's most influential national identity campaigns, one in 1929 for the London and North Eastern Rail system (LNER) using the Gill Sans typeface, and the other for the London *Times* in 1931. Sculptor and illustrator Eric Gill designed a 1928 version of Edward Johnston's 1913 type design commissioned by Frank Pick for the London Underground. The company named this face the Gill Sans. Initially, Frank Pick had used the 1913 design as "part of an overall Functionalist aesthetic policy" in the city transportation system. Pick had tried to build goodwill with customers through tasteful posters, beautifully designed by a number of American expatriate advertising artists, including McKnight Kauffer.[72]

Monotype's Gill Sans recut and repackaged the 1913 design, according to company literature. Gill's letters are formed along more architectural models, whereas Johnston's had been perfectly round, homey, even chubby when cast in a boldface, thick-line version. The Sans letter forms possessed classical architectural roots: Morison wrote that the original letter designs had been discovered on the cornerstones of ancient buildings in Greece and Rome. It's probably safe to say, though, that the same readers who accepted the plain-stroke, readable letter form as symbolic of modern commercial culture knew little about antiquity or neoclassicism and cared far more about current fashions and conventions. B.W. later concluded that the historical importance of the Gill Sans came from its being the first jobbing face to "challenge the German" reputation for inventiveness.[73]

At first Monotype could only offer the Gill Sans in capitals (Series 231). Then a lowercase alphabet (Series 262) followed, along with routine display and composition sizes. Subsequently Monotype developed other weights: Bold 272, Light 362, and display

Beatrice Warde, ca. 1928, as "Paul Beaujon,"
her pseudonym as a printing history scholar
and internationally respected trade writer.
Photograph courtesy of Alicia Street.

faces Cameo 233, Shadow 406, Bold Condensed titles, No. 1, and
Series 373. All these developments occurred rapidly. Eventually,
the Monotype Sans evolved into a family of seventeen related designs.[74]

Gill's next innovation, a relatively unpopular book face called Perpetua, took thirteen years to complete. Compared with the rapid
Sans development, the book face took twice as long as the display
face. The fact that Stanley Morison was developing his own design,
the "New Roman" face, at the same time may account for some of
the delay in producing Gill's Perpetua.[75] Trade critics judged Perpetua's "spindliness" and "delicacy" to be a "severe handicap" stylistically that made it too expensive to use.[76]

Warde, Gill, Morison, and others wanted to educate the public
about modern design through the use of historical type forms. The
company wanted to establish its identity through symbols. Morison
attempted to explain the tug and pull between the high aesthetic
aims of commercial art and the middle-market economic necessities
of having to attract a crowd to justify advertising expenditures. He
wrote that it would be a mistake to think that journalists' preference
for bold sans-serif letters came from a "concern for the proletariat,"
when, in fact, it came from the need to catch the eye of readers.[77]
He noted that the newspaper in the stall had to be visible to passers-
by against a welter of images that made up the surroundings. The
morning and evening news should have different looks, as Morison
observed: simply put, readers wanted to buy something familiar
yet fresh.

Morison called the sans serif the chief product of typographic
modernism. Widely used by mid-nineteenth-century advertisers because the plain form of the letters could be thickened or enlarged for
emphasis, the sans serif was thought by serious artists and the modern literati to be tainted by its long association with commercial
messages and advertising. The Sans face came to dominate the advertising industry so completely that there were critics who complained that modern printing suffered from "sansitis," which had become a formula, "an expensive word for rut."[78] Use of sans-serif
block letters in display advertising increased from not quite 10 percent of all goods produced in 1928 to nearly 60 percent in 1940; in

1953, the sans cornered 75 percent of the market, and by 1960, it dominated close to 87 percent, with twenty-two block-letter faces, "virtually indistinguishable" except for their various names. Every typefounder in France, Germany, Holland, and the United States offered some version of the character, while in Britain, "it was virtually all one face, not twenty-two," although Monotype's Super Caster technology had made modernization and refinements possible.[79]

Ruskin and Morris predicted that the modern forces of industrialism would undermine art. Yet during revolutionary movements in the twentieth century artists attempted to disseminate ideology to integrate industrial life within a society organized for the public good. When the sans serif dominated commercial letters, Morison thought that manufacturers of printed goods felt a social responsibility to integrate art and industry and redeem the mass market from its unlettered state.[80] The sans serif became synonymous in the public mind with publicity type. Its popular appeal lay in its timeliness and seeming contemporaneity rather than its history. Yet distinguished printing scholars like Morison found it necessary to use historical evidence to explain its development. Morison wrote, "The Bauhaus attitude towards the sans serif of John Nash in 1830, of Aubrey Beardsley . . . in 1893 and of Stefan George . . . in 1905 . . . [was] different from that of Wassily Kandinsky in 1924 and Paul Klee in 1925, and El Lissitsky in 1926. . . . the sans serif which began c. 1820 as a by-product of a gentlemanly survey of the monuments of ancient Greece, next adopted by advertisers because it was a novelty, used by engineers and draughtsmen because it was easily thickened, finally progressed to acceptance as a norm by artists and intellectuals."[81]

Although the mass market came to accept the sans-serif design as a convention of advertising, this followed initial resistance from the printing industry. Morison wrote that so widespread did the use of a sans-style typeface become that "the artistic forces in industry" tried to make it a book composition face; publishers wanted to use the upper- and lowercase versions of the letters in books. Serious authors and publishers of academic works and belles lettres objected to the use of sans in book production. Under her pseudonym, B.W.

Recutting Monotype's English Faces, 1922–1932

wrote that "a touch of unusualness, even of snobbishness, helps an advertising face; but it damns a book face, and it is by books and not by ephemera that future judges will assess the degree to which our printing reflects the use of our intelligence and how nearly our reading matter reflected the spirit of our times."[82] According to Morison, the serif or ornamental typefaces rather than the sans style continued to "monopolize the text of books intended as permanent possessions" or anything that was meant to be read more than once, despite the dominance of the sans serif in advertising.[83] The use of ornamental styles for books and plain style for advertising might signal a difference between the producers' perception of the common reader's intelligence and emotions. According to Morison, the book composition types seemed to value historical form, sometimes without regard for popular legibility, whereas the advertising or display types seemed enthralled by the idea of typographic freedom "proper to ephemeral matter addressed to the emotions" of the masses.[84]

The advertising boom of the early twenties precipitated an unprecedented demand for sans-style lettering of all types, sizes, and ranges. According to Morison, this brought printers more business than the "total sum" of "biblical, liturgical, literary, educational, journalistic, periodical, official or traditional media."[85] Advertising expenditures in the United States in the early 1920s, estimated to be about a third of that spent in Britain, may have been nearly $15 million annually.[86] Advertising images beckoned alluringly to consumers from packages, magazine pages, and posters in the London Underground. B.W. wrote that they "imperceptibly" educated the public eye "to look for grace and breeding and proportion in printed matter" by innovative marketing and advertising schemes for the family of faces.[87] The character, size, and what was called the personality of letters used on transport signs, newspapers, railroad schedules, menus, and souvenirs recut and recast to suit modern tastes resulted from what the publicist called "a more respectful attitude" toward the common reader.[88] Yet mass production seemed to threaten what B.W. had called "leaving the artist out."[89] The Monotype firm positioned itself in the debate about the competitive values of public utility, artistic individuality, and engineering genius as an advocate of "integrated design," the planning of aesthetics prior to

Recutting Monotype's English Faces, 1922–1932

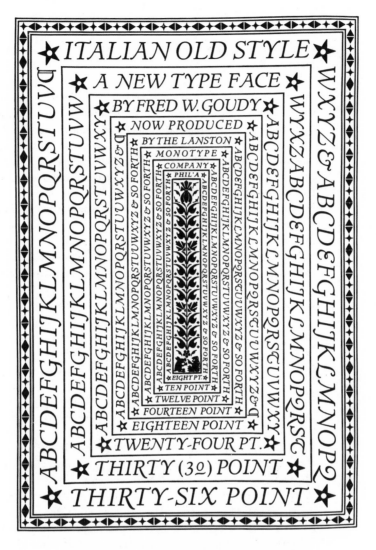

*Lanston Monotype advertisement, Philadelphia, ca. 1926,
for Frederic Goudy's Italian Old Style. Designed and printed by
Bruce Rogers's Rudge Press, Mount Vernon, New York. Rogers used
traditional lettering in an innovative fashion; 11,600 copies were
printed to publicize Goudy's face for the American branch of Monotype.*
Courtesy of John M. Wing Foundation, Ransom Papers, Newberry Library.

manufacturing, taking the customer's needs into account before production began.

Monotype unveiled the updated Gill Sans typeface to the printing industry at the 1928 Federation of Master Printers' conference in Blackpool, a meeting Beatrice Warde described as "a gorgeous row, fought out in high good humour for the most part."[90] Attendance figures for the conference have not been found, but eight thousand master printers belonged to the organization at the time.[91] Two specimens of the Sans typeface used for routine publications at the meeting created a storm of controversy. The first one, the conference program, stirred the Congress. It was designed by Stanley Morison and Beatrice Warde "in a deliberately anti-conventional style" in a bold Gollanz-yellow. Then there was a red-line, black-letter publicity brochure titled "Publicity and Selling" (possibly designed by B.W.) with a two-page program insert, "The Two Kinds of Effectiveness," which was placed on each printer's chair.[92] B.W. recounted that these ephemeral pieces of Sans printing provoked the older printers to attack the letters as inartistic, while it provoked the younger ones to call publicity and jobbing typography unconventional, seeking novelty and effectiveness without counting the cost.[93] She wrote that "the printer who specializes in publicity printing, whether for commercial firms, theatrical or film companies, travel agencies or societies of Christian or Froth-blowing endeavors, cannot afford to get stabilized in any one style, however good . . . to be effective, you must surprise—startle."[94]

From the podium, Morison spoke to the federation members about the modern forces that conspired "to rob the printer" (184). "It is not," he argued, "that advertising men have more brains" but that printers had their heads in the sand and did "not see the fight going on" (182). Morison argued for greater competitiveness with the advertising industry, the kind of competitiveness demonstrated by Monotype's 235-font Super Caster technology that made innovations in modern letters possible. Morison's disingenuous remark, that as a consultant to Cambridge University Press and Monotype he did not merit the title of master printer, did little to soften opposition. Many at the Blackpool meeting seemed to consider the new Monotype face to be "sans" everything but ugly (184–85).

Recutting Monotype's English Faces, 1922–1932

Capitalizing on printers' animosity toward advertising agents and professional stylists, Morison suggested that these forces robbed printers of the bread-and-butter pamphlet, leaflet, and brochure that had sustained them for years. Spiraling price competition created by the influx of thousands of amateur printers, "a veritable army of one-man shops," remained among the several sore points with the federation, as its members listened (184–85). With the influx of "mere" machinists, Morison said, playing to the darker sentiments of the group, much of the public had "lost faith in the printer," a state of affairs that threatened to reverse the professional advances printers had made during the previous decade (183–86).

To counter this trend, Morison said, printers needed to "raise the level" of the common intelligence among readers, so that they would demand a level of excellence that only printers could provide. If printers wished to do more than survive, Morison argued, they had to relinquish obsolete typefaces and meet the advertising agents and maverick experts head on. "As long as we have cigarette makers shouting across the pages we have to have new types and various types, in order to see that one cigarette advertisement may not look like another" (184–85). Admitting that printing had to respond to a complex of market forces, Morison argued that styling was part of the competitiveness that made modernism aware of its place in history. Although competition from advertising forces may seem "depressing," he admitted, it was "part of the capitalist system." Those who tried to fit one standard typeface to every kind of job would soon enough find themselves "robbed" through the competition with advertising agents, industrial artists, and maverick typographic design experts: "You have to have an enormous number of styles. You have to have individuality" (183–86).

At this point a printer from Leeds (A. E. Wigley) stood up, interrupted Morison, and disagreed with what he had heard, saying that the speech sounded like "teaching your grandmother to suck eggs"—although he hesitated to call printers' competitors parasites as Morison had. Another printer (Howard Hazell) defied the speaker to point out what was beautiful about the yellow program printed in Monotype Sans. Morison's response, that he couldn't answer him "in the least" because it was "somebody else" who bore re-

Recutting Monotype's English Faces, 1922–1932

sponsibility for the program, seems more than disingenuous: "I think my programme has its uses. I saw Mr. Hazell kill a fly with his copy. I think it has other uses. It must have been more of a sensation than ever I expected. I thought it might be quite mildly interesting. . . . had it not been that I was shown a letter. . . . [which] describes it as 'an abomination that ought not to have seen the light of day'" (183–86). As the exchange between Morison and Hazell became more heated, the distinguished speaker charged that his audience's dislike of the modern face arose not from any qualities of design but from printers' reluctance to try anything new "unless they could be tricked into thinking they had been doing it for years" (183–86). Following Hazell's retort, that the typeface, although undoubtedly original, would decidedly attract attention, another printer (Bertram Evans) countered that originality was something very different from truth. Making a comparison with a five-legged horse, Evans pointed out that although the Sans typeface might attract a lot of attention, it had, like the horse, limited use. Further, Evans observed, lecturing the eminent guest from the floor of the assembly, successful attention-getting resulted from persuasion rather than provocation: "If it is not worth reading, it is not worth printing." Near the end of the conference, another printer (Austen-Leigh) told the assembly that if they objected to the look of the program they should blame the federation itself, which ought to do its own publicity printing instead of letting a "cock-robin shop" (a swipe at Monotype) do its publicity work (183–86).

Within months of the Blackpool meeting, Monotype garnered a national market niche for the Gill Sans when the London and North Eastern Railway (LNER) attempted to establish a national transportation system. To create a unified corporate identity in the public mind, the system settled on the Monotype Gill Sans for use throughout the nation. The LNER system wanted to "speak" to the British public in "one unified voice."[95]

The Gill Sans design aimed to achieve one special effect for only a few purposes, although B.W. later reported that "no poetical arguments" arose in the design and production process at Monotype.[96] Instead, the firm's image of the common reader as a passenger deter-

mined the design. She wrote of "being jostled on a crowded platform on a winter evening, and trying with one eye on the station
clock to verify the connections of a given train; a picture of another
passenger running his eye over fifteen excursion leaflets that are
printed perhaps by fifteen different printers; glancing from there to
the station announcement, to the destination board of the train, to a
16-sheet poster issued by the company, and being given in every
case a sense of continuity and consistency, a sense that something
had been said to him with as little fuss and distraction as possible."[97]
Over the next fifty years, according to Monotype's sales ledgers,
more than eighteen thousand "sets" sold worldwide along with the
Monotype machinery designed according to its specifications. Pre-
sumably one "set" included several sizes of one face. Though some
scholars conclude that its critical reputation suffered from overexpo-
sure, the Gill Sans remains the standard face used throughout the
national British transportation system today.[98]

The process of standardizing all typefaces associated with the system occurred over a period of several years. In order to carry out the
LNER nationalization, nearly a hundred small print shops were required to produce the more than forty million copies needed annually of handbills, leaflets, pamphlets, and publicity materials. The
selling point for the Sans, according to B.W., had to do not only with
its simplified modernistic look but also with the fact that it could
be used easily and with little training by printers of varying abilities
in geographically disparate shops. The LNER annual report alone
would keep five or six different printers busy; their output would be
assembled and the signatures collated and bound together in one
book.

The LNER owned two thousand stations, ten steamship and
twenty bus lines, restaurants in dining cars that fed thousands of
people from daily menus, in addition to continually changing timetables, rate cards, stationery, bills, menus, and keepsakes for the system's twenty-three hotels. That would mean the Sans, benefiting
from the 235-character and size range of the Super Caster, could be
used on small ticket stubs, directional signs in stations, on bronze or
enamel letters for outdoor use, and in newspaper advertisements,

Recutting Monotype's English Faces, 1922–1932

Lanston Monotype broadside for Frank Goudy's Italian Old Style
uses both Bradley and Monotype materials in a one-page flyer;
designed and printed by Bruce Rogers's Rudge Press, ca. 1926.
Courtesy of John M. Wing Foundation, Ransom Papers, Newberry Library.

on station posters, and souvenir match boxes. In the rail system, B.W. reasoned, she had a customer to whom standardization made perfect sense.

The Monotype sans serif—the distinctive typeface, as she put it—so "simple and free from artiness" that "it was practically fool-proof," made it possible for local sign painters and printers to work with minimal training. B.W. thought printers would buy the equipment and typeface inventory and the resulting product "could to a great extent look after itself" when "a huge public service company had a real conviction" to a specific style. The LNER products would be uniform, according to Warde, conveying to the public one idea about the identity of the new transport system.[99] She wrote that

> the traveller entering King's Cross or any one of the two thousand other stations of the line, or boarding the Vienna or the other L.N.E.R. passenger or freight vessels, is able to "hear the Company talking" in one recognizable voice. It is a crisp, unsentimental voice that can be raised or softened by the weight of the letter. But above all it is recurrent. It sets up a rhythm in the mind. . . . In standardizing its typography, the London and North Eastern Railway has not only made possible a number of economies, but has given the public at large a *visual image of one "group personality"* which is even more valuable than the emerald green livery borne Northward by the iron dragons of King's Cross.[100]

Enthusiastic about its success, Monotype developed the full range of sizes and weights for the Gill Sans and then created a range of complementary faces, including Baskerville and Plantin.

While Eric Gill undoubtedly profited from the Sans, Monotype profited from his reputation. B.W. called him the company's chief publicity asset, "a living artist," but some might argue that she herself was the greater publicity asset, and that her skills made the Sans "catch on."[101] Gill fancied himself a thinking man's Beardsley. Although his unorthodox personal behavior often contradicted the Roman Catholic beliefs he espoused, his unabashed irritability about the role of the artist in industry became as much a part of his persona as the imitation monk's habit he wore. Gill denounced the print-publicity trades while yearning for the "sans" life of his family farm,

Recutting Monotype's English Faces, 1922–1932

all the while working with tremendous diligence and energy.[102] He produced a number of type designs and also sculpted, engraved, cut letters, wrote, and published to support his extended family.[103] There is no doubt that his skills were considerable, but some have regarded his "glamour" the result of B.W.'s "brilliant" press-agentry for Monotype.[104]

As Gill's fame grew because of the LNER campaign, so did his involvement with the publicity processes that he told B.W. he despised. He posed for product-launch photographs, hanging the rail company's standardized logo in the Sans face on the front engine. He also received an increasing number of public commissions for his sculpture, including one for a piece in the lobby of the British Broadcasting Corporation and one for the stations of the cross in the Catholic Westminster Cathedral. Nevertheless, despite his prosperity, Gill bitterly denounced advertising as the cause of what he regarded to be the breakdown of industrialized society.[105]

To a degree, he seemed almost to blame B.W. for his success. He wrote to her heatedly, "Tell me—do you honestly think advertising (i.e., publicity as it is at present practised . . .) is not a filthy business? I think it absolutely stinking. . . . You kid yourself all the time. . . . I love you dearly but I loathe your silly job."[106] In correspondence that suggests their relationship became equally impatient on both sides, Warde made the following rejoinder to Gill's charges that he found the publicity blurbs for his new book on typography "disgusting," "fatuous muck," "shy-making and shame making":

> If you think Holy Church alone should have the missionaries and the sermons, then you really think my persuasive powers are admirable but mis-placed—wasted. I think that's what I'm to answer, for I can't believe you think one shouldn't advocate with all one's power, any force for good. Nor can I believe that your fastidious, patrician dislike of my work in the vernacular—amongst the typographical publicans and sinners—is as representative of you as it would be of a pagan. No, I believe you think I am advocating an unworthy cause. . . . But . . . we book-hungry people, we who brought about first the press and then the composing machine—we are not absolutely blind

Recutting Monotype's English Faces, 1922–1932

to the clothes that words wear. Lots of wealthy collectors of "fine books" in the renaissance times would have hooted at Jenson for trying to print a "beautiful" letter on his abominable machine, the press. "Leave Beauty to the scribe, and get on with your mass-production, you mechanized slave!" Yet the printers kept trying to see how good in appearance they could make a mass-produced article. Was that a fatuous desire?[107]

While Gill denounced commercial modernism as a corrupter of the artist-printer, B.W. retorted that the refinement of the Kelmscott-style limited edition did a disservice to the common reader by diverting energy from the effort to make well-printed trade editions designed for the mass-market reader more affordable. She labored for the good of the many, she argued, while Gill's "fine" press work for the book beautiful labored for the good of the few. She wrote that she believed

it is GOOD that many books should be printed: text-books, Bibles, pamphlets, *The Times*, *Lady Chatterly*. . . . If all the books which might contribute to man's understanding had to be set and printed by hand, there would be a decided fall in the standards of book-making. . . . It is unfair to make any one piece of reading be luxurious when the cost of that book is the cost of 3 ordinary books. . . . Most of my propaganda consists of making unvarnished statements in print as to what the Monotype alone can do. . . . The people who create 250 copies for 250 collectors don't need me. The slug companies can't use me, for my arguments are not theirs and I don't lie or cheat. . . . My real job is in preventing the slug salesman from unloading on a printer a machine which for years afterwards will produce distinctly bad work for him.[108]

Knowing that Gill's opinion carried weight, she tried to quiet his public outbursts against her work. She pleaded with him to take a balanced view of the ideological value represented by the artist and the machine in the Kelmscott era. "You could not possibly do us more harm . . . than by saying . . . leave us the fine work, and let the machines do . . . cheap, lifeless, efficient and nasty settings . . . without any guidance from real designers. . . . We, the artists, will be handicraftsmen. . . . should you bid "the machines" be satisfied

Recutting Monotype's English Faces, 1922–1932

with cheap and unambitious designs, you will be knocking the props out from under me. Please don't damn the machine that produces the finest face you or anyone else ever cut."[109]

TIMES NEW ROMAN

In 1931, "another wall" in the progress of printing, as B.W. put it, gave way when the London *Times* decided to adopt Morison's design for a new typeface, the Monotype New Roman. The company's best-selling typeface of the century, the New Roman sold close to forty thousand sets over the next fifty years.[110] While the LNER account provided Monotype an opportunity for increased visibility among the masses, the *Times* provided the firm an opportunity to be associated with elites. As the Sans face for the LNER had operated on the principle of utility and a unified identity, the New Roman improved legibility for the news industry.

In summarizing the impact of the *Times* typeface change on the social status of printers, Warde concluded that neither *Burke's Peerage* nor *Who's Who* offered such an opportunity for associating the Monotype brand name with the "prestige" of the country's leading newspaper. "All the readers of the *Times*" were "people who count," she wrote, executives and "rulers in every walk of life." Even among the mass-market nonreaders, those who got their news secondhand, by "infiltration" or word of mouth, the *Times* occupied a status as a public symbol, "not unlike the monarchy," as the most complete newspaper representative of all that was regal about British culture. Readers thought of the newspaper as theirs by virtue of an array of identities: bylines, signed editorials, and letters to the editor. The newspaper acquired the characteristics of a group personality by introducing a standardized look.[111]

Apparently, the *Times* New Roman adoption occurred slowly. Even after five years, when many in the industry regarded its introduction as "the most important development in modern type design," Daniel Berkeley Updike's 1937 volume *Printing Types* did not include Morison's New Roman typeface, because Updike "suspected that a face intended for a newspaper would have limited use in printing books." Yet Updike's Merrymount Press soon ordered Morison's New Roman from Monotype and used it regularly for

Cover, Monotype Recorder, *ca. 1928; Coat of Arms, Cardinal Richelieu,
founder of the French national printing office. Begun by Stanley Morison
and edited by Beatrice Warde between 1926 and 1965, the monthly*
Recorder *magazine was distributed free to customers by Monotype-UK.
Courtesy of the John M. Wing Foundation, Newberry Library.*

bookmaking. Extensive use of the New Roman typeface in British war propaganda accelerated its dissemination by newspaper and book printers in India, Africa, Germany, Poland, and Switzerland, extending Monotype's influence in the worldwide communications industry.[112]

The New Roman innovation began in the summer of 1929 when the *Times* approached Monotype and urged the corporation to take out a full-page advertisement as it had in 1912.[113] Once the paper's initial draft of the advertisement reached Morison, he was so appalled by the layout, copy, and design that he told Monotype to pay the *Times* £1,000 to "keep its hands off" the advertisement. He then told the newspaper's directors that they should completely reform the paper's typography.[114] His exhaustive thirty-four-page essay about the typographic history of the London newspaper since its first issue in 1788, titled *Memorandum on a Proposal to Revise the Typography of the Times*, persuaded them to adopt his reforms. The *Times*'s typographic change became so popular that other newspapers and periodicals on the Continent and in the United States adopted the Monotype New Roman face.

Responding to a subsequent invitation from the *Times* to join its staff as a typographic consultant, Morison agreed he would but only on the condition that they remove the period after the paper's name on the masthead.[115] Initially, Morison believed that the paper's readers would be interested by things typographical. Unlike the readers of an American newspaper, he argued, who took the paper to look at rather than to read, the *Times*'s public took the paper to read rather than as read. He wrote, "The clean, sharp impression of the Monotyped newspapers gives the highest satisfaction to advertisers and readers alike. It is a mistaken impression that readers of newspapers and periodicals are indifferent to the quality of the printing, for quite often a potential purchaser is as much influenced by the clean and orderly typographical presentation . . . as by the prospect of the contents being interesting, which, after all is mere speculation."[116] He declared that *Times* readers were "above class" and resisted easy categorization as an audience "attracted only by legal, clerical, scholastic, sporting, political," or other categories.[117] Morison argued that a new typeface would change public perception of the newspaper industry, although generally, when serious printers thought about the rotary press, they thought it had "little to do with the aesthetic concerns" of printing. The curved plate of the rotary machine could never compete with the crispness produced by the fast-running flatbed press, Morison wrote, and the average book, magazine, or sales catalog in the twenties "hopelessly outclassed" newspaper printing.[118]

A move by a major newspaper to take its typography seriously would persuade others, Morison wrote, to upgrade the quality of their printing and still others to think about news and the print process as parts of the same allied industry. In his lengthy historical treatise, Morison traced the conversion of private intelligence or correspondence into public news. As reporting became professionalized, commercial news came to be regarded as public property, and the common reader's hunger for information grew steadily in response to war. The *Times's* typeface had originated in 1830, Morison demonstrated, and as the public appetite for news had grown, so had its appreciation for typography.[119]

The way in which the public generally thought about news and advertising differed. As Morison saw it, whereas the LNER campaign had been effective—using national standardization to associate a corporate "personality" with a single unified public image through systematic design of publications, advertising, and typographic arrangements—the *Times's* adoption of a new look did little to change readers' perception of the paper but greatly changed their view of the news industry.[120] Once readers began to distinguish news from advertising, other newspapers followed the *Times's* typographic lead. The net effect of public opinion exerted a force for change in the industry; in the newspaper business, companies followed rather than led public opinion. In contrast, the rail system tried to create a unified corporate identity by enlisting nearly a hundred small printers to carry out the planned campaign.

Morison believed that the success of any newspaper depended on readers' abilities to feel ownership of the opinions expressed by the paper, and to feel familiar with the names of the staff members who made up the newspaper's group personality in bylines, editorials, and columns, as representative of a "ruling class of elites."[121] From a

Recutting Monotype's English Faces, 1922–1932

printer's standpoint, though, newspapers traditionally had been the lowest rung on the ladder for a printer trying to break into the typographic design industry.

Monotype's proposed change in typography would improve the status of the printers who worked in the *Times* organization and elsewhere in the news industry, Beatrice Warde believed. None of the progress of the past decade, she wrote, created an advantage to printers on the scale of the *Times*'s change of typeface. In her opinion, the publicity that accompanied the change should "prepare the public to deal" with printers as "men of prestige," not as "cheapjacks."[122] Because of the nature of its public, the *Times* account raised by association the prestige of the brand name of Monotype, and that resulted in an improved professional regard for printing generally. The *Times*'s identity, synonymous, Warde asserted, with "what we call 'England' in our more sanguine moments," stood, for the mark of civilized intelligence and good breeding. A *Times* reader turned to the paper out of "respect for the self-respect of its conductors," and they remained "above class." According to the paper's slogan, "Top People Read the Times."[123] Setting itself up to be the paper "best worth reading," the *Times* became known as the "paper easiest to read" through Monotype's promotions. Because the Monotype Corporation had asserted its dominance and cultural authority over the mass market between 1922 and 1929 and publicized its program of innovations, by the thirties tradesmen consistently looked to Monotype for leadership.

The modern value generally placed on visual literacy went well beyond sales rhetoric. It had to do with the spreading realization that political power derived from the perceived authority of public opinion, and that authority was a sense of how the powerful styled themselves through the language they used. It could be said that in a pervasively material culture, all language—especially aesthetic language—was taken at face value, forced to be more concrete rather than allusive, to speak in a vernacular of things that could be consumed rather than to construct a realm of the purely imaginary. Over time, widespread public acceptance of commercial letters as convention rather than as innovation led to the growing use of print propaganda in a war of ideas. The political use of the printing press had long been commonplace, but it was modern warfare that enlisted the tools of mass communications, film, broadcast, and print. Twentieth-century military history changed public perception about mass communication as a weapon in a war of ideas.[124]

What made the public perception of print *modern* prior to 1940, however, was not its use as propaganda but the philosophical principles of the producers who contributed their social convictions to the public arena. They wanted their work to benefit the reading public.[125] In the mass-communications industry, both printing houses and plants had an unprecedented opportunity to shape twentieth-century culture. They could boast of being connected to the nation's historical and literary identity, a connection to culture that modern technology did not offer. Marketers in the early-twentieth-century communications industry sought to reassure common readers that modern commercial products both possessed the progressive qualities represented by new technology and reiterated historical values by adapting inherited forms to suit contemporary tastes. Regard for modern mass-communication technology as a powerful instrument that could shape public taste spanned the period of commercial modernism during the interwar years from the promotion of Frank Pick and the typography of Edward Johnston to the advertising art of McKnight Kauffer, to the ambitious reach of John Reith of the British Broadcasting Corporation.[126]

The effectiveness of the national campaigns that flourished during the interwar years would be difficult to measure. Monotype's promotional skills with modern letter form designs between 1922 and 1932 illustrate how philosophical conviction successfully applied to commerce resulted in a capacity to nationalize style. At the same time, uncertainty about the investment value of product designs based on contemporaneity rather than history gave rise to tensions among artists. They were concerned that the desire for greater efficiency in manufacturing and marketing might diminish the value of individual expression and that efforts to define a nation's commercial culture might lead to a national cultural standard. Homogeneous standards for public taste would undermine the values of permanence and utility so highly prized by the artistic revolutionaries.

Recutting Monotype's English Faces, 1922–1932

Beatrice Warde and T. S. Eliot launch the
Books across the Sea Campaign, ca. 1938.
Photograph courtesy of the English Speaking Union, London.

As propaganda permeated the mass market, the importance of inherited styles in classic letter forms declined. The common reader became increasingly indifferent to print, whether beautified or modernized, and turned to film and other new technologies, even to illustrated daily newspapers. At the beginning of the century, printers discussed the social relevance of fine printing, and by mid-century, they had become the fine print, a footnote in modern mass-communication history.[127] According to Morison, the change came about through the sudden appearance of the target common reader who shifted from middle to lower-middle class. As events developed, the public wanted to be shown, not told; they wanted to see rather than read. Morison accepted these realities. He believed that the public rather than the trade should decide whether more attention should be given to print than to pictures.[128]

By the end of the Second World War, the role of public educator and arbiter of taste had been passed from the industrial corporation to government propagandists through entities such as the Creel Committee in the United States. With the growing importance of the state as a public communicator, the role of the artist shifted from a servant of the masses employed by the corporation or factory to a role as conduit of "public information" aesthetically neutralized by government regulations, social conventions, or economic climates. The modern artist tried to accommodate the individualism equated with historical traditions and the values of an increasingly public culture, to perpetuate the ideals, goals, and vernacular of those in power, whether in business, government or the media. This shift proved critical in the formation of modern aesthetic values that involved the artist in both high and low culture to reach a mass-market common reader. Many might argue that this turn of events represented a regression, to the days when artists had to please patrons to survive.

While historically European artists had accommodated themselves to the tastes of royalty or the church, American artists had longed for utopian experiments that expressed their individualism. Whether or not such experiments lasted, or thrived, for a short time mattered little to American individualists. What did matter to Henry May and other literary critics was the artists' attempt to cre-

Recutting Monotype's English Faces, 1922–1932

ate a new Eden.[129] Similarly, commercial modernists tried to create a perfect market, where ideology and aesthetic concerns improved the social order and printing elevated the public mind through the beauty of its designs. After 1940 the time for innovation and the attention to historical precedent in contemporary styling had passed.

Recutting Monotype's English Faces, 1922–1932

*

DEFINING
·
R. R. DONNELLEY'S
·
AMERICAN
·
CULTURE
·
1926–1935

Here is a temple which was built to make business sacred.
—James Weber Linn, letter to the editor, *Chicago Tribune*, 1931

The full-service publicity firm emerged around 1905 as an amalgam of print-product and message-placement managers and typographic experts. Once it did, *agency* meant not an occupation but an organizational structure.[1] It described a group or network of individuals skilled in writing, layout and design, illustration, and typography. These new experts broadcast persuasive commercial messages in public spaces. Specializing in well-designed ephemera, such full-service agencies posed a competitive threat to large family-owned commercial printing houses. One of them, the R. R. Donnelley & Sons of Chicago printing firm, had dominated the regional market for brochures, catalogs, annual reports, company biographies, and the like since its founding in 1864.

Competition between family-owned firms like Donnelley and the maverick design experts in publicity agencies during the heyday of commercial ephemera in the United States expanded the capability of printers to publicize their products.[2] Modern publicity advisors developed ten major generic print-product lines. Each had clear rules for design and use. Souvenir booklets, posters, and brochures, along with the other products in wide distribution since the eighteenth century (dodgers, broadsides, and catalogs) proliferated in record numbers. Chicago and New York each boasted being the "world's leader" in the production of such pieces. A single plant—each city had several—could pump out these products in the millions. In addition, they offered services including advice about typography, layout, copywriting, illustration, printing, and distribution. When first introduced, alternatives to advertisements in newspapers siphoned revenues from the dailies, and the legal right to advertise in public spaces became a matter fought out in the courts.

THE CULTURE OF THE PRINTING FIRM

Donnelley responded to the challenge of the agencies by establishing a new department staffed by William Kittredge and other specialists in typographic design and setting up at the University of Chicago a program whereby apprentice craftsmen could become "printing engineers." Promising lifetime employment, progressive management, and training, along with integrated design and production, the Donnelley company hoped to elevate printing industry standards by initiating a bold publicity campaign targeting mass-market publishers. Company officials called it "The Four American Books" campaign.

The R. R. Donnelley & Sons Company became the country's largest commercial printer in the twentieth century and today remains one of the world's largest. According to company advertisements, the firm manufactured catalogs, broadsides, booklets, newsletters, and other publicity ephemera at the turn of the century "by the trainload." Donnelley's early clients included Sears, Roebuck & Co., Montgomery Ward, and Marshall Field's. Donnelley's Lakeside Press printed commercial books, including the *Chicago City Directory*, telephone books, and the *Encyclopaedia Britannica*. Taking advantage of the burgeoning mass-market appetite for popular business literature of every description, the company's department

Defining R. R. Donnelley's American Culture, 1926–1935

of design and typography initiated the Four Books campaign in 1925, which was designed to attract new book-printing business, assert the quality of its print technology, and foster company morale. R. R. Donnelley's campaign, according to company literature, aspired to position the company as "one with taste, skill, know-how, and ambition."[3]

The Four American Books were Herman Melville's *Moby Dick*, illustrated by Rockwell Kent; the *Tales of Edgar Allan Poe*, illustrated by W. A. Dwiggins; *Walden*, by Henry David Thoreau, illustrated by Rudolph Ruzicka; and Richard Henry Dana's *Two Years Before the Mast*, illustrated by Edward Wilson. The campaign attempted to improve American book-production standards by demonstrating that large machinery could achieve fine impressions for books, giving them the appearance of having been typeset by hand on a smaller private press. The Four American Books raised book-production standards to compete with the finely printed advertisements that had proliferated since the arts-and-crafts decades of the 1890s. The details of this campaign illustrate Daniel Boorstin's well-known comment that the "blurring" of shadow and substance that characterized modern American culture resulted from the importance modern society placed on public opinion.[4] The blurring of class distinctions among products in the emerging communication industries resulted from other market forces and cultural currents in addition to public opinion.

Three market factors shaped the book trade: the overproduction of books, the emergence of advertising as the most significant force determining sales, and the proliferation of small bookstores.[5] The shrinking margin between the cost of producing books and their selling price placed publishing in a precarious condition between 1925 and 1935. According to Alfred McIntyre, president of Little, Brown Company in the twenties, "The business of selling books at retail is still growing and its weakness lies more in the margin of profit than in the amount of sale."[6] Publishers wanted to sell more copies of books and print fewer titles. Advertising costs rose steadily, and the increased cost of obtaining publicity for individual titles pitted booksellers and publishers against each other. Publishers needed to bypass the inflationary force of booksellers, who raised

Defining R. R. Donnelley's American Culture, 1926–1935

the price of books for consumers without any increased profits for publishers.

By the twenties, with the blurring of product distinctions and the increasing use of books as company advertisements, the distinction between publishing and commercial printing also became less clear. Donnelley had separated its publishing and printing businesses, as a matter of company policy, and had taken care to avoid turf battles with book and magazine editors. Donnelley's corporate clients placed large commercial orders for publicity and advertisements, catalogs, and multivolume works, including company biographies such as those of Henry Ford, William Wrigley, Albert Blake Dick, and Harvey S. Firestone, club directories, travel journals, genealogies, and magazines including *Time*, *Life*, and *Esquire* for Henry Luce.

Richard Robert Donnelley, the company founder, was born in Brantford, Ontario, on November 15, 1836. He became an apprentice printer in grammar school, and by age sixteen, he received full journeyman's wages. In 1857 he traveled to New Orleans for the *True Delta* newspaper, working with John Hand, a Canadian typesetter. When the Civil War broke out, he returned to Canada. Donnelley moved to Chicago in 1864 with his new wife, Naomi Shenstone, and became a partner in Church, Goodman and Donnelley, a firm specializing in educational, religious, and historical printing. One of the most prosperous commercial printing houses of its day, the company had incorporated to allow the expansion of the original printing operations as Lakeside Publishing and Printing Company.

The Chicago fire of 1871 destroyed most of Richard Donnelley's assets, including a building then under construction for Lakeside. At that point, he went to New York for new printing equipment, then reopened the business in Chicago under the name of R. R. Donnelley, Steam Printer. Facing widespread economic depression as well as a general decline in commercial printing after the war, Donnelley and his partners attempted to diversify, forming a subsidiary—Williams, Donnelley and Company—to publish the *Edwards Chicago City Directory*. Then in 1875 Williams, Donnelley

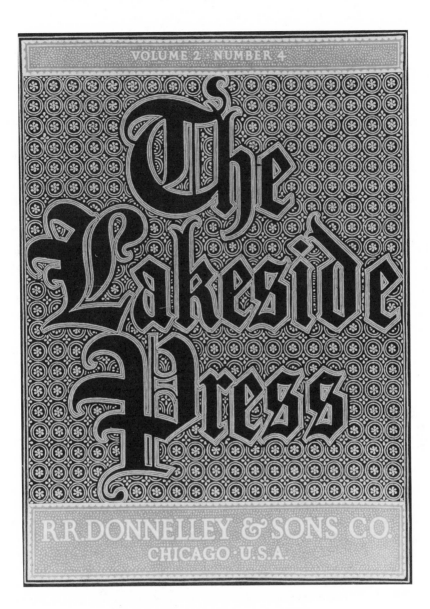

The
Lakeside
Press

RR DONNELLEY & SONS CO.
CHICAGO · U.S.A.

Cover, publicity brochure for Lakeside Press,
R. R. Donnelley, ca. 1920, in the Kelmscott style.
Courtesy of the John M. Wing Foundation, Newberry Library.

and Company successfully published a limited edition of two hundred copies of classic reprints called the Lakeside Library.

When these and other attempts failed to establish a profitable publishing business by 1880, a reconstituted partnership called Donnelley, Lloyd & Company bought the printing equipment at the Lakeside Publishing and Printing plant. At that time Richard Donnelley created the Chicago Directory Company as another corporate entity to handle book publishing ventures and keep them separate from commercial printing orders for corporate clients, long the base for the company's prosperity. In 1882 the directors of another reconstituted entity called Donnelley, Gassett & Lloyd voted to change the name of the printing firm again, this time introducing the firm as a family enterprise named R. R. Donnelley & Sons Company. At the close of the company's most successful decade, Richard Robert Donnelley died in April 1899. After the founder's death, his sons managed the firm, electing Thomas Elliott Donnelley as company president. Thomas Donnelley's older son, Reuben H. Donnelley, managed the publishing subsidiary, no longer called the Chicago Directory Company, but retitled Reuben H. Donnelley Corporation. When Reuben died in 1929, the publishing operation became a separate company.

In many respects, the Donnelley company embodied the Kelmscott industrial ideal, a spiritualized industry that aspired to turn work into worship and the factory into a shrine for beautifully manufactured goods. The Donnelley organization responded to the competitive market forces of the day, including the rise of maverick typographic design experts in advertising agencies. The company also subscribed to the Taylor Scientific Method, which permitted employees "to earn as they produce and as they possess superior skill and ability." According to the firm's 1923 publicity brochure, the company developed a unique organization. They described themselves as a factory where "printing is not only an art but a science," stating that their engineers and mechanics "have perfected methods and machines, labor saving devices and processes not available elsewhere." The company also touted its achievements in education, reporting that 192 members of the organization had a college education.[7]

Defining R. R. Donnelley's American Culture, 1926–1935

Between 1904 and 1908 the Lakeside Press faced the national strikes that took place throughout the printing industry. According to company literature, management's response was to organize the R. R. Donnelley Lakeside School of Apprenticeship—in order to remain union free and "build up an organization trained in the ideals of the institution and have loyal employees free from outside control and satisfied with their relations with management."[8] According to the company's advertisement brochure for prospective employees and clients, the Lakeside School for Apprentices accepted fourteen-year-old Chicago boys "of special promise and ability" and put them through a seven-year course in "craftsmanship combined with cultural studies."[9] Many remained with the company for the whole of their working lives and were promoted throughout the company's ranks. The school harmoniously combined the Kelmscott ideas of "genius" with the trade standards for fine "workmanship" in design and printing. One of its brochures described the program: "An organization of hundreds of compositors, trained from boyhood in a world-famous apprentice school, may well develop more men with talent than a shop with few workmen, especially if the larger group has an organization whose chief job is to find and develop unusual talent."[10]

In the tower of the company printing plant, a training library contained fine specimens of book production spanning several centuries, designed to "influence the taste" of Donnelley printers. In a 1931 letter to the editor of the *Chicago Tribune*, a University of Chicago English professor described the Memorial Library's appeal as spiritualized industry where "work and worship," art and craft combined to manufacture beautiful products. Donnelley reprinted the article as a publicity brochure in Kelmscott style. Using red and black ink, the piece praised the company's "beauty as well as scholarship," where the professor found "the same splendor and the same Gothic in a printing office." He even found spiritual meaning in the entrance to the plant, which he described as "simple," "powerful," and as "suggestive" as "some mighty museum." The professor offered his experience of touring the Donnelley factory and library as an example that spiritualization in industry was "feasible," writing that he

Defining R. R. Donnelley's American Culture, 1926–1935

came upon a library, a genuine library . . . one of the two or three most beautiful rooms I have ever seen in these parts. Later I went down and down, through floor after floor of machines, linotyping . . . printing . . . assembling . . . binding . . . turning out books, catalogs, magazines, directories by the thousands and hundreds of hundreds. The ingenuity that had devised them was awe-inspiring. . . . But ingenuity and executive ability I am used to in American business. . . . My most vivid memory is of the devotion to an ideal, the inspiration engendered perhaps by devotion to a memory, which is symbolized by one beautiful room, a room so beautiful that it turns work into worship and a factory into a shrine.[11]

To influence the taste of apprentices and workmen, according to company officers, Donnelley established art galleries "ventilated with washed and refrigerated air," where employees could enjoy regular exhibits. These expositions of the "great things" currently being produced in the publicity, printing, and publishing industries also attracted the Chicago public. According to company literature, Donnelley's gallery rooms, on the same floor as the library, were the equal if not the rival of similar exhibition spaces of the major American art museums of the time, including the Metropolitan Museum in New York. In the fall of 1930, the company's exhibition space heralded the production of the Four Books.[12] Donnelley printed a souvenir catalog, and the Caxton Club, the Society of Typographic Art, and other professional groups praised the show.

The concept of book design in nineteenth-century American publishing usually was confined to the text of the printed page alone. After the 1890s, the printing trade began to publish mass-market magazines that paid particular attention to typographic arts, including Charles Francis Brown's magazine *Brush and Pencil* and Herbert S. Stone's *House Beautiful*. As commercial printers became more design conscious, the Donnelley company used a number of book illustrators, typographers, and advertising artists employed by full-service agencies as freelancers in its department of design.[13]

In 1918, when Pittsburgh Plate Glass placed an order for a $300,000 institutional advertising booklet, taking advantage of a World War I tax law loophole, Rudolph Ruzicka, one of the several freelance designers Donnelley employed, found the prospect of producing a six-figure advertising booklet somewhat daunting. To manage the PPG order, Donnelley formed the Department of Design and Typography, supervised by C. G. Littell, the firm's senior vice president. In 1920, William Kittredge became the first manager of the new department staffed by five to seven employees.[14] According to Herbert Zimmermann, a company vice president during these years, Kittredge's "instinctive feel for promotion" resulted in the immediate and long-range influence of the Design Department on company operations. Zimmermann explained that Kittredge "stimulated an increase in our own publicity activities and used all his talents in improving the appearance of our advertising matter and setting the high standard for our exhibits and the printed publicity that went with them." Kittredge and the other Donnelley officers worked to assert leadership in typographic design for commercial printing from their "feeling that The Lakeside Press was the finest institution in the graphics arts industry."[15]

As company lore recorded it, Littell gave Kittredge carte blanche to design the announcement of his own arrival at the Lakeside Press. He produced an impressive tabloid brochure patterned after the early-nineteenth-century work by the French designer Gille. Kittredge produced an eight-page tabloid with blue paper covers, printed on ivory Italian paper (Tuscany) in eighteen-point Bodoni type, and French-Empire borders, a format later imitated by George Macy to promote membership in The Limited Editions Club. He titled the booklet *Authoritative Design and Typography in Printing*, and in it he summarized the history of the Lakeside Press and described its guiding principles and readiness to take on modern challenges "through craftsmanship with mechanical excellence." He spoke rather grandly about himself, as "Mr. Kittredge," who was "eminently fitted for work here." He came to the Lakeside Press with more than ten years' experience, first with the Riverside Press in Cambridge, then as art director "for a leading house" in Philadelphia with clients like the Victor Talking Machine Co. and Packard Motor Car Company.[16] Kittredge's patience and enthusiasm for the work of fine printing by large printers, as well as his instinctive feel for publicity, sustained the Four American Books campaign through more than five years' production.

Defining R. R. Donnelley's American Culture, 1926–1935

According to Herbert Zimmermann's unpublished notes, the company's senior vice president, C. G. Littell, consulted Kittredge and generally obtained approval for decisions. The company officers made the final selection of type, paper, and binding materials. Kittredge's correspondence in the Newberry Library's Wing Foundation Collection suggests that Kittredge was more influential than Littell in production matters, although the senior executive made decisions about distribution and sales. The two worked well together: Kittredge had an amiable disposition and dedicated himself to detail, whereas Littell was blunt; he usually scribbled his directives in pencil right above Kittredge's carefully phrased, orderly, internal memoranda typed on beautifully printed office forms that Kittredge had designed. According to company records, Kittredge's wholehearted commitment to the use of design in every aspect of the organization, even interoffice memoranda, influenced the general appreciation for fine printing and established his department quickly as an integral part of the company. Littell believed that the Donnelley firm should lead the graphic-arts industry, and in his external relations with vendors, illustrators, and suppliers as well as his internal relations with salesmen, pressmen, binders, and typographers, he worked to make the goal a reality.

Littell, a collector of rare early-American books, stressed that the Four Books campaign should market only "what the Lakeside Press could do for the book publishers" and that the printers would stick to what they could do best. The Four American Books, he argued, should be printed in runs of one thousand only "to touch as lightly as possible" on publishing, enough to whet the appetite of book publishers who would send their printing to the Donnelley corporation.[17] Further, he thought the company should oppose limited editions as being anti-democratic. The Four Books effort, to produce fine editions within the reach of all, under American manufacturing conditions, did not cater "to people who speculate in books and who are so wealthy that money is no object."[18]

The company's earlier ventures into book publishing also had integrated some publishing as part of a marketing plan. In 1903, the company president began printing a series of Christmas gift books for employees, customers, and vendors. Called the Lakeside Classics, these volumes, according to the company's publicity materials, produced regional and national classics that "normal" businessmen would want to read if they could have affordable copies made available. The Lakeside Classics aimed to represent American literary culture to the common reader and show by excellence in mechanical detail the expertise of the Lakeside Press in "workaday bookmaking."[19] The Four American Books were produced "at cost" and "only as a publicity scheme," but their production grew from the company tradition of publishing gift books for corporate anniversaries.

The Four American Books project meant to assert American competitiveness in printing, papermaking, bookbinding, and illustrated books, and to advertise the ability of modern American printing technology to meet the most demanding European standards. The company prescribed that "a book must be within the reach of the world."[20] The campaign intended to persuade mass-market publishers that Donnelley had the taste to do book printing as well as the marketing skill to advertise the business. The campaign aspired to establish the company's reputation among bibliophiles, book collectors, and "people generally interested in the cultural status of American graphic arts" as the leading American printer capable of producing museum-quality typographic design. As it repositioned itself, the company that had largely been known as a printer of commercial catalogs and ephemera announced that "some of our tonnage work may be artistic."[21]

For Littell and Kittredge, the goal of the campaign was to produce "definitively" illustrated works of American literature, so that "it would be a mistake for anyone to attempt to illustrate them again."[22] Kittredge pressed the idea with characteristic enthusiasm, asking Rockwell Kent, "Do you think this is too bold or too forward?"[23] For Kent, Kittredge, and the others involved in the 1926 campaign, making editions "definitive" meant the books would be indigenous texts printed on American-made paper, with typefaces designed by American typographers, intended for a vast new democratic audience. Littell described to Kittredge that the company was to remain a printer, not a publisher. He wrote that they wanted to produce books that would be read as well as admired, and that they would differentiate their efforts from others publishing "limited"

Defining R. R. Donnelley's American Culture, 1926–1935

*Lanston Monotype press operators at work in the
R. R. Donnelley & Sons Company, Chicago, ca. 1925.*
Courtesy of the John M. Wing Foundation, Newberry Library.

editions.[24] The Four American Books would be limited editions because the printing company did not want to "stir up" the publishers, as Littell warned against doing. When the immediate popularity of *Moby Dick* warranted a trade edition and Kittredge also proposed a "small, fat volume" of Thoreau's *Walden*, Littell advised against it, writing, "I do not want to monkey with any more trade editions at the present time. Let's don't stir them up. After we have all our books out, then we can consider it."[25]

Typesetting, presswork, and binding for the Four Books were to be done by graduates of the Lakeside Press Apprentice School. Refinements in style, design, typography, and production details would reflect the quality of the training program Donnelley had established in-house. Caught up as much by enthusiasm as by wishful thinking, Littell, Kittredge, and others at Donnelley speculated that they might do more after they had produced the Four Books to print additional definitively illustrated editions of all the recognized masterpieces of American literature. In the planning stages, Littell suggested that as long as they were about it, they might as well go one step further, into bibliography. They should draw up a conclusive list of all the definitively illustrated books that had ever been done in the English language, which could be integrated into the campaign as a publicity device. He suggested that a small but comprehensive bibliography might be taken "by competent judges" as a natural standard for editions definitively illustrated. Because the main publishing enterprise of the Lakeside Press had been multivolume works of all types—encyclopedias, city directories, and telephone books, as well as the series of Lakeside Library Classics—the philosophy of this new venture to offer the public a complete set of illustrated editions of American literary masterpieces was in keeping with the company's historical tradition.

In 1926, what did Littell and Kittredge have in mind as being definitive? If they believed that a "man's reach must exceed his grasp," how then did their sense of public value, of aesthetic standards, measure up against their need to cater to popular taste? The books themselves represent the scope of their ambitions, in the graceful fall of the pages, the softness of the endpapers, the rich color, the various qualities of black in the inks for Rockwell Kent's illustrations

Defining R. R. Donnelley's American Culture, 1926–1935

and all-black title pages, the simplicity of Ruzicka's wood-grain landscape, and the three-dimensional quality of stamped bindings. Littell sought to achieve what Kittredge thought would add something to the philosophy of bookmaking and make printing and publishing history.[26]

Ambitions for achieving cultural definition through the campaign went beyond the books themselves and included an exhibit and a direct-mail invitation to potential subscribers. In 1928 Donnelley sent an eleven-page prospectus to nearly eight thousand potential subscribers for the four books. The two men planned the campaign in great detail. Littell carefully noted that they would prepare a complete provenance for each publication that "should serve publishers as a guide when they contemplate bringing out new illustrated editions." Urging Kittredge to keep the idea confidential for the moment, he thought the list would "establish our serious purpose in this work, and leave no doubt."[27]

When news of the plan reached Rudolph Ruzicka, he suggested that they avoid absolute statements about productions being "definitive"; many such overwrought so-called masterpieces of design incorporated every available printer's device and nuance of luxurious detail. Ruzicka opposed these as what he called "precious de looks" books, the "meretricious" editions that were the hallmark of the day. He urged that the artist wait for others to say whether or not future generations of illustrators should think of "redefining" the meaning of books.[28]

From August through October 1931, the Donnelleys, Littell, and Kittredge mounted an exhibit and printed a catalog titled "An Exhibition of Illustrated Books, of 242 Definitively Illustrated Works, Drawn from All Cultures Worldwide." The illustrated items included pre-1500 wood engravings, copper-plate engraved books from France, and sporting books with color plates from England. Many of the books came from the company's training library; collectors lent others. The Art Institute of Chicago lent hand-colored engraved plates done by William Blake for Dante's *Inferno* and examples by Redon, Goya, and Turner. A private collector contributed a copy of the *Nuremberg Chronicle*. The Donnelley company wanted to exhibit its Four Books illustrations alongside drawings by Hans

Holbein and Albrecht Dürer, Sandro Botticelli's vision of Dante's *Divine Comedy*, printed in Berlin in 1925, Eric Gill's *Canterbury Tales*, Kate Greenaway's *Pied Piper* and *Language of Flowers*, and Frederic Remington's *Old Sante Fe Trail* and the 1892 edition of *Oregon Trail*. Littell, Kittredge, and the Donnelleys wanted to place their books in the company of William Blake's engravings for editions of Milton and Dante, of George Cruickshank's *Seven League Boots*, *Cinderella*, and *Jack and the Beanstalk*, of Aubrey Beardsley's *Le Morte D'Arthur* and *Salome*, and of John Tenniel's illustrated Aesop's *Fables* and *Alice in Wonderland*. The exhibit also included a number of works from English illustrators of the 1860s through 1900.[29]

PRODUCING THE ILLUSTRATIONS

The Donnelley company approached about a dozen possible illustrators, including Rockwell Kent, Rudolph Ruzicka, William Dwiggins, and Edward Wilson. Each time Littell wrote to a potential illustrator, he sent a list of titles he had selected including those by Melville, Thoreau, Dana, and Poe. Additional possibilities on Littell's original list included Mark Twain's *Huckleberry Finn*, Owen Wister's *The Virginian*, Jack London's *Call of the Wild*, Joel Chandler Harris's *Uncle Remus*, and Nathaniel Hawthorne's *The Scarlet Letter*. Littell had "definitive" criteria for selecting the literature: the text had to have been written by an American author, and it must not have been illustrated previously. Further, he wrote, the text must lend itself to illustration and tell something about American lives in a historical setting.[30]

Each edition possessed its own idiosyncratic production problems, and Kittredge negotiated every aspect, from production and packaging, to illustration, to getting the top quality from suppliers and from his pressmen. The selection of paper and typeface proved one major production obstacle. For each volume, the illustrator helped in these design decisions before he began the drawings. Everyone involved believed that the illustrations had to be congruent with the aesthetic principles of the typeface, and vice versa. The illustrators also helped decide other equally important matters, such as the quality of ink used in the book; whether the illustrations would be tipped in, printed on blank pages, or on pages with type on the verso side; and whether illustrations should be integrated with the text, placed on half or quarter pages, or used simply to highlight the chapter headings.

The campaign would be a labor of love for the illustrators eventually selected, Rockwell Kent, William Dwiggins, Rudolph Ruzicka, and Edward Wilson. Even though Kittredge's offer approached the standard rate for book illustrations, any of the four men could have earned more as an advertising illustrator. Generally, a well-known illustrator like Dwiggins might receive from a mainstream publisher like Alfred A. Knopf about $450 per book for a set of illustrations plus headnotes. Although fine-book publishers might pay artists slightly more than trade-book houses, Goodspeed reportedly paid $75 a drawing. The same work might have brought $200 to $250 per drawing in advertising.

Each artist agreed to make all the drawings for his volume for $2,000. Kent eventually made nearly 300 drawings, for which he received $6,000 or about $20 per drawing. Type designer W. A. Dwiggins, who illustrated Poe's *Tales*, including chapter headnotes, called the Lakeside rates "sacrificial." He wrote to Kittredge that the book trade "cannot compete with the advertising trade."[31] Because the artists engaged as illustrators had to earn their living from other projects, their drawings took second priority, slowing the project's completion.

While all four illustrators struggled to make ends meet, Edward Wilson complained to Kittredge most vociferously. Initially Wilson's direct-mail civic advertisement, "The Miracle of Coral Gables," had attracted Kittredge, who wrote to Wilson that "these are exceedingly lovely, and I wonder if they are not in the spirit suitable to one of these books we are considering."[32] Wilson replied that he thought "the scheme" had "the right ring to it" but that omitting *Robinson Crusoe* he thought an "oversight." Here Wilson seems to have missed Kittredge's point about producing definitive works. Daniel Defoe's *Crusoe*, a British novel, already had been illustrated.[33]

Wilson wanted to work on either Defoe's *Crusoe* or Melville's *Moby Dick*. Rockwell Kent, however, had cabled from Ireland that he wanted to illustrate the Melville, and that settled the matter from Donnelley's point of view: Wilson had illustrated about a dozen books before taking on the Donnelley project, but Kent had illustrated fifty. Finally, Wilson agreed to illustrate Richard Henry Dana's *Two Years Before the Mast*. In December 1926 both Wilson and Kittredge felt confident that the book would be on the market in time for Christmas the following year, although it would take another form.

Family and financial problems slowed Wilson's work in the first part of 1927. Wilson was a man given to wanderlust. One month after the two struck the deal to do the book, he reassured Kittredge that as for enthusiasm, "I've got it," saying he would think seriously about Kittredge's suggestion that he reconsider plans for a holiday in the West Indies. Kittredge suggested Wilson go to Carmel, California, instead, where he could remain in closer touch with him. Wilson replied that he would think about it.

Kittredge used a variety of other ploys to get Wilson moving on the drawings, including flattery and competition, as he pointed to the accomplishments of the other illustrators. Attempting to cajole Wilson into a better temper, he wrote:

> I have enjoyed seeing new works from your brush and pen. I can always tell your drawings a long way off, and do not have to look for your signature. . . . Every once in a while they ask me about the work, and I still stick to my story. However, I realize that I cannot do this forever, and am writing to ask if you will frankly write and tell me whether the work still appeals to you and whether you can commence it some time soon. . . . Rockwell Kent is doing the best work I have ever seen him do. . . . we have set the type for the Poe which Dwiggins is doing."[34]

In 1929–30, Wilson illustrated four other books, although none of these projects was as "fully illustrated" as the sixteen full-page and ten half-page illustrations required for Donnelley's *Two Years*. In January 1929 Littell authorized Wilson's $2,000 advance in response to the artist's complaints: "It's one hell of a job to try and do as much advertising work as I do and do anything else believe me! The Victor people insisted on having the whole year's campaign completed by the fifteenth of May."[35]

Defining R. R. Donnelley's American Culture, 1926–1935

Rockwell Kent's enthusiasm also seemed to get in his way. With his reputation as a book illustrator well established, he reluctantly continued to illustrate advertising, although he did enjoy the income. By the winter of 1928, Kent had completed 157 drawings for *Moby Dick*. He and his wife wrote Kittredge asking for thirty yards of "the paper you use in printing . . . that has the wide blurred stripe in it" for their 14-by-6½-foot hallway.[36] They liked the overall effect so much that Kent requested an additional thirty yards for their upstairs hall. Kittredge found Kent's enthusiasm contagious, offering to have a special paper made and named in Kent's honor; although honored, the artist declined. Kittredge's November 1928 letter to Kent was similarly effusive. He wrote that the latest "drawings have excited the greatest interest and approval of everyone who has seen them here. They exceed our highest expectation of how you would do this work. As works of art, reflecting the spirit of Melville's book, they could not be finer."[37] Kittredge's high spirits about the importance of the Four Books enterprise proved justified; among the four, Rockwell Kent's *Moby Dick* came closest to meeting the definitive standard to which Kittredge aspired.

The enthusiasm shared by Kent and Kittredge also infused an impractical or unrealistic quality into their thinking about the grandeur of their scheme. That Kittredge in the spring of 1927 thought it would be possible to complete Kent's *Moby Dick* in time for the Christmas market demonstrated his inexperience with book production. As his sense of the project's importance increased, an along with it his thinking that this would be a "first" in the entire history of American bookmaking, Kittredge no longer concerned himself with marketing seasons. Ignoring schedules that suited commercial markets, he devoted himself to production details. Both Kittredge and Littell referred to the project as "the greatest books of this generation," and Kittredge informed Kent: "The book will be so good—one of the finest illustrated books of all time—that it will probably not matter whether it comes out at a holiday season or not."[38]

The advertising illustrator and type designer William Addison Dwiggins of Hingham, Massachusetts, was another idealist. The *Fleuron* called Dwiggins "a deliberate modernist," and Kittredge

William A. Kittredge, who led the Department of
Design and Typography for Donnelley, ca. 1926,
and inspired the Four American Books Campaign.
Courtesy of the John M. Wing Foundation, Newberry Library.

knew his work before hiring him for the Poe. Dwiggins wrote to Kittredge, saying he thought the Four Books idea "thrilling" to "the starved book-artists," and believed that Kittredge was "on the right track," if he would be careful not to be "too precious." The books should reflect the tastes of the year in which they were produced, not of the time when they were written, Dwiggins believed. The illustrator expressed a decided interest in a "bit of the whimsical and a bit of the grotesque." They settled on his illustrating Edgar Allan Poe "with some extraordinary ominous flowers," "straight from the gardens of Hell."[39]

At first, Dwiggins estimated that he would need one month to finish the eight full-page drawings and eight chapter headings and, if fitted in around other projects, the illustrations might take him six months. Two years later, Kittredge was still pushing Dwiggins for a summer completion and a fall release date. The Poe illustrations remained unfinished. Dwiggins's report to Kittredge explaining the delay echoed Wilson's: although he had no trouble with "inspiration" and was "full of material," Dwiggins referred to a "jungle" of "damn little hurry-up jobs," and "casual junk" done for money, which was "maddening." "The Poe racket is the thing that I am keenest about," Dwiggins confided to Kittredge: "We will get her through if we bust a backstay. . . . Stall with your insistent staff-members for all you are worth, and pray like a Methodist. I think I have a clear two weeks in sight, and I will get a bale of them done."[40]

Like Wilson, Dwiggins counted on work as an advertising illustrator to provide income. At the same time, he worked on other book-illustration projects: fifty-eight full-page illustrations (plus eight vignettes for the text) for George Macy's two-volume edition of Alphonse Daudet's *Tartarin of Tarascon*, published in 1930, as well as illustrations for Balzac's *Droll Stories*, which Macy published in three volumes in 1931, and H. G. Wells's *The Time Machine*, published by Random House in 1931. Advertising represented the "tame" or artistically unimaginative to Dwiggins, the "Strathmore Stuff" or rubbish that he thought "no good," a life he wanted to get away from.[41] He hoped the illustrated Poe would help his career as a book illustrator. Dwiggins wrote to Kittredge that although the project would "save" illustrators, the Donnelley company would also benefit and "put itself on a high level." He thought the "book crowd should rise to it," basing his conclusions on "what I have seen lately of the market's appetite for limited editions" (referring to his work for George Macy).[42]

Rudolph Ruzicka, an experienced designer who had illustrated fifteen books, published his first for the Grolier Club in 1915. He had already completed work for Donnelley on editions of the Lakeside Classics and for the Pittsburgh Plate Glass campaign. His woodcuts for *Walden* so interested Kittredge and Littell that they offered to increase his payment, as they had for Kent, in order to get a few more drawings: "We are so much in love with your wood engravings in color," Kittredge wrote to him.[43] The press also arranged a house for Ruzicka in Concord, Massachusetts, near Walden Pond, so that he could complete his work over the summer of 1929, and he did do so. The increased compensation was a recognition that Kent and Ruzicka had achieved a level of superior craftsmanship, something that approached the aspiration for "definitive" illustrations.[44]

Public reception and sales of the Four Books served as a comment on changing standards of popular American taste in the 1930s. The bridge "between book and publicity printing" called for in the *Fleuron* of 1928 meant discarding the theatricality of advertising, including illustrations, in favor of more authentic styles. Two years later, Beatrice Warde, writing in the *Fleuron*, declared that the styles that reflected showmanship—"the whole apparatus of the arabesque and rococo" so popular in the post-Exposition era—should be abandoned in favor of a more "sober style."[45] As she later tried to define the American feel for print, B.W. associated showmanship more often with American display type than with British book composition.

The textual values illustrated in Kent's *Moby Dick* and Ruzicka's *Walden*, as opposed to those illustrated by Wilson in *Two Years Before the Mast*, and by Dwiggins in Poe's *Tales*, may serve as a partial explanation for the discrepancy in popularity and in sales for the books. Kent's illustrations succeeded because the aesthetics of the *Moby Dick* text lent themselves to drawings that represented a philosophical depth. Melville's book is a story of Old Testament dimensions. A human soul combats profound forces that cannot be understood in natural terms. Kent drew the great white whale that sounded the ocean depths against a backdrop of high stars in a pitch black sky. Rockwell Kent said his title pages were "The only black title pages that ever were" and called *Moby Dick* "the most beautiful book ever published in America."[46] The sculptural, solitary human figures on each of the title pages of the three volumes are in postures of supplication, fleeing, and falling headlong through limitless space.

Ruzicka's illustrations for *Walden*, on the other hand, are as domestic as Kent's are exotic; they seem to convey a sense that people, rather than events, make history. He showed Thoreau, the individual philosopher, in repose. Similarly, Thoreau's text conveyed both the strength of the individual and the power of observation.

Unlike Kent and Ruzicka, Dwiggins designed his chapter heads and flowers as abstractions from engineering, full of the mystification of nuts and bolts, ratchets, gadgets, and a demonic potential attributed to autonomous machinery.[47] Dwiggins's illustrations of Poe's narratives are the essence of the theatrical. The outlines of expressionless, blank-eyed human figures blurred by a spatter-paint technique, with captions in calligraphy heighten a cartoonlike effect. The soft focus of his sketches contrast with the razor-edged black-and-white mechanical drawings he used in his chapter heads.

If Dwiggins's illustrations could be said to represent the abstract interpretive value of inanimate objects, Wilson's drawings represented the homogenized world of goods represented by advertisers—the "soap smiths" of so-called Strathmore Town, the artistic mediocrity that Dwiggins abhorred. Wilson's pastel palette and pale characterizations never got very far away from those figures of "insistent cajolery" that typified the publicity printing of the day. Wilson's sailors seem to smell more of soap than of the sea. Although advertising illustration had a broader experimental field than book illustration, the style that typified the "hired square inches" lacked the ability to inspire, to "initiate a movement."[48]

Late in the production process, in the spring of 1930, it took six more months for Kittredge to settle textual matters. Then, when the company finally prepared to go to press after almost six years in the preproduction stages, Kittredge found himself scrambling for authoritative texts for his pressmen to use. For a reliable first edition of Poe's text, they had gone to Prof. Thomas O. Mabbott, a Poe scholar, who owned an imperfect copy of the first edition of 1840 with two pages lacking. Mabbott first asked for a 10 percent royalty on the Poe volume, which he dropped to 8 percent after the company flatly rejected his initial demand. Mabbot also requested six free copies of the book, but even Richard Henry Dana Jr.'s grandson and Littell himself had to purchase copies; the only free copies went to the illustrators, with fewer than ten promotional copies distributed.[49] Given the tight-purse-strings approach that had delayed production, giving in to Mabbott's demands could have provoked outright rebellion from the illustrators. When he heard of Mabbott's proposition, Littell's response was "Forget him. Let's print the stories from the first edition and reproduce it without notes."[50] After nearly a year's investigation and extensive correspondence about the states and variants of the texts of Poe's *Tales of the Grotesque and Arabesque*, R. R. Donnelley finally settled on the 1840 edition as the one to follow, using a perfect edition from the University of Texas.

The company asked Prof. Raymond Adams of the University of North Carolina to write a brief introduction to *Walden* for a flat rate of $250. Kittredge fully expected the professor to be responsible for determining the authoritative text, but Adams misunderstood. He replied to an inquiry from Kittredge that he would check with reluctant collectors and scholars to get a copy of the text for printing. With an apparent knack for saying the wrong thing, Professor Adams suggested to Kittredge, while making excuses for not being able to get a copy of Thoreau's corrected text, that "your edition is not to be a definitive text as much as an example of fine bookmaking with a classic American book used as the vehicle."[51] Finally, the textual matter apparently was settled, when Kittredge happened to find a used copy of the so-called Bixby edition, named after a St. Louis collector, in a bookshop. In the Bixby edition, a scholarly editor named F. B. Sanborn had restored twelve thousand words that Thoreau originally deleted to improve the first draft of the original manuscript. Understandably unsettled, Kittredge did not know what he had stumbled across. He immediately sought reassurance from

Defining R. R. Donnelley's American Culture, 1926–1935

MOBY DICK

OR

THE WHALE

BY HERMAN MELVILLE

VOLUME III

ILLUSTRATED BY ROCKWELL KENT

CHICAGO THE LAKESIDE PRESS 1930

Title page, Moby Dick, by Rockwell Kent, 1930. The most popular
of the Donnelley "Four Books" intended to reposition the printer with
mass-market book publishers, the one-volume trade edition launched
Bennett Cerf's Book-of-the-Month Club for Random House.
Courtesy of the John M. Wing Foundation, Newberry Library.

Adams about the authority of the text, which Adams promptly supplied.[52]

In their selection of paper and type for the Melville project, Kittredge and Kent compromised their goal of producing entirely American-made books. This change of plan came about because the first eighty-thousand-sheet paper shipment for *Moby Dick* arrived damaged, and questions arose about whether various types of paper could absorb the heavy ink used in reproducing Kent's all-black title pages and heavily shadowed etchings. In the end, they decided on Arnold Unbleached White Wove, imported from England.

Kent thought "homeliness" the dominant characteristic of Melville's book. He believed the character of the type for the text should also be "homely rather than refined and elegant." Instructing Kittredge about the Melville style, and how to integrate illustrations with the text, he wrote that

> one does, to be sure, associate "starkness" and "coldness," as you have with the theme of the sea; but *Moby Dick* is decidedly not of that character. Its prose is ample, voluminous, rich, warm; it is above all not refined, not studied; it blunders through to triumphant success by the dramatic intensity of the visionary mind it serves. It is a literary woodcutting not engraving. . . . The color, so far as I can see, is determined: night, the midnight darkness enveloping human existence, the darkness of the human soul, the abyss, such is the mood of *Moby Dick*.[53]

Kent thought a Caslon more suitable than a Bodoni for the typeface, but none could be found in the United States that Kittredge judged appropriate. They had tried specimen pages of eighteen-point American Monotype Fournier, which appeared flawed. In Kent's opinion, on a page consisting of type without leads separating the lines, and on others where letters ran together, the page looked "spotty," resembling "dirty fingerprints."[54]

Kent also judged an italic produced for American Monotype inferior. In fact, using it would have obliged the printers to set all the italic type by hand, because machine Italic fit so badly that "ugly gaps" appeared. In Kent's opinion, this drawback could not be rectified simply by putting leads between the lines; the Italic typeface should resemble the written line and be set as close together as possible. Kittredge solved the problem by importing eighteen-point English Monotype, Caslon Old Style, printed on Arnold Unbleached White Wove Antique. Although the American character of the production would suffer somewhat, importing type seemed less of a compromise than setting type for the book by hand if the company had insisted on American type foundry productions.

Dwiggins's book design required additional attention because his illustrations proved to be full of curves, and type could be set vertically or sideways, but not at a 45-degree angle. The series of individually hand-stamped images that characterized Dwiggins's abstract flowers decorating Poe's *Tales* resembled, in the opinion of Beatrice Warde writing in the *Fleuron*, "the naturalism of a Chinese plate."[55] Although stenciling would have been an alternative, Kittredge thought it was too commercial a technique. He wanted original illustrations that could not be duplicated. Dwiggins first suggested using very thick antique book paper similar to the rag used for the permanent edition of the *New York Times*. He wanted the illustrations French folded so that both the back of the illustration and the opposite page would be blank, with the paper folded at the top or side; Dwiggins's drawings were very intricate, and the transparency of all-rag book paper would have caused a shadow of the type to show through from the verso of the illustrated page.

After running specimen pages, Kittredge judged that the effect of the illustration would be ruined by the ink on the verso of the illustration, and tipped-in drawings on blank pages would be too expensive. Both Kittredge and Dwiggins decided the solution lay in selecting a high-quality paper. Pure linen and spring water produced good paper, but it was insufficiently opaque. Kittredge wrote Dwiggins in 1928, "So far we have been unable to locate a paper so that the type will not be observed through the sheet."[56] Both men disliked the trial specimen pages set with sixteen-point Bernhard Script, and they agreed that its daily use in advertising had made it too "common" for book composition. When they finally printed the book, they ended up using Linotype Original Old Style twelve-point type, on 100 percent rag book paper.

Defining R. R. Donnelley's American Culture, 1926–1935

In producing *Walden*, Kittredge and Ruzicka rejected what they called the "elegance" of Scotch Roman English Monotype Baskerville. Instead, they chose twelve-point Monotype Fournier printed on Aurelian Natural Wove Dull paper, and they decided to bind the book in a decorative cloth from one of Ruzicka's designs. Ruzicka wanted to produce drawings by a stone lithographic process, rather than by using woodcut techniques, but Kittredge dissuaded him from that idea. He conveyed Littell's feeling that modern technology should be employed in the production of the books, rather than any mode considered antique, and that the purpose of the campaign was to demonstrate to mass-market book publishers Donnelley's latest technology and design capability. Kittredge observed that although Wilson's *Two Years* had been imitative of Dana's first edition, they used a modern Scotch Roman Monotype printed on Aurelian Natural Wove Dull book paper, bound in blue cloth with linen backbone enclosed in a slipcase. Both Littell and Kittredge wished to capitalize on Ruzicka's reputation as a wood engraver, but they did not want him to pursue what Dwiggins would have called "period stuff." They wanted Ruzicka to provide definitive illustrations that epitomized his own artistic sense of *Walden*, not Thoreau's.[57]

After Kittredge had solved the major production problems, he threw off all restraints, praising the illustrators, saying Dwiggins should have been a "Planner Of Cities and Dictator of Aesthetics, there was so much common sense, logic and reason in his aesthetic choices."[58] He praised the artist's sense of color, saying he "wished he might go to school with him, and stir some of the American manufacturers to follow his lead." Whatever production problems Kittredge had faced, he had stuck to his core marketing concept, design purpose, and goals, to produce definitively illustrated editions.

The demands of the company's first line of business, commercial printing, contributed to production delays as much as the schedules and demands of the illustrators did. Kittredge wrote to Kent in April 1930, "In spite of the fact that we have four presses doing the work, it will probably take another five weeks to complete." After five years of coordinating production decisions involving artists, craftsmen, and Donnelley management, Kittredge remained optimistic that the project represented an opportunity to advance American industrial techniques. In a letter to Ruzicka in 1929, he bluntly stated, "In spite of the fact that I have been wrestling with things here for five years and not getting any place in particular, I have lost no whit of my vision of what the real thing may be and what printing may become in the hands of honest and talented craftsmen."[59]

The original marketing plan required subscribers to order all four books at once. Although the anticipated volumes met a robust response, due to the unanticipated delays, Kittredge and Littell decided to treat each edition as a separate sale. As production was delayed, costs rose, and deliberations about type, paper, and authoritative text seemed even more drawn out. *Moby Dick* quickly became oversubscribed at fifty-two dollars for the three-volume edition, but the other editions remained undersubscribed at fifteen and twenty dollars per volume. Half of Kent's edition sold before the illustrated prospectus ran out. Littell explained later to Kittredge, "The main thing is to be sure and sell them all. If we get out 1,000 Rockwell Kents, and they go in a heck of a hurry, it would be easier to sell the rest of them."[60]

Once Kent submitted some of his drawings and it became clear how important the *Moby Dick* would be, Kittredge appealed to Littell to expand the first run to twenty-five hundred. Littell rejected the idea because it deviated from the original plan; he felt that it would "look like we varied on Rockwell Kent simply because we could get more for them." Then as early as 1927, Kent suggested to Kittredge that they plan for a "pocket-size" one-volume trade edition, and Kittredge approved the idea immediately.[61] Consequently, each subscriber to Kent's three-volume edition received a four-page pamphlet fully explaining the differences between the trade and the special edition, with an offer to refund their money or to transfer their orders from the special to the trade edition, but no one canceled the three-volume for the one-volume edition. By production time in 1930, the trade edition of *Moby Dick* had been printed and bound—ten thousand copies for distribution by Random House for the Book-of-the-Month Club—even before Donnelley's three-volume limited edition was off the press.

Rockwell Kent illustration for Moby Dick, *1930.*
Courtesy of the John M. Wing Foundation, Newberry Library.

DISTRIBUTION AND SALES

R. R. Donnelley distributed the Four Books, and Littell handled all orders himself, assuming the responsibility for sales and for accounts receivable. Littell limited the availability of free copies to those in the book trades who might put Donnelley's presses to work. Even Rockwell Kent was told by Kittredge when he appealed for more copies of his own book that "Mr. Littell has, under lock and key, a few copies with which he may be willing to part when he returns. . . . Orders for sets of the books are coming in so rapidly that it looks as though some people are going to get left out in regard to orders for single volumes."[62]

Booksellers such as Weyhe of New York publicized the books and distributed the prospectus, a finely printed booklet with a tipped-in title plate for each book. Persuasive as a sales piece, it was coveted by collectors. Weyhe also mounted an exhibit of the illustrations in their shop. Kent feared that Donnelley's move to handle distribution itself, cutting out the booksellers, would be misunderstood, appearing as though "you are declaring war on them. . . . It would be considered a first threat to the booksellers' existence."[63]

As events developed, the booksellers were not a problem, but the matter of copyright and ownership of plates was a point of contention between the company and each illustrator. Kittredge insisted that although the artists could own their plates, Donnelley owned the reproduction rights. No additional imprints should be made of the illustrations, "in fairness to those who subscribed."[64] Over the next twenty years, this policy was observed, with exceptions: George Macy produced a commemorative volume of the work of Edward Wilson, and in 1951 a Czech edition of five thousand copies appeared of the Czech-American Ruzicka's *Walden*.[65] Wilson complained, "I am quite anxious to get some return on my investment, and I don't see why I shouldn't. You people admit that you are making your ten percent but I am so far in the red illustrating books that it's no joke. Now what the hell? Give a fellow a break! Do I have to land in Littell's office à la Kent out of a flying machine to get anything? If so I'll do it."[66]

Kittredge replied to Wilson, as he did to Dwiggins and Ruzicka, that reproduction rights and the decision to take the book into a trade edition had to be defensible from a business standpoint. When each illustrator in turn pushed for the same opportunity, Kittredge questioned them: "How can a trade edition . . . be made sufficiently different from the special edition to warrant the probable difference in price?"[67] Wilson lobbied hard for a trade edition, enlisting the support of an associate editor of John Day Co., but had difficulty when sales lagged for *Two Years*. Littell comforted Wilson, saying that "it is certainly no fault of yours that they are unsold. It is a darn good book." Littell admitted that Donnelley had "never published anything before," and probably "never will publish again." He also acknowledged that the campaign had been one conducted as a public-relations scheme to cajole mass-market publishers through direct mail. They had bypassed advertisers as well as book-sellers, with only some very plain advertisements placed in *Publishers Weekly.*[68]

To dispose of the remaining books, the company launched a "Three American Books" campaign. A 1935 balance sheet suggests that it did little to alter the original figures. Approximately $7,000 had been spent on preliminary promotional expenses, including the printing of prospectus booklets to advertise the campaign and Donnelley exhibition in 1930. Over the 1930–35 period, total sales for the Four American Books came to $95,085, and production and promotion costs were $87,264. This included a 15 percent markup because of the extra quality requirements demanded by Kittredge's Department of Design and Typography.[69]

The uneven company sales records for the Four Books between 1930 and 1935 confirm Littell's admission about the publishing venture being a first for the company. Though Ruzicka and Kent achieved national trade recognition in the 1931 American Institute of Graphic Arts (AIGA) Fifty Books competition, the tremendous popularity of *Moby Dick* overshadowed the three other titles. Each of the Four Books had been slightly overprinted: Melville by 27 copies, Dana by 25, Thoreau by 26, and Poe by 34. Subscriptions remained strong for all the volumes: 998 copies of the Melville sold by subscription, 975 of the Dana, 901 of the Thoreau, and 786 of the Poe. According to company records, the total distribution for the Melville was 1,020 copies; for the Dana, 1,008; for the Thoreau,

Defining R. R. Donnelley's American Culture, 1926–1935

930; and for the Poe, 820. The company sent no more than ten copies per title for promotional purposes to reviewers, with a few other copies allowed for copyright deposit, for accessions in the Donnelley Memorial Library, for the AIGA Fifty Books of the Year competition, and the like.[70]

By the winter of 1930, proceeds on sales of 2,567 copies of the Four Books totaled $61,302. Advance orders for the *Moby Dick* came to 997; for *Walden*, 716; for Poe's *Tales*, 713; and for *Two Years*, 774. *Moby Dick* was yielding the largest net profit: $12,380. The following year, *Moby Dick* exceeded earlier sales estimates by $1,000; sales for *Two Years* improved slightly, and the figures for the Thoreau and Poe remained about the same. Production costs relative to sales value in 1930 showed *Moby Dick* as the most profitable, with more than a $12,000 profit. With *Walden* and Poe's *Tales*, the company broke even: Ruzicka's *Walden* yielded a profit of less than $100, and the Poe recorded a loss of $11. Edward Wilson's book represented the greatest loss, of $4,280. Book auction records show that between 1933 and 1938—the depths of the Great Depression (none were auctioned before 1933)—twenty sets were sold at auction, but for far less than the original publication price.

The low point was 1935, when three complete sets of the Four Books sold for $8, $25, and $27. On the average, the Melville volumes brought only $35 during the thirties, with one three-volume set, apparently inscribed by Rockwell Kent, bringing $50 in 1938. Another dozen sets sold between 1941 and 1945, with an average cash value approximately close to the original purchase price. One volume, rebound in pigskin, with letters from Kent tipped in, sold for $165 in 1945. Through the late forties and fifties, the auction value seldom exceeded an average of $60. By 1987, however, a three-volume Rockwell Kent *Moby Dick* in good condition with the original aluminum slipcase fetched $1,000. After two decades, the company still had the volumes on hand: in 1951, only 7 surplus copies of *Moby Dick*, 17 of *Two Years*, 96 of *Walden*, whereas 214 of Poe's *Tales* remained. These went for half price to Donnelley employees. *Publishers Weekly* estimated the value of the remaining books to be $4,000. Even after the sales to employees, 15 copies of *Two Years*, 90 copies of *Walden*, and 207 copies of Poe's *Tales* remained.

Defining R. R. Donnelley's American Culture, 1926–1935

These went by job lots to book dealers and yet another half-price offer to employees.

The Four American Books campaign succeeded not only in producing definitively illustrated editions of Melville and Thoreau, but also in meeting the company's marketing aims. The *Moby Dick* issued in 1930 led to an increase in Donnelley's printing orders from book publishers. Random House asked the company to manufacture its edition of *Wuthering Heights*. Donnelley also printed Rockwell Kent's *N by E* for the Literary Guild and *Salamina* for Harcourt, Brace. "All of these helped us to maintain our position as good book manufacturers," according to company president Herbert Zimmermann.[71] The first trade edition of Kent's *Moby Dick*, ready in time for the Christmas season of 1930, ran to 69,167 copies, of which the Book of the Month Club distributed 50,000. Random House and Cassell & Company, Ltd., in England, published 2,000. Donnelley & Sons favored the trade edition because it lent importance to the three-volume limited edition. It provided what Littell called "a good size job of book making" over which they could maintain complete artistic control. The popular success of the illustrated edition of Moby Dick caused an increase in printing orders from other book publishers.

In 1937 Garden City Publishing Company reprinted the 1930 trade edition of *Moby Dick* after upgrading the production quality of the book. The company demanded that they use finer paper and materials than they had at first intended. Garden City published 20,500 copies, of which the Book of the Month Club issued 2,621. Following the entry of the U.S. into World War II, the War Production Board ordered another edition. In response to the demand for this issue, Bennett Cerf of Random House profitably printed their Modern Library Giant series, publishing 15,000 copies in 1943, 10,000 in 1946, 6,000 in 1948, and 10,000 in 1949. Random House gave the order to print nearly 100,000 copies of the *Moby Dick* trade edition to R. R. Donnelley.[72]

The Four Book illustrators shared the ambition of Littell and Kittredge that the books would represent an ideal of graphic beauty. This sustained their intense concern for the book's physical properties—type, paper, binding, and packaging. Kittredge explained to

Kent that "when we first thought of making these special books, we thought of doing them according to machine conditions of today. They were, first of all, American books, American texts, illuminated by American illustrators, printed on American-made paper. It seems to me that in this country we should have a paper adequate to the work of this book, made by machine in a sheet large enough so that we can print with reasonable economy."[73] Combining higher standards of artistic beauty with social goals, R. R. Donnelley aimed to produce affordable volumes for the masses. According to the company's policy of bookmaking, volumes should fit comfortably in the hand of the reader, the binding should be done with the grain of the paper so that pages would fall open easily and stay open, and the books would be printed in a regular book pressroom on cylinder presses.[74]

Even the packaging and wrapping of the completed editions involved everyone's opinion. The illustrators provided drawings for the spine and cover binding, and even the design in the paper. Kittredge and the artists determined the best method of tying the ribbon to wrap the edition, as well as the design of the label to go on the outside of the cardboard packages used to ship the books. Months of labor and testing of specimens and materials went into the design and production of the special aluminum slipcase for Kent's *Moby Dick*, considered highly innovative at the time. Kittredge wrote to all the illustrators, saying that this would not be "just another commercial transaction," but the packaging itself would be an "event."[75]

Sales and distribution figures for the Four American Books do not accurately measure the success of the campaign, nor its impact on Donnelley's expanding client base among book publishers. They do suggest the extent to which Kittredge's feel for publicity and Littell's long-range marketing strategy would influence the way illustrated books would be thought about in the mass market over the next several decades. Although only the Kent edition achieved its projected sales potential, Donnelley & Sons accomplished the long-range marketing goal of the campaign: to reposition the company so that it would become known as a printing house with the capability of handling illustrated editions of books for the mass market.

Publicity can be thought about as a market force with an effect of

Defining R. R. Donnelley's American Culture, 1926–1935

homogenizing culture. The Four Books Campaign demonstrated that from the earliest years of the modern mass market where an advertising effort involved individualists, artists, and craftsmen, publicity served to position the market leader and advance quality and standards of the industry. At a critical point in the company history of R. R. Donnelley, men of intelligence, with near-giddy enthusiasm, great patience, and skill, who lived in the heyday of ephemeral messages, aspired to reach out and claim as definitive something that they thought would become a permanent part of America's cultural record. Theirs was a labor of love for the intrinsic beauty and integrity of the literary product; they were excited by their own persuasive power. In the end, it was the combination of their intention, imagination, and appreciation of design that made the Four Books, along with the publicity scheme that led to their production, an important exercise of the American business imagination.

Defining R. R. Donnelley's American Culture, 1926–1935

*

LIMITING EDITIONS

·

AND

·

ILLUSTRATING

·

BOOKS

·

1929–1939

*Lying is a gift, and the best liars are as truly
born to their trade as the best poets are to theirs.*
—Carl Van Doren, "On Lying"

The American "feel" for printed products in the twenties and thirties demonstrated how advertising and illustrated books served the
iconoclastic impulse of the aesthetic individualist.[1] The constructivists, dadaists, and futurists had believed that the modern book
should be seen as well as read; they introduced images into texts, using photographs, drawings, and superimposing type on film. In the
1930s two publishing experiments also attempted to redefine the
modern book genre, and the principles upon which its style was
based, by balancing market demand for images and integrated typographic design. Both the Limited Editions Club, a mass-market
book subscription plan, and the *Colophon*, a subscription quarterly
for connoisseurs of fine printing, began publishing one month before the 1929 Wall Street crash. George Macy's Limited Editions
Club approached book design and illustration from a modern American advertising perspective, whereas Burton Emmett and Elmer

C · H · A · P · T · E · R // F · I · V · E

Adler, editors of the *Colophon*, upheld the conservative traditions of the British private press. The Limited Editions Club flourished during the Depression, but the *Colophon* struggled for five years and published only sporadically through 1939, when it went out of business.

MANUFACTURING PUBLIC APPEAL

The distinction between a printing and publishing corporation as print managers and the news corporation as a disseminator of price value information is an important one in the story of the Limited Editions Club and the *Colophon* experiments. As Macy and Adler and Emmett identified their market niche, they also tried to differentiate their publications from a crowd of competitors and imitators. The Limited Editions Club and the *Colophon* used similar public appeals but employed different marketing techniques.

The success of Macy's club and the demise of Adler and Emmett's quarterly explain what Beatrice Warde meant when she wrote about an American "feel" for printed goods, although each publishing experiment fell short of defining what the British would call a national style.[2] Whereas the British accepted stylistic convention as part of their national culture, American printers tended to regard aesthetic protocol as confining. American printers, publishers, and advertisers preferred individualism in printing styles, and they saw illustrated books and limited editions as an exercise of their freedom from inhibitions—what Warde characterized as a "why not" attitude.[3]

The illustrated books published by the Limited Edition Club represented George Macy's iconoclastic individualism—what might be called his "antistyle."[4] The *Penrose Annual*, among the leading British printing trade journals, praised Macy as "the greatest single influence on American printing."[5] His "why not" attitude epitomized the language merchant of the advertising age. Said to have an average mind, he took these observations as a compliment.[6]

Unencumbered by typographic principles or aesthetic convictions, Macy approached readers directly through the mail. He believed in appearances, in packaging, and in marketing techniques. The Limited Editions Club enterprise integrated public appeal

with print planning. The *Colophon*, published by Adler and Emmett at the Pynson Press, housed in the back offices of the *New York
Times*, held more traditional attitudes associated with the private
press movement. They wanted to publish beautiful printing without bothering to sell, and they preferred to imagine they had an audience rather than going out and finding one.

Using a mix of marketing, mass psychology, and advertising,
Macy persuaded readers that his books possessed an investment
value at a time when few prices were holding steady. His direct-mail
letter appeal to subscribers advised, "Your investment . . . is permanently assured, more certainly than almost anything else in this
naughty speculative world."[7] At first, the editors at the *Colophon* dis-
paraged Macy's publicity hype and the promotional schemes used to
promote the Limited Editions Club. The idealistic *Colophon* editors saw their publication as a book news experiment. The London
Times praised the *Colophon*, a quarterly limited to a run of five hundred to one thousand copies per issue, as America's "most beautiful
magazine."[8] For each issue, the editors bound a half dozen signatures printed separately between hard covers, using different paper,
inks, and typefaces, printed by different private presses. Leading typographers and illustrators designed the covers.

To differentiate its status as "real book news" from the publicity
hype decried by journalists of the day, the *Colophon* editors announced that they should not "spend themselves" on the "expensive
and indiscriminate business of creating a public" because "a good
piece of work has its natural public." The editors declared that the
Colophon was "not to be a vehicle for collecting propaganda" but
should interest "an audience of people who collect books." Eventually, though, in order to survive, the editors of the *Colophon* had to
turn to Macy's highly successful mass-marketing techniques, but
they were far less successful at it.[9] Despite their initial prosperity,
Macy's books did not hold their auction value as the issues of the failing quarterly did: the *Colophon*'s first issues quadrupled in price almost immediately and continued to increase in resale value; the complete set of sixteen numbers originally priced at $10 each fetched
more than $600 in 1990.

Merely one among many language merchants during the 1930s, a

P. T. Barnum in Kelmscott clothing, George Macy had a singular zeal for packaging and marketing skills that did not extend to a concern for literature. Quite simply, he thought the public would prefer a good American book to a fine English one, and that the modern reader should be able to spot a good book by its cover.[10] Macy commented in one of his monthly newsletters that many fine books "have not been good books at all, have not been intended for reading or for inclusion in one's library of friendly, companionable volumes. Many have been objects d'art [sic] full of pictorial beauties which completely obscured the words of the authors; many have been printers' exercises. . . . a good book is harder to achieve than a fine book."[11]

Macy brought what he called "taste and beauty" to the production of American books, in styles derived from the advertising pages of American magazines.[12] Although he complained of being "harried by the conviction," he thought "more art existed in the advertising pages of America's magazines than in the pages of America's illustrated books."[13] Believing that artistic talent and creative genius would emanate from the advertising rather than from the printing or publishing sectors, he concluded that "many fine books have appeared in this world in the last three decades, books which were meant to be works of art, which were meant to be beautiful; it is a question whether many of them have had style."[14] While Macy devoted himself to creating and building an international style for a global market, Adler and Emmett spent themselves on raising standards of production.

As book designers in the Anglo-American publishing industry tried to upgrade trade production standards to equal those of the British private press "fine" edition, many illustrators and type designers had to accept assignments indiscriminately in advertising to make ends meet. Type designer William Dwiggins explained that he had "to keep the advertising stuff going in order to pay taxes . . . because the book trade cannot compete with the advertising trade."[15] Beatrice Warde concluded that an affordable trade edition became a reality in Britain before Americans accepted the idea.[16] Through B.W.'s promotional activity for Monotype, the British public met the idea of the book beautiful, she wrote, "on a thousand public

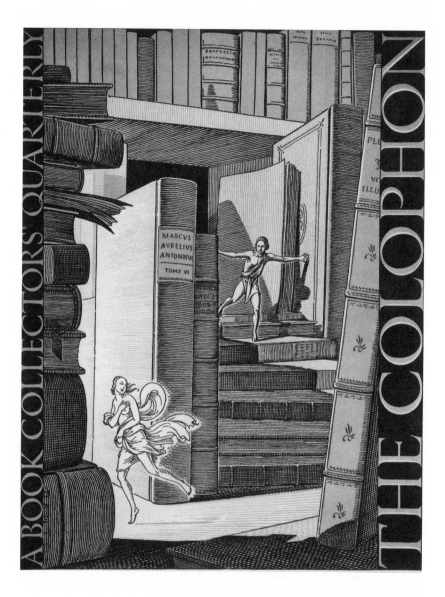

Colophon *cover, no. 2, May 1930.*
Designed by Joseph Sinec.
Courtesy of the John M. Wing Foundation, Newberry Library.

thoroughfares" as early as 1922.[17] Burton Emmett initiated formal efforts in the trade as president of the American Institute of Graphic Artists in the late 1920s through the AIGA Fifty Books of the Year competition, a competition the British later adopted. Under Emmett, the idealistic *Colophon* aspired to improve United States printing standards in 1930 by example.

Macy advertised that he, too, performed a public service by bringing beautifully fashioned trade books to the average buyer. Macy's advertising appealed to buyers' snobbery, though, whereas Emmett and Adler appealed to their aesthetic judgment. Macy wrote that "the book trade has been sitting on a gold mine and not known it. The various 'clubs' and 'unions' represent tentative efforts to find other ways of applying mass-production to books. . . . People want a solid background to give some coherence to the newspapers' scintillating confusion of day-to-day events."[18]

Although Macy made every effort to differentiate his enterprise from competitors, he did not hesitate to imitate or borrow techniques from other successful schemes. He urged members to imagine themselves in an armchair in a bona fide bookmen's Club, the Grolier in New York, or the Rowfant in Cleveland. He wrote that the "land is full of talk about the Book-of-the-Month Club and the Literary Guild; they are accused of standardizing the literary tastes of America. . . . Yet there is not one point of similarity between us."[19] Claiming for himself a special role as an "educator and arbiter of public taste," Macy tried to capitalize on a growing American appetite for the deluxe edition while differentiating his club from others trying to take advantage of the same trend.[20] He distinguished membership in his club from belonging to the Book-of-the-Month Club or Literary Guild and, in advertisements, he reassured readers that "the Limited Editions Club has no connection whatever with any of these firms and knows nothing about any or all of them other than what you see in the papers."[21]

In direct-mail messages tailored to the mass market, he offered his books not only to collectors "of means" but also to the ordinary reader.[22] In his advertising, Macy defended his use of the term *limited*. A trade publisher's run could be anywhere from five hundred to three thousand books and still be "limited." To the fine printer, the term meant a press run of not more than two hundred fifty. Macy justified his use of the term *limited*, saying that nature imposed a limit on the materials and equipment involved in producing his fifteen hundred books each month.

The modern literary marketplace made the definition of artificial and authentic scarcity less exact.[23] The term *limited* had indicated special manufacturing conditions such as handmade paper or ink, or publishing by hand-set letterpress, by which process only a few volumes of a particular title could be produced. Private-press editions were authentically limited; artificial scarcity occurred when the print run of a book had been limited to create the illusion of demand.[24] In defending his limited editions as authentic, Macy accused his contemporaries who issued large runs of limited editions of doing so "because people are accustomed to paying higher prices for limited editions than for unlimited." Based on his sense of the market, he added that "more than twenty-five thousand people in the United States . . . more . . . in the United States than in England" are ready to buy limited editions.[25] Relying on the styles devised for Kittredge's Four Books campaign, Macy boasted that the titles he selected had "never before" been "definitively" illustrated. His Macy-Masius publishing company in New York brought zeal for the mass market together with ambitions to be taken seriously by connoisseurs of fine printing and book design.[26]

Macy capitalized on the public appeal among American middle-class readers for luxurious printed goods associated with the British aristocracy. Creating affordable luxury for the workingman had been the basis for a number of marketing schemes in the Anglo-American printing industry over the years. The idea of marketing a series of great books published under one imprint served J. M. Dent's Everyman's Library, the Modern Library, Riverside Editions in the United States, and Allen Lane at Penguin in Great Britain.[27] In a 1936 advertisement for the Heritage Press, one of Macy's subsidiaries, he urged buyers to become the envy of friends and be taken for a "person of sound taste" by putting certain titles in high-quality bindings on their personal library shelves. By using works already in the public domain, he avoided having to pay royalties. Macy wrote that "a certain number of fundamental books—always the same books—lie at the base of our culture, and form part of our spirit's very texture. These are not necessarily the most grave and solemn works. . . . The publisher's and the artist's chief function [is] to preserve only what warrants preservation."[28] Macy's idea of a classic had less to do with a literary canon than with creating an impression of financial advantage. In a candid appeal to his subscribers, Macy admitted that "the ideal library always has been, and, for many years will continue to be, the subject of prolonged discussion." He invited subscribers into that discussion by involving them in the selection of titles for future publication. He also asked for their opinion of his books as he published them.[29]

It was Bennett Cerf who first developed the marketing approach later adopted by Macy and Emmett. Cerf's Random House developed a middle-class market for finely printed British books that were moderately priced. As the leading American distributor of British private-press books between 1927 and 1932, Random House boasted on its company letterhead that its mission was "to further creation and distribution of books of typographic interest in America."[30] Cerf had involved Macy at Random House as a director of a scheme called the Readers' Club in 1929. There Macy worked as part of a committee that included Clifton Fadiman, Sinclair Lewis, Carl Van Doren, and Alexander Woollcott.[31] Random House discounted by one-third to one-half or more the list prices of British deluxe editions produced on private presses between 1927 and 1932. Elmer Adler also worked with Cerf at Random House. Cerf wrote that "as agents for the Nonesuch Press and the Golden Cockerel Press, both Mr. Adler and I feel that Random House has secured the American market for the first moderately priced press books being turned out in England today."[32] Calling itself a price discount specialist, Random House traded on the investment value of the private-press books.

For Macy, Emmett, and many other publishers at the time, Random House set the American trade standard for book production by bringing British fine-press books before the American public. According to Macy, most books manufactured in the United States looked "shoddy and commercial" in comparison. He also found that Random House had proposed a solution to the inflationary force of

Limiting Editions and Illustrating Books, 1929–1939

booksellers who drove up the price of all books "beyond the reach of the common reader."[33] According to industry reports for the years 1929–31, the anticipated profit margin in 1931 for publishers amounted to less than 3 percent industrywide, and in 1932, the industry reported a decrease of 12½ percent in profits. Against these economic realities, Macy's success seems more impressive, and the demise of Adler and Emmett's *Colophon* less surprising.

The volatile markets of the 1922–32 decade helped to differentiate authentic book trade news from publicity hype. R. R. Donnelley's Four American Books, for example, made news because of their quality. Attracting attention from the public, press, and industry, the books brought Donnelley the business it sought and positioned the company as a stylistic leader in mass-market publishing. In the late twenties and early thirties, publishers often tried to get free publicity in the newspapers by employing the practice of "farming out to newspapers what passed for book news" in the form of press releases. Some authors and publishing houses also solicited and paid for favorable reviews of new titles. Printing corporations tended to take a dim view of the practice, calling it "educating the public" when it pertained to manufactured product lines, but "hype" when it pertained to publishers' books. Competitive booksellers, who could lose money if publishers marketed directly to consumers, also used the term *publicity hype*.[34]

The distinction between "real trade news" and promotional schemes helped position a journalistic experiment as different from a marketing scheme. George Macy declared that his own annual, the *Dolphin*, in folio-size hardcover, launched in 1933 at a cost of approximately $1,500 per issue, should be considered the "inheritor" of the short-lived *Imprint*, edited by Gerard Meynell, and the *Fleuron*, edited by Oliver Simon and Stanley Morison. The *Fleuron* published seven issues between 1923 and 1933; the *Dolphin*, four between 1933 and 1941, failing when it became a quarterly.[35] Based on its editorial content, Macy's *Dolphin* can be categorized as a "publicity hype" publication.

The *Fleuron* mixed trade news with promotional objectives, whereas Macy's *Dolphin* appears to have been published purely to promote subscriptions to the Limited Editions Club. However,

Colophon *cover, distributed as an advertisement,*
no. 6, June 1931. Designed by T. M. Cleland.
Courtesy of the John M. Wing Foundation, Newberry Library.

some trade critics did regard volume three of the *Dolphin*, *The History of the Book*, as a contribution to printing and publishing trade literature; it included articles on fifteenth- through nineteenth-century manuscripts and on the invention of printing, bookmaking, type, paper, presses, and the like. Although the first two volumes of the *Dolphin* contain little that would constitute bona fide trade news, volume one does have an article by Frederic Goudy on designing typefaces, one by the British Museum librarian Alfred Pollard titled "Margins," and others on ink, paper, and bookbinding. Volume two contains a similar number of trade-related articles, most written by the same eminent typographic specialists. In the last sections of volumes one and two, though, in two-part chapters titled "A Survey of Recent Books in Europe and the United States," only those books by George Macy's firm are discussed in the historical-critical survey. Even in volume three, the "history" of the illustrated book, the last section is a thinly cloaked essay about the historical significance of his own enterprise, promoting the titles on his current list.

The *Dolphin* and the *Colophon* expressed contrary views of the printing and publishing businesses. In their gravity, Colophonians naively believed the American private press could still "make real book news" as late as 1930. Meanwhile, Macy made his own news, engaging several "most respected experts" to write promotional and advertising copy.[36] Daniel Berkeley Updike of the Merrymount Press, for example, wrote copy for Macy's promotional brochures patterned on those designed by William Kittredge for R. R. Donnelley and Sons.[37] Carl Purington Rollins, the printer for Yale University Press, contributed several critical columns that invariably concluded with a statement about the historical importance of Macy's enterprise.[38]

Macy's first venture, a wholly owned subsidiary called the Brown House, Inc., begun in 1929, failed because he did not advertise. He lost nearly $6,000 in his best year at Brown House, according to annual reports for the eight months ending September 30, 1930. Alexander King illustrated the first three books—Fielding's *Tom Jones*, Gustave Flaubert's *Salammbô*, and Fyodor Dostoyevsky's *The Brothers Karamazov*—for a fee of $4,500. Enlisting the same illustrator for the first three books may have contributed to sluggish sales, because the reader would have been acquainted with the texts and would have expected some originality in the illustrations. Macy's entire sales effort would have had to depend on packaging. Originally *Tom Jones* and *The Brothers Karamazov* came in two volumes, boxed, for $25 or $35 or, as with *Salammbô*, in one cased volume for $18. When the books did sell, they went for well below the original prices. This contributed to the perception that Brown House books were "discounted" from the start.[39]

Macy's sales records show that some of the 157 copies of *Salammbô* sold for as little as $16 each. The records also show that only 4 of the 129 copies of *Tom Jones* fetched the full price of $25, and none of the 133 copies of *Karamazov* brought the full price. Production costs for 800 copies of each title ranged from $7 per set for *Tom Jones* to $5 per copy for *Salammbô*, and $9 per set for *The Brothers Karamazov*. Macy recorded advertising expenses of $3,000 against operating and production expenses of $30,300. His advertisements claimed that he had vigorous sales, but only 300 copies of each title were bought, with an additional 100 sold at a 20 percent discount.

Half the copies of each title sold to booksellers went for a 30 to 40 percent discount. Of his potential profits of $16,000 from *Tom Jones*, $11,520 from *Salammbô*, and $19,200 from *The Brothers Karamazov*, nearly one-third went to the booksellers. After reporting losses of $1,000 annually over four years, at an estimated liability to the parent company of between $10,500 and nearly $13,000 in the years 1930–32, with profits as low as $41 and sales as little as $230 per title, the Brown House "surrendered its charter," according to the Heaton Company accountant's report of March 13, 1934.[40] The Limited Editions Club acquired 186 unsold copies of *Salammbô* for $2,134 and all the outstanding capital stock for $250. Another of Macy's subsidiaries, the Print Club, incorporated on May 2, 1934, offered reproductions of prints and drawings and proved to be more profitable than the Brown House.[41]

When he incorporated under the laws of New York State as the Limited Editions Club on March 19, 1929, Macy served as president, J. O. Straus as vice president and treasurer, and Harold Riegelman and George Hecht as secretary. According to corporate documents, Straus provided start-up capital. Macy's club sold books to

1,500 subscribers through the mail for a $10 monthly fee. By eliminating costs involved in retail distribution, he could price his books so low that "the unscrupulous among American publishers would be put to shame."[42] Although subscribers could obtain the books at cost, Macy also assigned a list price to each volume to set a resale value and recommend a price to booksellers.

Among his marketing devices, Macy created a newsletter column, which he called a "department," titled "Book Exchange." In it he offered to link subscribers who wished to "resell any books they do not like directly with other purchasers" so members could remain "out of the clutches of the booksellers."[43] Macy confronted candidly the image of his books as discounted. He wrote that "if we had to follow the regular plan of giving a large discount to the bookseller, and a commission to the traveling salesman, and so on, such books would have to be sold in the bookshops for twenty-five dollars apiece. As a matter of fact, the books we have issued have been resold in the bookshops for sums ranging from eighteen dollars up to forty dollars. . . . we sent out all our books for ten dollars each."[44] In the first two years of operation, in spite of the generally bleak economic conditions, all 404 shares of the first issue of common no par value stock sold quickly.[45]

Learning a lesson from the dismal Brown House sales records, Macy invested more in marketing and publicity for his next venture, established simultaneously, as the Limited Editions Club. Using the example set by Bennett Cerf at Random House, Macy's advertisements for the Limited Editions Club relied on two pitches—the affordable price of the books and their fine production quality. Macy chided readers in advertisements, saying they paid too much for books: "You paid $25 to $250 per copy for limited editions made by Daniel Berkeley Updike, Bruce Rogers, William Addison Dwiggins, Frederic Warde, Jan Van Krimpen, Rudolph Koch, Thomas M. Cleland." Macy admonished that "in former years, you did not hesitate to pay these prices (or even more!) for the books you wanted. You knew that the works of these men would stand the test of time; that—aside from the aesthetic satisfaction in owning rare and beautiful volumes—the books themselves represented an assured investment."[46]

Limiting Editions and Illustrating Books, 1929–1939

The Limited Editions Club prospered after a slow start, issuing stock that paid dividends of $10 and $20 in 1932, and was worth as much as $200 per share by 1934. As the chief executive, Macy paid himself $12,000 a year, investing about one-quarter of his salary in new ventures and subsidiaries over the next four years. During the first six weeks, six hundred members enrolled in the Limited Editions Club. By the third month, Macy boasted of having a "waiting list." By 1931, he claimed the list numbered two hundred.[47] At least eleven major literary publications covered the Limited Editions Club debut as "book news." The *Saturday Review* and the *New York Times Book Review* charged that Macy's experiment might be a force for standardization in American literary culture. In reply, Macy wrote that he "shuddered" at the thought. To his subscribers, he fumed,

> In eleven major literary publications, extended articles were printed about us. Nine of these pleased us. Two did not. In the *Saturday Review* appeared a piece in which the writer pointed the finger of almost hysterical scorn at us; it is, said he, another attempt to "standardize" America, through the medium of the book collector; this damned Club, he hinted, is forsaking literature for book-making. . . . The *Times Book Review* . . . played upon this last theme. . . . The *Saturday Review*'s gentleman horrified us by saying that we were under-emphasizing the literature itself. . . . Under-emphasis, we feel, your grandmother![48]

With typical brashness, Macy was able to turn even negative publicity into opportunity.

In September 1931, Macy spent $32,449 on all promotion expenses for direct mail, advertising, and every other form of publicity; and $21,714 on recruiting the first one thousand memberships. He spent an additional $6,043 in the second year of business and $4,691 in his third for the other five hundred members, plus a waiting list of more than two hundred. According to the company's annual reports, Macy spent $4,392 for monthly letters, notices, and circulars for 1931, of which $2,555 covered printing and the rest was distributed among costs for paper, addressing envelopes, and postage. In 1932, he spent $21,234 for direct mail and $18,729 for display advertising.[49] As a result of Macy's aggressive direct-marketing campaign, his advertising and publicity costs amounted to three times his other operating expenses. In addition to his general expenses—salaries, operations, entertainment expenses, direct mail, display advertising—he also paid sales commissions to solicitors, and distribution of free copies for promotional purposes averaged about $400 per year.[50]

In June 1933, the corporation acquired a printing plant in Westport, Connecticut, to print the club's publicity materials; as a branch of the corporation, it had a value of $3,268. Profit and loss statements in the corporation records show that the printing office paid for itself in the first year, with neither a profit nor a loss. The Connecticut plant greatly reduced Macy's publicity costs and made possible an expanded version of his already-large direct-mail operation. The Connecticut office initially did not produce club books, although Macy and his wife, Helen, later designed several books printed at the press for members. In 1933, monthly direct mailings cost $3,179, of which $1,920 represented printing alone. In 1934, the cost of direct mail dropped to $2,152, of which $1,066 represented printing alone. In a summary statement prepared in 1933, promotional expenses dropped to $8,711 annually, down from the first year's figure of $21,714.[51]

Macy expanded his publicity through a broad-based network that incorporated a variety of printed ephemera including monthly letters, notices, and stationery that had been handled by outside printers. He asked his readers to serve as critics. He used polls, newsletters, essay contests, direct-mail appeals, and other means of soliciting direct feedback to find out which books readers would buy and in which styles they wanted to see them illustrated, before they were produced.[52] He promoted each volume in advance in the club's monthly newsletters. He also published readers' responses to earlier publications, reporting both average resale prices of earlier club books and the results of opinion polls about future titles. Selling the club as exclusive, he also marketed the enterprise as democratic.

Macy sometimes tried too hard. Although he seemed to lack real aesthetic or ideological conviction, he developed an ethical manifesto for subscribers, published as a finely printed limited edition. An individual's library "is the mirror of the personality," he declared in the preface to "A Code for the Collector of Beautiful Books," which was sent to all prospective subscribers as a hardcover gift book. He drew up the code as a manifesto of fundamental principles for the modern bibliophile, including four admonitions to purchasers, seven to publishers, and five to illustrators. He advised illustrators, for example, that they "must be able to read."[53]

When members failed to resubscribe, he advertised openings through the newsletter's Book Exchange Department. According to the company's annual reports, this department served as a medium for exchanging and selling books, "created for the convenience of subscribers." The Book Exchange Department touted the resale value of the books members no longer wanted. On August 31, 1933, the department reported having six hundred copies available of the first nine titles from the third year at an estimated value of $3,118, offering various discounts. In his monthly newsletter, Macy wrote that "thirteen of the subscribers to the second series have not as yet renewed their subscriptions. . . . Any vacancies in the membership remaining at the time this advertisement appears will be filled strictly in the order of receipt of application."[54] Macy's balance sheet for 1933 shows a gross profit of $1,112 for the Book Exchange Department, but his expenses were twice that. The department's net loss for the year totaled $993, which he used to offset the annual profits of the Limited Editions Club and subsidiaries.

Prize money and the cost of printing monthly newsletters added slightly to Macy's expenses. He staged contests to expand his appeal. A call for essays about the ideal book drew responses from around the world, according to his newsletter. He published the two best in finely printed pamphlets.[55] When he invited subscribers to name the titles they most wanted to have him publish, he reported receiving a similar response. To illustrate the winning titles, he opened another contest within weeks, inviting illustrators and designers throughout the world to submit drawings. When the design contest closed after several months, 311 sets of illustrations had been submitted. Macy reported receiving 1 from China, 14 from

Limiting Editions and Illustrating Books, 1929–1939

Colophon *cover, no. 10, May 1932.*
Designed by Boris Artzybasheff.
Courtesy of the John M. Wing Foundation, Newberry Library.

Russia, 20 from Germany, 3 from England, 11 from France, and others from Czechoslovakia, Italy, Holland, Canada, and Romania.

Macy published the names and accomplishments of the winners in his newsletter. First place went to Nicholas Lapshin of Moscow, who won a $2,500 contract for his illustrations of *Marco Polo*. The second prize was won by Thomas M. Cleland, for illustrations for *Tristram Shandy*, which earned $1,500. Richard Flothe of New York took the third-place prize of $1,000 for illustrating *Tyl Ulenspiegl*. Rene Ben Sussan won fourth place and a prize of $1,000 for illustrating *The School for Scandal*.

Despite the fact that academic critics remained unimpressed with all this publicity, Macy's club succeeded because he organized his enterprise around popular rather than critical opinion, appealing to readers' snobbery. He recognized that common readers wanted to buy an image of themselves as educated people rather than the critical opinion of "cultural aristocrats."[56]

Each year between 1929 and 1939, the Limited Editions Club constructed its list around a different theme established to enhance its public appeal. Macy responded directly to subscribers' ideas and suggestions gleaned through his monthly newsletters in polls, letters, contests, and articles. The Limited Editions Club sales showed positive results. In a summary statement for 1930–33, he reported operating profits as high as 17.4 percent for the first two years, and a low of 9.59 percent for the third.[57]

Macy's production expenses represent typical ones for the publishers of the day. By 1932, he reported net profits of $14,903 and total assets of nearly $100,000. By using literature already in the public domain, he saved the expenses of original authorship and avoided paying royalties. Fees paid to illustrators ranged from $500 to $1,500, contingent on the number of designs in the book, and critics received between $150 and $250 for a favorably written introduction. Gross sales per title as reported on the annual statement totaled $15,000, against production expenses for each title of $9,000, including import duty, wrapping and shipping, translations, introductions, illustrations, and the like. Thackeray's *Vanity Fair* represents the most costly book he produced, at $14,639, and Thomas Carlyle's *Sartor Resartus*, the least costly, at $5,771.[58]

Limiting Editions and Illustrating Books, 1929–1939

PRODUCING AN ANTISTYLE

Among the club's first 250 volumes, three distinct schools took shape that expressed the thinking of the modern advertising intelligence at work in book illustration and design: a product-based, sentimental Strathmore style; a personality-based, contemporary, functional style; and an audience-based, avant-garde or bold, futurist style. The Strathmore style, best represented by the work of Edward Wilson, remained well within the bland conventions of good taste set by corporate product advertisements. The Strathmore Paper Company, well known for its pastel-colored papers titled charming green, smart modern yellow, mint, warm gray, rose, peach, and maple, defined the soft sell. The Strathmore style favored the arabesque rather than the undecorated line, the painterly genres of costume prints, and human figures caught as if in a still life. Within this honeyed restraint, calligraphy prevailed over typography, creating an overall effect of a surplus of character shielded by a bland personality.

The second school, or contemporary style, is best represented by the work of Eric Gill. In this style, letters formed a personality on the page while sculptural human figures boasted more strength than sensation. Both the human image and typographical design existed in a syntactical relationship. With all letter edges forming justified margins, elements reflected careful planning on a medial axis.

The cubo-futurist style, represented by the advertising art of Rene Clark, Alexander King, and type designer William Dwiggins, among others, favored startling the reader with bold colors, exaggerated proportions, grotesques, even sinister shapes, showing humans in a state of agitated emotions. In this school, photographic realism replaced the still life, and the camera angle distorted proportion. Composition demonstrated psychological processes. Calligraphy rather than typography explained visual elements in captions. Factories, machinery, robots, and overt displays of technology intrigued the artist.

As Macy reminisced twenty-five years later, the best-known book illustrators, designers, and printers were engaged in his first year of business "to do only those books" that they "long wanted to illustrate or design."[59] The first list of Limited Editions Club books in-

Limiting Editions and Illustrating Books, 1929–1939

cluded a staid production of a two-volume edition of Boccaccio's *The Decameron*, illustrated and designed by Thomas M. Cleland and listed for $12.50; and Daniel Defoe's *Robinson Crusoe*, illustrated by Edward Wilson, with a preface by Ford Madox Ford, printed by the Grabhorn Press, and listed for $20. The club's earliest years, Macy admitted, contained "about an equal number of triumphs and mistakes." Among the "mistakes," Macy counted an unpopular edition of *Tartarin of Tarascon*, by Alphonse Daudet, printed by the Georgian Press, and illustrated by William A. Dwiggins, and listed for $9.

If Macy's books demonstrated the "why not" attitude that typified an antistyle, as Beatrice Warde implied, Dwiggins's work for Macy epitomized the look she intended to describe by the phrase. Dwiggins's self-conscious modernism, his romance with machinery, overshadowed any aesthetic convention or ideology. B.W. described Dwiggins's work as a "personality riding a book."[60] In 1932, for example, Dwiggins looked ahead in Orwellian fashion and speculated in *Towards a Reform of the Paper Currency*, published by the Limited Editions Club, that the year 1951 would see angry book illustrators and typographers attack and abolish the United States Bureau of Engraving and Printing in Washington, assassinate the director of the bureau, and massacre what he called the "Federal Art Experts" during the assault. Dwiggins's propaganda tract, finely printed in a limited edition between hard covers on special paper with engraved chapter headnotes, proposed redesigning American paper currency and stamps so that they would "report the tension of 1932."[61] Despite the political intensity he demonstrated during the Depression years, Dwiggins is best remembered as a type designer and specialist in advertising layout credited with "improving the typography of American magazines" by restyling *Harper's* covers.[62]

Dwiggins's book illustrations animated the grotesque and consistently romanticized modernism. He used machinery as fine printers once used flowers and printers' devices to decorate the page, and his synthesis of a romantic modernism with historical realism led him to create some stylistically contradictory works. Although his works might have been faulted for being too self-conscious, even eccentric, in a display of individual style, his aesthetic designs are neither

capricious nor whimsical. Nor does Dwiggins ever succeed in deriv-
ing a style that personalizes the reader.

A provocative, eccentric style that displeased critics may have
been more alluring to the public, though, than those books trying to
"define" a national identity through style. Possibly the appearance
of eccentricity in book design capitalized on the mass-market appetite for personalized luxury goods. Macy's *Snowbound*, by John
Greenleaf Whittier, designed by Carl Purington Rollins, is a good
example of a contrast to Dwiggins's eccentricity. Pairing an under-
stated typeface with monochromatic illustrations, Rollins's conventional restraint seems nonchalant compared to Dwiggins's self-
announcing style.[63] Yet both Dwiggins and Rollins show how the
idiosyncratic styles of designers with personality made Macy's list
ripe for critics, for those serious about modernism and the principles of the new typography, as well as those who clung to the values
of the private-press movement.

Although Dwiggins's books remained in Macy's opinion "among
the best fifty" that his Club published in its first twenty-five years,
they were unpopular with readers. The drawings in *Tartarin* ap-
pear unfinished; faces and figures meld without seeming to refer to
one another or to the reader. On one page, three illustrations render
three different scenes, and none bears any relation to another; they
are arranged like cartoons on a sketch pad without syntax or compositional axis. Captions are in calligraphy, not type, and the *Tartarin*
paper stock is so thick that pages do not lie flat when turned. In light
of the Lakeside Classics ideal, that a book should fit in an ordinary
business-suit pocket, the *Tartarin's* awkward size may explain its
unpopularity: it measured 3½ by 4½ inches in two volumes of approximately one hundred pages each. The 12-point typeface is difficult to read and appears even more cramped against the odd page dimensions. Dwiggins's paper-board covers—geometric patterns on a
pastel background—promise a well-planned design, but the inte-
rior of the book fails to follow through.

Once a designer's name became associated with a certain style,
his next book risked becoming a cliché because readers were easily
bored, and critics took a dim view of aesthetic predictability—
charging that it signaled what B.W. called a "creative rut."[64] La

Fontaine's *Fables*—illustrated by Rudolph Ruzicka, printed by the Merrymount Press, and listed for $7.50—represented such a "rut" to Macy. He called it "a most typical Updike job." Although the achievement and reputation of Daniel Berkeley Updike's Merrymount Press remained unchallenged, Macy thought Updike had ventured too little beyond the safety of his previous achievements in his *Fables* for the Limited Editions Club list. Macy seemed to find a safe harbor in proven formulas. That can be attributed to his marketing instinct. Designers were expected continually to try something new. Actually, any variation in Updike's style would have made book news, thus bringing the club more publicity.

So-called "stunt" books also could be counted on to make news. Raspe's *Travels of Baron Munchausen*, printed by the R. R. Donnelley Lakeside Press and designed by William Kittredge (listed for $10), did not impress Macy much. He thought it unsuccessful, even as a stunt, "redeemed" only by the introduction by Carl Van Doren, "On Lying," in which he described Munchausen as the "Euclid of liars." Advertising could be called the "genius of lying," of course, in a Swiftian sense. Van Doren wrote that "there is luck in lying. No liar is invariably lucky, any more than any poet is. Travelers do not lie from necessity . . . they lie for the joy they get from it and the fun they give by it. . . . If they are dull men they tell dull tales."[65]

Both the book covers and illustrations of Munchausen prove that stylistically, self-consciousness was easily confused with aesthetic "lies." The Munchausen covers are orange cloth on boards with dyed yellow spots, and gold-embossed, slack-jawed fish decorate the green leather spine. The illustrations are grotesque. The block-faced primitive human faces lack emotion, but the animals seem capable of appetite and surprise. In an illustration titled "I Gave Myself Up as Lost," the Munchausen figure surrenders, eyes to the heavens, in a self-dramatizing gesture. Meanwhile a lion gazes from the underbrush directly out at the reader beneath luminous eyes fringed by long lashes, and an alligator opens his jaws anticipating a bit of action.

Macy called Jonathan Swift's *Gulliver's Travels* a "triumph." This book was illustrated by one of Macy's favorite stylists, Alexander King, whom he called "the arch king of ugliness." He listed

Mailing envelope for Colophon *magazine.*
Courtesy of the John Johnson Collection, Bodleian Library, Oxford.

the book at $17.50 and gushed in his promotional copy that "for the first time, Dean Swift's roaring, savage and adult satire is taken out of the namby-pamby children's editions and made, unexpurgated, into the lusty and rugged volume it was always intended for" (238, 250).[66] King's illustrations try to mirror Swift's satirical view of humanity. He distorted dream and reality, made humans silent and beasts talkative. He cast tiny people alongside colossal clocks, spoons, and other household objects. Book illustrators, who took on advertising projects in order to survive, found an opportunity to exploit commercial themes in literary publishing, and King was no exception. An advertising illustrator like King could enjoy a freedom from the seriousness about commodities in book illustration that his work in commercial design did not allow.

More than one of the American "classics" Macy selected for the club list demonstrated a sentimental style. In addition to Whitman's *Leaves of Grass*, designed by Frederic Warde, and Whittier's *Snowbound*, designed by Carl P. Rollins, he also published a sentimental Robert Louis Stevenson's *Two Medieval Tales*, printed by the Marchbanks Press and listed at $5, and Washington Irving's *Rip Van Winkle* with an introduction by Mark Van Doren, designed by Frederic Goudy and listed at $7.50. Macy declared a "triumph" the Poe *Narrative of Arthur Gordon Pym*, illustrated by Rene Clark and listed at $5. Clark's *Pym*, however, popular as it might have been with readers, is an imitation of Rockwell Kent's *Moby Dick*. Macy basked in the popularity of Clark's illustrations and held them up to readers as the epitome of the advertising artist's talent. When Clark later became president of his own advertising firm, Calkins and Holden, he went on to design better books than *Pym*, for the Limited Editions Club and for others.

Macy concluded that, in the first year, he made only "two serious mistakes": in publishing the Walt Whitman, he used the "wrong text" and he asked Frederic Warde to design the book, including selecting the typeface. To Macy, Warde's style ended up seeming too delicate for its rough-hewn subject matter. He wrote, "The barbaric yawp of Walt Whitman is hushed by the meticulous, delicate, charming and inappropriate typography of Frederic Warde" (235).[67] In his second year, Macy changed his focus from American to European

Limiting Editions and Illustrating Books, 1929–1939

culture. Victor Hugo's *Notre Dame de Paris*, listed at $7.50, demonstrated French typography and illustration. Members protested, though, that they disliked the French style of binding the book in paper covers, because it seemed too delicate and lacked the rugged individualism associated with American bookmen. For disgruntled subscribers, Macy offered to rebind the two-volume edition in hard covers, and that silenced complaints.

The list represented work by the most outstanding "fine" British printers and illustrators. Thomas de Quincey's *Confessions of an English Opium Eater*, printed at Shakespeare Head Press, Oxford, was designed by B. H. Newdigate and listed at $10. Thomas Carlyle's *Sartor Resartus*, with an introduction by Bliss Perry, was designed by Oliver Simon, printed by the Curwen Press, and listed at $6. Although Simon's remained "among the ten best books" Macy thought he had published, he also counted it among the ten least popular. Simon's style disappointed some conservatives, and among those who preferred the advertising artists, Clark, Dwiggins, King, and Wilson, it seemed bland. John Johnson, the Oxford University Press printer, designed and printed Macy's two-volume edition of Thackeray's *Vanity Fair*, with a preface by G. K. Chesterton, which listed for $22.50. Macy enlisted Dutch printers (Enschede en Zonen, Haarlem) for a text of Homer's *Iliad* with the preface by Alexander Pope. Another of the "ten best, ten least popular" books was a very conservatively designed *Tartuffe*, by Moliere, which was produced by a German printer (Poeschel & Trepte), designed by Hugo Steiner-Prag in Leipzig, and listed at $6.

Macy admired the work of Czech and German printers. He engaged Rudolph Koch to illustrate a selected edition of *Grimm's Fairy Tales*, which was printed by the Wilhelm Gerstung press in Offenbach, Germany and listed at $13.50. The state printing office of Prague produced *Aucassin and Nicolette*, listed for $5, according to Macy, which the American public disliked because he used period costumes to illustrate the book.[68]

At the end of his second year in business, Macy polled his subscribers about their preferences. His subsequent advertisements claimed that the third series took shape "almost solely on the basis of the suggestions of the members." He announced that among mem-

Limiting Editions and Illustrating Books, 1929–1939

bers there had been "a surprising uniformity," and most "liked our own choices." Certainly the club's strong profits in a depressed economy bore out this impression. For the year ending 1932, Macy reported gross profits of $64,655.61, with average profits of $5,387 per book. Total production costs ran $45,000 over gross profits.[69]

As the Depression deepened, the club's style in both its book illustration and publicity became more flamboyant. Along with predictable selections such as Benjamin Franklin's *Autobiography* and an *Alice in Wonderland* designed by Frederic Warde, the club offered *The Last of the Mohicans* illustrated by Edward Wilson. William Dwiggins also illustrated Balzac's *Droll Stories*, and Japanese designer Yasumasa Fujita illustrated Lafcadio Hearn's *Kwaidan*, which was printed in Japan, set on handmade Japanese paper in traditional old-style type, and bound in brocade with a silk wraparound slipcase and tied closure.

Rene Clark illustrated Goethe's *Faust*. The flashy result, with gold-embossed illustrations and endpapers, represented what Macy called the "triumph" of the advertising style.[70] The volume also featured a new typeface designed by Dwiggins called Metro, a thinner version of the Sans popularized in the 1929 Montoype campaign for LNER. Macy wrote, "Once again, I went to the leading practitioner of advertising art, to ask him to illustrate. . . . I think he created a startlingly beautiful advertising brochure. When people tell me, with anger flashing from their eyes, how much they dislike it, I can only say in defense, and in weak defense, that it is not unpleasant, now and then, to have in one's library a startlingly beautiful advertising brochure."[71]

Clark's *Faust* is the most visually arresting of any of the books Macy produced in the first decade, even though Dwiggins's typeface and book design are incongruous with Clark's style of illustration. The pastedown endpapers have an embossed two-color reverse-pattern design, the title "Faust" occupies a full third of the frontispiece, the layout and text are engaging and airy enough for the reader to see each line of dialogue, and the illustrations, some of them embossed, are suitably operatic. Yet in turning away from the tableau vivant to a florid, action-filled drama, the devil comes across as a thoroughly modern fellow, a man on the go, a commoner in a

Limiting Editions and Illustrating Books, 1929–1939

royal costume. Clark, Dwiggins, and Macy seemed to enjoy remaking the classic at the same time they discovered critical objections about its self-conscious modernism.[72] Faust dazzles, without becoming beautiful. An ornamental parable not without its didactic moment, it retains a hint of glamour.

Reworking his already proven formula, Macy developed an international list, commissioning the following titles: *Don Quixote*, by Miguel de Cervantes, printed in Barcelona by Oliva de Vilanova, listed at $13.50; Dante Alighieri's *Divine Comedy*, from the Italian printers Officina Bodoni, Verona, designed by Hans Mardersteig, listed at $10; a version of the four Gospels from the Leipzig printers Poeschel and Trepte, listed at $4; and Aesop's *Fables*, with Florentine woodcuts redrawn by Bruce Rogers, printed at the Oxford University Press, listed at $13.50. The *Hamlet* designed and illustrated by Eric Gill listed at $7.50, and a two-volume edition of Charles Dickens's *Pickwick Papers*, printed and bound by John Johnson at Oxford, listed at $17.50.

Books printed abroad and delayed by important historical events held an element of news value and public appeal, which Macy exploited. Accustomed to stretching the boundaries of good taste, he always reached for what he thought the mass market would find novel and remarkable. For example, he bound *The Golden Ass*, by Lucius Apuleius, which listed for $9, in full natural ass's hide purchased from patent-leather shoemakers. Macy thought it "one of our best, though it does not fetch high prices when sold at auction." The *Analects* of Confucius, printed and bound in China, which Macy later judged flawed by bad presswork and type composition, was delayed by the Japanese bombing of Shanghai. Tolstoy's *Anna Karenina*, printed and bound in Moscow by Goznak Press, met similar delays. Macy explained to subscribers in his newsletter, "I was given the faithful promise that the books would be shipped within six months . . . the bindings would be stamped in pure gold even if the people had to take the gold teeth out of their mouths for the purpose. The books were not shipped for eighteen months, but the bindings are stamped in pure gold."[73]

The idea of a fifth series illustrated by those Macy called the best designers and printers of the day, "capturing the definitive qualities of modern commercial art," interested many illustrators who wanted to contribute. Macy designed a series of books that featured only well-known, celebrated names in book design and illustration, using titles long established as favorites. He reported in his monthly newsletter to subscribers that "someone approached him" with the idea that the club scheme be duplicated in a series of books illustrated by famous modern painters.[74] When Macy designed and printed books illustrated by Picasso and Matisse, the club's Westport Press became involved in book production. Picasso illustrated Aristophanes' *Lysistrata*, listed at $17.50, and Matisse illustrated James Joyce's *Ulysses* at $18, or $30 if signed by Joyce. Matisse's painterly lovers carry emotion lacking in their faces through the composition of their abstract figures. Several tissue sketches by Matisse are tipped in (separately printed, glued on one edge to the bound page) so that one sees the artist's imagination progressing toward the finished work in a series of overlays. Picasso's figures are sculptural, drawing on vignettes from the classical drama.

According to Macy, Picasso agreed to consider an assignment as a book illustrator, but only "for a stiff price." He paid what Picasso asked. Macy described his encounter with the artist in his ten-year report, writing, "I was in Paris again when Picasso had finished the plates, and sought to take them from his apartment. . . . He made me send to America for the money with which to pay him, he made me hand him the actual cash with my left hand while he handed me the plates with his left hand. They are, I think, wonderful illustrations; and this book will, I think, go down into history as one of our best."[75] Macy's personal involvement with book production intensified as the business matured. He declared himself a book designer among others he dubbed as the "greats," though he apparently did not design more than a half dozen books in the first ten years.

William Kittredge designed Anatole France's *The Sign of the Queen Pedaque*, which was printed and bound at the Lakeside Press and listed at $12.50. A *Brothers Karamazov*, illustrated by Alexander King, this time in three volumes, designed, printed, and bound by Daniel Berkeley Updike at the Merrymount Press, listed at $12.50. King's drawings are caricatures with exaggerated features and blank stares that imply rather than demonstrate a connection

Illustration for Faust, *commissioned by George Macy
from Rene Clark for the Limited Editions Club, 1932.
This represented the best of advertising style, in Macy's opinion.*
Courtesy of the John M. Wing Foundation, Newberry Library.

between the illustrations and the narrative. Mrs. Frederic Goudy designed an edition of Shelley's *Frankenstein*, priced at $5. The prestigious Golden Cockerel Press printed Dickens's *Cricket on the Hearth*, which was listed at $6. Rockwell Kent illustrated Samuel Butler's *Erewhon*, with an introduction by Aldous Huxley, listed at $7.50. Elmer Adler's Pynson Printers, the New York publisher of the *Colophon* magazine, also designed and printed the Limited Editions Club *Erewhon*. Macy commissioned Frederic Warde to "reengrave" Tenniel's illustrations for an edition of *Through the Looking Glass*, with an introduction by Carl Van Doren, printed by Rudge Press and priced at $15, or if signed by Alice Hargreaves, $20.[76] Among this list of distinguished and celebrated designers and illustrators, Macy reserved for himself the privilege of designing *The Book of a Thousand and One Nights*, printed by Rudge in six volumes and listed at $25.

As if such a list needed a star, Macy engaged Francis Meynell to design, print, and bind Richard Sheridan's *The School for Scandal* at the Oxford University Press, listed at $7.50. Rene Ben Sussan's colored illustrations of Sheridan are among the best drawings produced during the club's first decade. Each figure in the well-known British comedy—Sir Benjamin Backbite, Lady Teazle, Lady Sneerwell, Mrs. Candour—wore his or her habit as a trademark personality. In the world of costume, personality and character were one. Good and bad characters enacted a romantic comedy about personal illusion in a one-dimensional moral world. In Sheridan's world of foppish hypocrites, people wore their identities on their sleeves. In their frailties they remained caricatures of ideal virtue. In that sense, the tale achieves the same level of moral theatricality as *Faust*.

In his sixth series, Macy enlisted the conservative typographer Thomas M. Cleland to design and illustrate *Tristram Shandy*, which Macy hyped as "Cleland's first completely illustrated book." Cleland's style favored the use of ornamental borders, vignettes, and flower ornaments. The well-known printer Bruce Rogers designed Sir Thomas More's *Utopia*, with an introduction by H. G. Wells. Rogers's book is unsurprising, although he does seem to have used his complete inventory of printer's devices. The first title page, for example, is decorated by a brown filagree intaglio border, and on the second title page, letters are squeezed into a triangular box. Macy also commissioned Edward Wilson to illustrate W. H. Hudson's *Green Mansions*. Macy thought highly of Wilson, and he praised him publicly as a leading example of the excellence of commercial advertising illustration. Wilson is pure Strathmore school. His illustrations drip with sentiment. Human figures lack personality, and they are disconnected from the literal level of the text. The illustrations could have been used just as easily to market paper, soap, or any household product.

As Macy's publishing enterprise matured, his books came to have more gall than panache, and his seventh list proved unexceptional. Among several innovations in 1936, his five-volume edition of the King James Bible, priced at $20, is representative. Designed so that ordinary people "might enjoy the prose without benefit of clergy," Macy printed a Bible "not for scholars," eliminating chapter-and-verse separations and diacritical marks. In the process he also eliminated the opportunity to embellish the text through decorated capitals. Macy boasted that "bookish folk have been prevented from deriving a proper literary joy from a reading of the Bible only because of its usual physical presentation. Two-column pages of small type interspersed with complicated arrangements of chapter and verse numbers are not inviting to the leisurely eye."[77] In the early 1930s, competitors published a number of Bibles considered landmarks in the fine printing tradition. The finest of these was the *Four Gospels*, designed by Eric Gill. A lectern Bible designed by Bruce Rogers received equal critical acclaim. Macy advertised his Bible as being an "original," particularly the "list of names of the translators" and the Introduction to the Reader as "exclusive." Despite his claims, Macy's prefatory apparatus and introduction imitated Rogers's Bible verbatim.

Although none of the other books published that year approached the ambition of his Bible, Macy's seventh list advanced his definitive aesthetic. At that time he published a two-volume edition of Tobias Smollett's *Peregrine Pickle* with an introduction by G. K. Chesterton, designed and printed by John Johnson at Oxford University Press. Then he commissioned Theodore Dreiser to write an introduction to Samuel Butler's *The Way of All Flesh*, which was designed and printed by Carl Purington Rollins at Yale University Press. Daniel Berkeley Updike's Merrymount Press designed and printed *Walden*, illustrated by the photographer Edward Steichen, and the Marchbanks Press produced Edward Everett Hale's *A Man without a Country*, illustrated by Edward Wilson with an introduction by Carl Van Doren.

Employing the well-known Veronese printing house Officina Bodoni to print Walter Savage Landor's *Imaginary Conversations*, Macy used a typeface designed by Hans Mardersteig. In this volume, each chapter headnote combined complementary design elements. Unillustrated and selling for $6, the book combined the fine Continental classic traditions of bookmaking. The Westport Press printed the The *Rubaiyat of Omar Khayyam* designed by Valenti Angelo, listed for $17.50. Hawthorn House printed Edmond Rostand's *Cyrano de Bergerac*, which Sylvain Sauvage illustrated, priced at $13.50. Eric Gill designed and printed at Gill & Hague outside of London a copy of Laurence Sterne's *A Sentimental Journey*, illustrated by Denis Tegetmeier and listed at $7.50. Dwiggins illustrated and designed a five-volume edition of Rabelais's *Gargantua and Pantagruel* printed by Southworth-Anthoensen Press in Portland, Oregon, priced at $15, in which he played with themes of distortion and proportion similar to those that King had employed earlier in his illustrating of Swift.[78]

Although Macy addressed himself "to the making of fine editions of well-known texts," as his eighth year began, he declared he was "in the service of literature" and became increasingly involved in book design, the selection of illustrators and titles, as well as the marketing of the publications.[79] In a three-volume facsimile, Macy printed James Boswell's *Life of Samuel Johnson*, with Hester Thrale's preface and annotations. With this production, Macy announced his ambition to be taken seriously as a bookman as well as his ability to rework a stale genre that had been developed earlier by a number of the other subscription clubs, including the Book-of-the-Month Club.

Macy established an honorary medal award to be given each year to one of his own books "most likely to become a classic." He conferred the honor on Van Wyck Brooks, Ernest Hemingway, and on a distinctly lesser literary creation of his own design, a prose calendar titled *An Almanac for Moderns*. Not unlike Macy's Bible designed for those seeking philosophy without clergy, the almanac, written by Donald Peattie and printed by Judd and Detweiler of Washington, addressed the problem of secular philosophy in the age of atomic power. According to one entry, for example, "The weather-wisdom and the simple faith that cropped up ... are withered now. . . . To the terror that faces mice and men, a man at least can find an answer. This will be his religion."[80]

European classics dominated the eighth list. Among the most important were: Benvenuto Cellini's *Autobiography*, designed by Hans Mardersteig and printed in Verona at the Officina Bodoni, listed at $13.50; Oscar Wilde's *Ballad of Reading Gaol*, for $6; *Pinocchio*, with an introduction by Carl Van Doren for $7.50; John Payne Collier's *Punch and Judy*, with etchings by Cruickshank, published by the Princeton University Press and listed at $10; Dumas's *Camille*, designed and printed by Oliver Simon, listed at $10; John Gay's *Beggar's Opera*, designed by Count Guiseppe Govone and printed on his private press in Paris, which was listed at $7.50; and Dickens's *Great Expectations*, with a preface by George Bernard Shaw, designed by the Scottish printers R. and R. Clark, listed at $10.

Yale University printed what might be called the stunt book for the eighth year: Sir Richard Burton's *Kasidah*, designed and illustrated by Valenti Angelo. A tiny (four-by-three-inch), elegant book, *Kasidah* is bound in lavender morocco with a gilt title on the spine and nightingales tooled on the covers with an ornamental flower border. The book is printed on tissue-thin paper, doubled to prevent shadowing, with a gray intaglio floral border. The text is framed by blue pastel bars with gold on the rosettes. Macy recalled later that his editorial experience with the book helped him understand W. Somerset Maugham's remark that "the author should never talk to his illustrator."[81]

In Macy's ninth year he reached for more ambitious literary projects, those he thought "destined to immortality." Producing an equal number of titles by European and American authors, he published Harriet Beecher Stowe's *Uncle Tom's Cabin*, Maugham's *Of*

Human Bondage (with a preface by Theodore Dreiser), Flaubert's *Madame Bovary*, and Gray's *Elegy*, printed by the Raven Press, Middlesex, all listed for $10. Oscar Wilde's *Salome*, illustrated by Aubrey Beardsley and designed by Rene Ben Sussan, listed for $15, and Tolstoy's *War and Peace*, in a six-volume edition printed by the University of Glasgow Press, listed for $27.50.[82]

That year he also published Robert Louis Stevenson's *Kidnapped*, which was designed and printed by Elmer Adler of Pynson Press and listed at $15, and *Pride and Prejudice*, by Jane Austen, at $12.50, designed and printed by Daniel Berkeley Updike. Francis Meynell designed an eight-volume edition of Casanova's *Memoirs*, priced at $12.50. However, war delayed a French edition of Baudelaire's *Les Fleurs du mal*, listed at $12.50, for several years. At the close of his first decade of business, Macy admitted that his efforts had fallen short of his ambitions. He "tried hard enough," he thought, to create books that defined "a perfect illustrated book which everyone will accept."[83]

Few of Macy's books appreciated in value over the years. In fact, most declined by nearly half. Although a drop in auction value is to be expected immediately following publication, Macy advertised that the club books fetched up to 500 percent of their original cost. Contrary to Macy's claims, auction records for the years 1929–39 indicate just the opposite. Macy assured his subscribers that the price of the Limited Editions Club books would continue to increase over time. He wrote that "it is a remarkable thing that the existing depression in most businesses has not touched the productions of the Limited Editions Club. . . . such books would have to be sold in the bookshops for twenty-five dollars apiece. . . . the books we have issued have been re-sold in the bookshops for sums ranging from eighteen dollars up to forty dollars."[84] In fact, two copies of the 1929 *Gulliver's Travels*, which originally sold for $17.50, went for $14 and $19 in 1931. The five copies sold at auction over the next decade showed an average auction price of about $17. One copy sold in 1948 brought only $20. Three copies of *The Decameron* published in 1930 and originally sold for $12.50 went for $13, $17, and $19 the next year. By 1934, *The Decameron* was selling below the retail price at publication (one copy went for $11), and in the years 1937–

39, the selling price for two copies dropped to $11 and $8, respectively. *Grimm's Fairy Tales*, printed in 1931 and priced then at $13.50, fared no better: even within the year, two copies sold for $8 and $10, and in 1948, one copy sold for $13. *Aucassin and Nicolette*, printed in 1931, originally cost $5, but sold at auction for $8 in 1931, $7 in 1932, $6 in 1937–39. Balzac's *Droll Stories*, printed in 1932, and originally priced at $13.50, sold for $8 in 1934, $11 in 1935, and $9 in 1937–39. Only the *Lysistrata* illustrated by Picasso, which sold orginally for $17.50, then went for $10 in 1935, showed an appreciation in value by 1947: three copies sold for $27, $40, and $55.[85]

PRIVATE PRESS VALUES AT THE *COLOPHON*

Macy's hype about the resale value of his books was made with the realization that fine printing still held considerable public appeal. Back issues of the *Colophon* quadrupled in price at auction virtually overnight, undoubtedly because fine printing represented a stable investment in the turbulent days of the Depression. Within months of the *Colophon*'s first number, according to the magazine's editors, many thought it "safer to put their money into an issue of the *Colophon* than in the bank."[86] Back issues sold for $20, double the original price, and their price at auction increased steadily over the next eight years. Still prized in 1987, a perfect set of issues from 1930 through 1935 brought $600.

A dozen of the leading private presses and two of the distinguished university presses printed signatures of the first issues of the *Colophon* magazines.[87] Each article constituted a separate signature of four, eight, twelve, or sixteen pages, printed independently by various distinguished typographers and printers who were given creative freedom, limited only by the page size of 8½ by 11 inches. Each issue consisted of a dozen separate signatures bound together as one magazine between board covers and illustrated by the leading designers of the day.[88] Each signature differed in paper weight, weave, color, texture, ink, and typeface. Their richness and variety made every one of the twenty issues read "like a continuously changing specimen book" imaginatively and skillfully arranged. The editors enlisted a number of illustrators and typographers to write

Limiting Editions and Illustrating Books, 1929–1939

Illustration for Lysistrata, *commissioned by George Macy*
from Pablo Picasso for the Limited Editions Club, ca. 1934.
Courtesy of the John M. Wing Foundation, Newberry Library.

articles that would be "eventful." Rockwell Kent did the logo for the publication; Edward Wilson illustrated the first cover. H. L. Mencken, Sherwood Anderson, Edith Wharton, Theodore Dreiser, and other literary journalists contributed to a "Breaking Into Type" series, articles by established writers about their first experience getting published. "With half of this group," editor Burton Emmett commented, it would be possible to produce "a superb daily newspaper."[89] The Colophonians aspired to the highest cultural traditions of printing trade periodicals represented by *Penrose's Annual*, the *Inland Printer*, and the *American Printer*. The editors wanted the magazine to be a periodical that not only would be beautiful but also practical.

Begun boldly, as Emmett wrote, "in the lush days of 1928 and 1929," the *Colophon*'s "enthusiasm" for the beautiful and "amateur ideals" of the private press and arts-and-crafts movements "soon met cold reality."[90] When the idea first materialized in 1927, Vrest Orton thought Bennett Cerf should be the editor. Although Cerf reportedly thought "the idea had possibilities," according to Orton, he encouraged the editors to contact Elmer Adler. In turn, Adler recruited Burton Emmett as the *Colophon* editor. Emmett had worked for the Lord and Thomas advertising agency and had served as president of the American Institute for Graphic Arts for more than a decade. He edited what became known as the *Colophon*'s first series until his death in 1935. With Elmer Adler and John Winterich, Emmett launched an "idealistic journalism experiment" for the purpose of providing news to "connoisseurs of private printing." Emmett imagined that his readers already knew about the externalities that added to the investment value of a book. By featuring the work and commentaries of the best-known printers, typographers, type designers, and illustrators of the period, the *Colophon* reported on contemporary developments in fine printing.

The *Colophon* did not cultivate critics. Yet critics praised each issue as brilliant when it reached the public, as if every volume achieved a milestone of literary importance. The British press also thought highly of the experiment, and the *Times* of London quoted trade journalists in the *Book Collector's Quarterly* who had called it "one of the most astonishing successes in the recorded history of

American periodical publishing."[91] In addition to Elmer Adler, the initial list of distinguished contributing editors of the *Colophon* included author Thomas Beer; Pierce Butler, then curator of the Wing Collection at the Newberry Library in Chicago; William A. Dwiggins, the artist and type designer; Frederic Goudy, the designer for Monotype Philadelphia; Ruth Grannis, librarian of the Grolier Club, and its president, Henry Kent; Belle Da Costa Green, director of the J. Pierpont Morgan Library in New York; Dard Hunter, well known as a papermaker and printing historian; William Ivins, print curator of the Metropolitan Museum of Art; book illustrator and artist Rockwell Kent; the writer Christopher Morley; bibliographer Vrest Orton; book designer Bruce Rogers; Carl Purington Rollins, the Yale University printer; and writer Carolyn Wells.[92]

Emmett "relived his newspaper days" on the *Colophon*, according to his colleague John Winterich, who wrote that editorially "it was a stretch," because the experiment had more in common with the private press than with the back rooms of the *Times*, where its editorial offices were housed.[93] As a former journalist and nationally known publicist, Emmett thought "everyone should be a reporter." He had become interested in typography as a young newspaperman, and in his maturity he used his publicity skills to persuade the common reader of the merits of fine typography. Although his enterprise began in a hail of international publicity, Emmett and Adler counted on too small a pool of subscribers. When problems arose with advertisers in the first issues, the editors reacted with what became characteristic bravado, by "pitching" the use of any advertisements, even those finely printed, "out the window."[94] Later issues did include advertising; but in the spirit of the arts-and-crafts enthusiasm for purity of form and beautiful typography, Emmett insisted that all advertisements "conform to the highest typographical standards."[95] In fact, a finely printed advertising prospectus for the publication had its own number at auction.

In February 1930, the *Colophon*'s first issue, oversubscribed (at $15 per issue) by six hundred, printed a short run of two thousand at $10 per copy and still ran a deficit of $2.50 per copy.[96] An anonymous donor who had contributed the start-up capital covered the

Limiting Editions and Illustrating Books, 1929–1939

deficit. Emmett later recounted to a newspaper reporter that "there were no circulation problems during that first fruitful year. . . . We were receiving, as the rumor of our eminence waxed, an increasing stream of contributions." He added that "once Wall Street began to rain brokers" as the second issue went to press, less effort was spent on editorial matters than on "just keeping the magazine afloat" financially.[97]

The *Colophon* gained in national prestige, acknowledged by both the daily metropolitan and trade press; nevertheless, letters began to arrive canceling subscriptions. At this point, an installment plan was initiated to try to keep the publication going and, according to the editors, "many took advantage of it for a time."[98] After 1932, however, "circulation problems outweighed all else."[99] Even some of the most loyal readers felt they had to part with the back issues. The editors wrote that "a few of our oldest subscribers regretfully parted with their treasures, preferring bread and butter without the *Colophon* to starvation with it."[100] In an effort to retain subscribers and stave off financial disaster, the idealistic fine printing enterprise fought back by seeking the advertising advice of a publicity expert.

Alfred Stanford assumed total responsibility for promotion and publication for the magazine in 1932. He apparently had the necessary grit for the job: his motto was "Better fifteen bucks from Newark than a query from Cathay."[101] He launched the "Colophon Crier," a publicity hype broadside meant to increase subscriptions. A direct-mail piece from the editors to the magazine's two thousand subscribers, it offered an explanation of the rise in costs and announced the editors' intention of attracting another one thousand subscribers in order to keep the enterprise going. Although the editors insisted that "this is the minimum basis on which present standards can be maintained," a *New York Times* journalist commented that standards had slipped under the strain.[102] The *Times* reviewer wrote that "for once we may say freely that this is not the best number so far issued, nor is it the most attractive or the most interesting. As these volumes grow in numbers we must learn to recognize the sad truth that each newcomer cannot go on indefinitely improving the past. . . . there does seem to be some of that spark lacking in this volume that set several of the earlier numbers aglow with natural brilliance. But the *Colophon* is never dull."[103]

Nine hundred of the original two thousand subscribers remained throughout the Depression. To retain them and attract new subscribers, Stanford borrowed direct-mail techniques from George Macy, the master of public appeals.[104] Among Stanford's first endeavors was to borrow Macy's mailing list; then he targeted the club members as potential subscribers to the *Colophon*. Stanford's direct-mail letter took an aggressive approach. He wrote that "a short time ago Mr. George Macy . . . wrote letters expressing his enthusiasm for the *Colophon*. He suggested that your subscription for the four parts issued during 1931 at $15 would repay you many times in the added enjoyment of the books you now receive through the Club, and those that you may be acquiring through other sources. The response to this letter was extremely gratifying. Even in these times book collectors of knowing taste and discrimination are quick to appreciate the value of the *Colophon* to them. . . . So far we have not heard from you."[105] The magazine editors who once protested the tendency of people like Macy to "artificially limit" editions in order to stimulate demand now borrowed Macy's techniques to reach potential subscribers. In response to economic realities, they began to print only five hundred copies per issue. Explaining the compromise to subscribers as more Colophonian idealism, the editors wrote that "it is the present plan of the Editors to arrange for the production of special books which otherwise might not be published, and these volumes are to be offered first to *Colophon* subscribers . . . this brochure is the first of a series. . . . Will you kindly send us names?"[106] In a further compromise, the *Colophon* turned to holding a book auction of its own. Even though they printed a witty catalog, upside down, this must have been a sobering moment for them.

With an increasingly urgent need for subscriptions, the editors and publicist issued a series of direct-mail appeals. Stanford drafted the letters over Emmett's signature, writing that "in the midst of the nation's economic crisis . . . Roosevelt found time to see that his check to renew his subscription for 1933 reached us. So far, however, we have not heard from [you]."[107] The early editorial policies that had steered clear of advertising as unworthy of their high aspirations changed dramatically after Emmett died in 1935, and attempts to publish a second and third series began. The editors of the second series confidently expected to reach the fifteen thousand book collectors they "estimated were out there but who had not subscribed."[108] Advertisements promised a broader editorial policy and a lower issue price of $6.

The new editors promised to turn away from the idealism of 1929–30, the "utterly lavish and extravagant features of the past," by reducing the quality and size of the paper, doubling the number of pages in each issue, and permitting advertisements with less-stringent typographic restrictions.[109] In the direct-mail appeals, every effort was made to instill loyalty and a sense of belonging among readers, as if they were participating in an exclusive club. Using the approach that had been employed successfully by George Macy, the editors wrote that "our Readers are part of our adventure! You are not just a cold, external public. . . . We have never had money to engage in high pressure mail campaigns. We can't afford to advertise beyond mere announcements. . . . The check you will sign will be one bill you are glad to pay."[110]

When the periodical ceased publishing altogether in 1940, according to Adler, it was changed but "uncompromised." At this point, he attempted to resurrect a "new" *Colophon*.[111] When the next *Colophon* enterprise failed, the *New York Times*, the *Times* of London, and *Publishers Weekly* reported its demise. The magazine that had continued to call itself "the most distinguished periodical ever published covering its particular field" was replaced by *Print* after 1940. As *Publishers Weekly* noted, "Many mourned the loss of so distinguished a magazine in a decade that had many such casualties."[112]

The economic realities of the 1930s marketplace had separated the fine from the good book. As the ideal of the book beautiful faded to an anachronism, the antistyle that distinguished the Limited Editions Club from the private-press values of the *Colophon* persuaded readers to believe in the power of advertisements for books. A keen marketer of literary wares, Macy put the audience before the author. He used designers and printers as celebrities and employed the value of reputation more than literary creation in his continuous reach for the crowd. Part of an ideological landscape populated by ideas about state power, individualism, and the role of language, illustrated books offered a new avenue to the mass market which thrived on images of the future packaged as words from the past. The transformation of the modern literary economy had more to do with the producer's imagination about history than the consumer's knowledge of the classics. In manufacturing public appeal, Macy demonstrated the uses of the business imagination. In doing so, he contributed to popularizing a marketplace sense of literary style. In trading words as commodities, Macy counted equally valuable the reputation of goods, the language of commodities in advertising, and the packaging of popular images of culture. In the modern literary economy, as Macy and other publishers who flourished during the 1930s demonstrated, the cover of the book had achieved as much value in the literary trade as literature itself.

Limiting Editions and Illustrating Books, 1929–1939

★

READING

·

AND

·

COMMERCIAL

·

MODERNISM

The plain style feigns a candid observer.
Such is its great advantage for persuading.
—Hugh Kenner, "The Politics of the Plain Style"

"Mediated language," according to the communication theorists, is continuously negotiated between artists and printers on the one hand, and readers and critics on the other.[1] The campaigns discussed in this volume illustrate that process where the meaning of a public text is negotiated, as it took place among aesthetic revolutionaries in Russia, Italy, Germany, and England; the imagist poets in Chicago, Boston, and London; the new typographers at British Monotype; the printers of R. R. Donnelley's "definitive" Four American Books; and Macy's marketing of the "Limited" Editions Club.

For several reasons, these language-product appeals represent milestones in the history of Anglo-American commercial printing. They were made possible by improvements in machinery, especially the rotary printing press and Monotype's Super Caster. Aside from being signs of technical advance, they influenced ideas about literary tradition, aesthetic values, and the social role of the text. As economic forces, they contributed to the formation of a public language and shaped the cultural role of the book. By means of integrated campaigns and print planning, publicists and typographical-design experts diffused contemporary styles of brand-name print products worldwide; these campaigns thus demonstrated the emerging power of the "new advertising," which made traditional genres and class-based distinctions among printed goods obsolete. The campaigns represented an early stage in the history of modernism in print: they brought clear intention, plain style, and the triumph of middle-brow taste. They succeeded at their stated social objective, using subjective appeals to improve the literacy level of the common reader.

Publicists routinely claimed that every artist, poet, type designer, and book publisher needed an audience. The publicist was in the business of providing one. Writers and printers could educate readers about style by example, they argued, and thus persuade the public of the value of printed goods. Of course, it was the common reader who ultimately determined whether or not the goods were worth buying and at what price.

Meanwhile academic theorists, literary critics, and other "authorities" developed theories of mass communication and public-opinion engineering and an aesthetic rationale for the popularity of the plain style. Phrases like "new journalism," "new criticism," and "reception analysis" involving the "ethnography of audience" all grew out of the social currents that these campaigns reflected. Among the individuals prominent in the publicity campaigns for print products in the 1920s and 1930s, few agreed on matters of style, but everyone savored the debate over aesthetic values that modernism provoked.

Whether a text was intended for traditionally "bookish" purposes or for display advertising, one of the distinguishing features of modernity in language was its ability to shape public opinion on the subject of aesthetic values. Public appetite for all that was new and improved provided ample opportunity for innovations in product design[2] and accelerated the devaluation of older styles that marketers called obsolete. The definition of modernism in print products fell to those who said books simply had to "look like a book" rather

Reading and Commercial Modernism

than a finely printed seed catalogue. Constant changes of style—a language of "scrap and replace" made possible by new and improved machinery—became the trade standard.[3]

By midcentury, campaign language—hyperbolic, self-announcing, intentionally obvious—became familiar to readers and nearly synonymous with modern styling. The public began to anticipate that all printed material—rather than stories with textual content that could be neatly categorized as fiction or fact—simply conveyed well-designed messages. Imagistic poetry, letter forms with "personality," and illustrated books competed with film, images in advertising, world events, and sales news. All genres became conflated as sources of entertainment, thus flattening traditional distinctions between high and low culture. Poets, typographers, book designers, advertising illustrators, printers, publicists, and journalists shared a common purpose in the modern literary economy—persuasion linked with sales.

PERSUASION AND PUBLIC CULTURE

Modernism challenged the traditional, or "class," distinction between commerce and art, which contemporary theory calls the "space" between information and fiction.[4] Turn-of-the-century revolutionaries had created an antitraditionalist aesthetic that they hoped would consolidate mass communications along radical principles and eliminate genres associated with the classics in favor of social utility or functionalism in the design of language products. Commercial modernists shared these ambitions for power over the reading public. They, too, located reasons for linked pragmatic design in a philosophy of social utilitarianism. They also experimented with layout, paper, the cine-book, and typophoto.

Avant-garde printers refined strategies for the sake of corporate profit. Some designs—such as the Gill Sans and Times New Roman—proved exceptional in their versatility, although both faces suited the communication industry rather than books. Clean lines, spare form, and a plain style became the basis for an international language of symbols. The style succeeded because it remained uncluttered. Separated by a continent and a decade, imagism (ca.

Reading and Commercial Modernism

1912) and the new typography (ca. 1922) employed the concept of international appeal as part of their rationale for spare design. Although Pound, Monroe, Lowell, and others argued their case with great dedication for more than two decades, imagism failed to convince readers of its social utility. Imagism's infamous spokesman whose verse often seemed purposefully designed to offend, Pound saw the mass-market reader as a nuisance and literature as a tool for totalitarian control. Even the publicity skills of Monroe and Lowell failed to gain an audience for imagism, whose practitioners proved to be better publicists than poets: like the revolutionaries, they failed precisely because the public thought they lacked social utility.

Modernist aesthetes romanticized printing and inflated the political power of individuals in civic life. Modernists glamorized the common because it contained elements of social realism. Both the avant-garde and the modernist represented a romanticized search for the prosaic, what William Dean Howells called the "natural gas man" in literature.[5] Each searched for a plain style that could appeal to a universal reader or (the central principle of commercial modernism) to a globally adaptable system of signs.[6] Social realism became equated with popular and middle-brow culture through products designed according to the once-revolutionary functionalist principles of aesthetic and literary elites.

The design experts who prospered in the 1920s and 30s exploited the lessons others had learned earlier in the century by making political uses of print and publicity. Iconoclasm became central to popular modernism. It permeated the design of literary products. In the mass-market literary economy, publicists for printing and publishing corporations became as important as typographers, designers, advertisers, or booksellers. The well-dressed message spoke to the common reader in an identifiable public voice. The commercial modernist became as influential in shaping public taste as classical aesthetes once had dreamed of being.

THE MEMORABLE TEXT

The glue that held the literary economy together was the readers' responsiveness to innovative texts, whether seriously literary or purely

Reading and Commercial Modernism

commercial. Regardless of their literacy level, readers needed to be able quickly to glean the intention and meaning of messages, which therefore had to present a self-announcing facade of image, word, and story. In the new marketplace, transparancy of intention formed modern literary values. Clarity drove the design and styling of type-faces, textual succinctness, and public expectations of literary wares and commercial texts alike.

Before an increasingly saturated audience and in an intensely competitive, interdependent literary marketplace, all language products had to communicate in a way that the audience would remember. The modern look had to surprise without startling. It had to be familiar yet innovative, comfortable without being cozy. If the look of the future had to reinvent the past, it had to do so without appearing to borrow from it. "Modern" in Warde's observation, denoted "some contemporary thing that has been re-fashioned, or specially fashioned, to meet new needs."[7] The modern look placed heavy demands on one's creativity, whatever the raw materials of his or her refashioning. The mood of the early twentieth century, according to William Addison Dwiggins—encompassing as it did (or encumbered as it was by) speed, electricity, the use of air as a highway, the realization of a universe of appalling size—had to be transmitted "not in pictures" but by "implication and through atmosphere."[8]

To succeed in reaching a universal audience, capturing public attention, and entering collective cultural memory, designs had to adapt the plain-style principles, becoming translucent or in a sense porous. All classes and literacy levels had to gain access to print. On the surface, they encountered messages. Print planners, indulging themselves in principles of social psychology and public-opinion engineering, counted on the readers' response to the very design of letters, their typographical style and arrangement on the page. In the hands of typographical-design experts and publicity mavericks, the sentimental arts-and-crafts style modernized as a combination of historical book-design elements (including flowers and rubricated letters) and the "clean shaven" letter face that came to typify the early-twentieth-century printing renaissance.[9]

Reading and Commercial Modernism

Whether set in baroque or plain style, delivering sermon or advertisement, telling fact or fiction, the page was the "place" where language became commodified.[10] The page itself became an object of attention, a place to demonstrate language rather than merely print
letters. In this demonstration, publicists cast readers in the leading
role and watched their every response, just as readers served as
the targets of campaigns that hawked literary texts. In the process
of commodifying language, the meaning of texts became less important than their readability or accessibility—the quality that ac-
counted for their public appeal; the marketplace value of a text depended simply on how well it stood out from a host of others and
could be recalled by readers/customers.

The 1890s ideal of beautiful letters—singular, handmade, crafted
using old-fashioned techniques—changed in response to demand.
There were objections. Contemporaries of the new typographers
who lamented the passing of traditional print products wondered
whether all the emphasis on design had not turned printing into ge-
ometry "in an economy bounded by the page."[11] Others in the trades
thought excessive attention to sales through innovative styling
would "feminize" the printing industry, turning it into a service.
Printers feared that economic forces associated with modern styling
in language products would sink their industry forever into the business of advertising. Critics of modernism later questioned whether
the absence of style could in fact be called a style at all.

In a crowded marketplace of imitators, hacks, and pseudoevents,
product differentiation became an imperative with cultural con-
squences. What appeared to be the zeal to innovate, to be noticed,
matured into the ideal of the memorable text, whereby readers of all
types and descriptions shared a language of cultural memory. Literary products, whether commercial or classical, stood a chance of entering that collective memory.[12] To modernists this competitive process was far preferable to having a canon imposed by authorities
whom they considered objectionable and outdated—clergy, academy, or critic. Beatrice Warde believed that modern books fell into a
different category of product from "what we ordinarily call books."
They were neither elitist "reading matter" nor the "feverish and hyp-

Reading and Commercial Modernism

notic gestures of a salesman."[13] Yet for unschooled commercial writers, artists, and printers, modernism meant the simple boldness associated with effective sales techniques.

Styling public appeals for brand names in the modern literary economy traded a centuries-old belief in classes of literature as culturally definitive for a modern creed of readable objects in a democracy of goods.[14]

NOTES

INTRODUCTION:
THE IMAGINATION IN BUSINESS

1. Stanley Morison, *Politics and Script: Aspects of Authority and Freedom in the Development of Greco-Latin Script from the Sixth Century B.C. to the Twentieth Century A.D.* (Oxford: Clarendon Press, 1972); *Letter Forms Typographical and Scriptorial: Two Essays on Their Classification, History, and Bibliography* (London: Nattali & Maurice, 1963); *On Type Designs Past and Present* (London: Ernest Benn, 1962), first published in *The Fleuron*, 1926.

2. Sherwood Anderson, "A Writer's Conception of Realism," *The Writer*, January 1941. Typescript, Anderson Collection, Newberry Library.

3. Jules Verne, interview, *London Daily Mail*, reprinted in *North American Review*, September 1902, 289.

4. Sherwood Anderson's "Rot or Reason" column (1903–5) in

Agricultural Advertising, the publicity magazine for the Long and Critchfield Agency of Chicago.

5. Anderson, "The Silent Man," *Agricultural Advertising*, February 1904, 19; *Perhaps Women* (New York: Horace Liveright, 1931), 66–74.

6. Sinclair Lewis, "The American Fear of Literature," Nobel Prize speech, Stockholm, December 1930.

7. Edwin Cady, *Realist at War: The Mature Years 1885–1920 of William Dean Howells* (Syracuse: Syracuse University Press, 1958).

8. Harriett Monroe manuscripts, Regenstein Library.

9. Lewis, "American Fear of Literature"; Anderson, *Perhaps Women* (New York: Horace Liveright, 1931), 66–74; William Dean Howells, *A Hazard of New Fortunes*, ed. D. Nordloh (Bloomington: Indiana University Press, 1976), 213.

10. Anderson, "Rot or Reason."

11. Barnum, the celebrated father of the Tom Thumb spectacle, died shortly before the 1893 World's Fair opened; he suggested that Chicagoans pay to exhume an Egyptian pharoah to display for publicity purposes at the entrance.

12. Walter Lippmann, *Public Opinion* (New York: Harcourt, 1922), 286.

13. Walter Lippmann, *The Phantom Public* (New York: Macmillan, 1927), 14, 16, 42.

14. Edward Bernays, "Recent Trends in PR Activities," *Public Opinion Quarterly*, January 1937, 147–52.

CHAPTER 1:
UTOPIAN TYPOGRAPHY AND THE PUBLIC EYE, 1890–1915

1. Carl S. Smith. *Chicago and the American Literary Imagination, 1880–1920* (Chicago: University of Chicago Press, 1984); Alan Raucher, *Public Relations and Business, 1900–1929* (Baltimore: Johns Hopkins University Press, 1968); Stanley Kelley, *Professional Public Relations and Political Power* (Baltimore: Johns Hopkins University Press, 1956); Monroe Friedman, *A "Brand" New Language: Commercial Influences in Literature and Culture* (Westport, Conn.: Greenwood, 1991); JoAnne Yates, *Control through*

Communication: The Rise of System in American Management
(Baltimore: Johns Hopkins University Press, 1989); Richard Ted-
low, *New and Improved: The Story of Mass Marketing in America*
(New York: Basic Books, 1990); Jerome McGann, *Black Riders:
The Visible Language of Modernism* (Princeton: Princeton Univer-
sity Press, 1993).

2. Virginia Woolf, quoting Samuel Johnson, "The Life of Gray,"
in *The Common Reader* (New York: Harcourt Brace, 1925), ii.

3. Timothy Materer, *Vortex: Pound, Eliot and Lewis* (Ithaca:
Cornell University Press, 1979), 20–21; Wyndham Lewis, *Blasting
and Bombadeering* (London, 1937); Exhibition Catalog, Hayward
Gallery, London, *Vorticism and Its Allies*, 1974; Michael H. Leven-
son, *A Genealogy of Modernism, A Study of English Literary Doctrine 1908–1922* (Cambridge: Cambridge University Press, 1984),
63–74; Lothar Lang, *Expressionist Book Illustration in Germany
1907–1927*, trans. Janet Seligman (London: Thames & Hudson,
1976), 71–81, 82–92; Hans L. C. Jaffe, *De Stijl* (London: Thames
& Hudson, 1970); Herschel B. Chipp, *Theories of Modern Art: A
Sourcebook by Artists and Critics* (Berkeley: University of California Press, 1968). See also E. R. Hagemann, *German and Austrian
Expressionism in the United States, 1900–1939; Chronology and Bib-
liography* (Westport, Conn.: Greenwood, 1985); Francesco Lengo,
Cultura E Citta Dei Manifesti del Primo Futurismo (1909–1915)
(Rome: Vecchio Faggio, 1986); Claudio Salaris, *Marinetti Editorie*
(Bologna: Societa Editrice il Mulino, 1990); "The Origin of Futur-
ism," "Futurism and Ourselves," "Futurism," "Futurist Number of
Poetry and Drama," *Poetry and Drama* 1 (1913): 389–90, 262, 136;
Exhibition Catalog, *Constructivism and Futurism: Russian and
Other* (New York: Ex Libris, 1978); Hugh Kenner, *Ezra Pound*
(Berkeley: University of California Press, 1971).

4. Will B. Wilder, "Advertising One's Personality," *Fame*, Sep-
tember 1905, 197; "On Municipal Advertising: How Cities Get Rep-
utations," *Fame*, January 1905, 56–57; Joan Shelley Rubin, *The
Making of Middlebrow Culture* (Chapel Hill: University of North
Carolina Press, 1992); Cathy N. Davidson, ed., *Reading in
America: Literature and Social History* (Baltimore: Johns Hopkins
University Press, 1989); Roland Marchand, *Advertising the Ameri-*

can Dream: Making Way for Modernity, 1920–1940 (Berkeley: University of California Press, 1985); Michael Schudson, *Advertising, the Uneasy Persuasion: Its Dubious Impact on American Society* (New York: Basic Books, 1984); Neil Harris, "Iconography and Intellectual History," in *New Directions in American Intellectual History*, ed. John Higham and Paul Conkin (Racine, Wisc.: Wingspread, 1977).

5. Donald Piper, "Aspects of Modern Drawing," *Signature* 7 (November 1937): 36; Szymon Bojko, *New Graphic Design in Revolutionary Russia* (London: Lund Humphries, 1972); Nicholas Pevsner, *Pioneers of the Modern Movement: From William Morris to Walter Gropius* (New York: F. A. Stokes Co., 1937); Paul Nash, "Surrealism and the Illustrated Book: A Paper Read to the Double Crown Club," *Signature* 5 (March 1937): 2–4; see also Alan Young, *Dada and After* (N.J.: Humanities Press, 1981), 110–23; Ralph Jentsch, *Illustrierte Bücher des deutschen Expressionismus*, catalog for exhibition, November 16, 1989 (Stuttgart: Edition Cantz, Exhibition Catalogue, 1990); Staatliche Museen preussischer Kulturbeseit, *europäische moderne: Buch und Grapik aus berliner Kunstverlangen 1890–1933* (Berlin: Dietrick Reimer Verlag, 1989).

6. Edmund Wilson, *Axel's Castle* (New York: Scribners, 1931), 309.

7. Sophie Lissitzky-Kupper, *El Lissitzky* (London: Thames & Hudson, 1967), 330.

8. Oliver Zunz, *Making America Corporate 1870–1920* (Baltimore: Johns Hopkins University Press, 1990); Alfred D. Chandler, Jr., *The Visible Hand: The Managerial Revolution in American Business* (Cambridge: Harvard University Press, 1977); David Lowenthal, *The Past Is a Foreign Country* (Cambridge: Cambridge University Press, 1985); John Clive, *Not by Fact Alone* (New York: Knopf, 1989).

9. Stanley Morison, "Picture Printing and Word Printing," pamphlet, Newberry Library Archives, James Wells Papers, 21; E. Mergatroyd, "The Artist in the World of Commerce," *Print* 23 (January–February 1969): 30–34.

10. Piper, "Aspects," 36.

11. Beatrice Warde, "On Decorative Printing in America," *The Fleuron VI* (1928): 69–93; Piper, "Aspects," 38.

12. John Ruskin, *The Political Economy of Art: Being the Substance (with Additions) of Two Lectures at Manchester July 10–13, 1857* (London: Smith, Elder & Co., 1857), 29; see also Peter D. Anthony, *John Ruskin's Labor: A Study of Ruskin's Social Theory* (Cambridge: Cambridge University Press, 1983); Eileen Boris, *Art and Labour: Ruskin, Morris and the Craftsman Ideal in America* (Philadelphia: Temple University Press, 1986).

13. Ruskin, *Political Economy*, 49.

14. Ibid., 50–52.

15. Ibid., 53.

16. Ruskin, *On the Nature of Gothic Architecture* (London: 1854); William James, *The Will to Believe* (1899) and "Great Men Great Thoughts," *Atlantic Monthly*, October 1880; John Fiske, "Sociology and Hero-Worship," *Atlantic Monthly*, January 1881; Grant Allen, "The Genesis of Genius," *American Mercury*, March 1881.

17. William Morris, *The Political Writings of William Morris*, ed. A. L. Morton (London: Lawrence and Wishart, 1979), 59.

18. Ibid., 3.

19. Ibid., 33–34, 74.

20. Werner Schweiger, *The Wiener Werkstätte: Design in Vienna* (London: Thames & Hudson, 1984), 13–15.

21. Gillian Naylor, *The Bauhaus Reassessed* (London: The Herbert Press, 1985), 7.

22. Naylor, *The Bauhaus*, 31; Schweiger, *Wiener Werkstätte*, 13–15; Morris, *Political Writings*, 33–34, 74.

23. Josef Muller-Brockman, "Herbert Bayer: The Bauhaus Tradition" and Gyorgy Kepes, "Laszlo Moholy-Nagy: The Bauhaus Tradition," *Print* 23 (January–February 1969): 40–41, 35–37; Marcel Francisco, *Walter Gropius and the Creation of the Bauhaus in Weimar: The Ideals and Artistic Theories of Its Founding Years* (Urbana: University of Illinois Press, 1971), 30–35; Alan Windsor, *Peter Behrens, Architect & Designer, 1868–1940* (London: the Architectural Press, 1981). Preparations for the founding of the group began earlier than 1915 and flourished during the twenties,

until the Nazis closed the school in 1933. A Bauhaus school of printing gradually evolved to include the publicity arts, and between 1920 and 1930, the school of commercial design became known as the "school of functional design."

24. Kepes, "Laszlo Moholy-Nagy," 36–37. Although no typography or advertising workshop had existed previously at the Bauhaus, Laszlo Moholy-Nagy (1895–1946) and others had experimented with type forms and arrangements.

25. Ibid., 36–37.

26. Moholy-Nagy, "Modern Typography. Aims, Practice, Criticism," *Offset Buch und Webekunst* (Offset, Book and Commercial Art), Leipzig, 1926, no. 7. Translated in Bauhaus documents, Wing.

27. Kepes, "Laszlo Moholy-Nagy," 36–37.

28. Ibid.

29. "Bauhaus," *New Graphic Design* 17–18 (February 1965): 44–51.

30. Moholy-Nagy, "Modern Typography."

31. Rurai McLean, *Jan Tschichold: Typographer* (London: Lund Humphries, 1975).

32. Rand, *New Life in Print*, 45–47.

33. Ibid.

34. Ibid.

35. McLean, *Tschichold*.

36. Ibid.

37. James Moran, *Printing in the Twentieth Century* (London: Northwood, 1974), 145–51.

38. Ibid.

39. Ibid.

40. Ann Ferrebee, "El Lissitzky: Design, Technology and the Social Context," *Print* (n.d.): 25–28.

41. Ibid.

42. Lissitzky-Kupper, *El Lissitzky*, 328.

43. Ibid., 336.

44. Ibid., 344.

45. Bojko, *New Graphic Design*, 13.

46. Ferrebee, "El Lissitzky," 25–28.

47. Catalogue of Books Printed in the USSR 1930–1936, for exhibition by First Edition Club, Francis Meynell (London: Pelican Press, 1930); Giovanni Lista, *Le Livre Futuristi de la libération du mot au poem tactile* (Modena: Edizioni Panini, 1984).

48. Lissitzky-Kupper, *El Lissitzky*, 358–59. To distinguish themselves from the Italians, the Russians labeled themselves "futuristy" in 1913. Marinetti expected to promote his book *Zang Tumb Tuum* with a lecture tour just when Khlebnikov wanted to release his book titled *Te li le*. "Both were looking for an irrational art—but unlike the Italian, the Russian title has no onomatopoeic references. Marinetti's book was typeset, albeit with typographical innovations; Kruchenykh's was handwritten with decoration . . . by a primitive gelatine process. . . . if the language experiments were lost on Marinetti, he praised the originality of the book which was totally unlike anything being produced in Italy."

49. Bojko, *New Graphic Design*, 27.

50. Lissitzky-Kupper, *El Lissitzky*, 355–56; Susan Compton, *The World Backwards: Russian Futurist Books, 1912–1916* (London: The British Library Board, 1978), 1.

51. Lissitzky-Kupper, *El Lissitzky*, 357.

52. Bojko, *New Graphic Design*, 25.

53. Lissitzky-Kupper, *El Lissitzky*, 357.

54. Bojko, *New Graphic Design*, 25.

55. Compton, *World Backwards*, 18.

56. Compton, *World Backwards*, 18, 35. The public received with interest the seventy issues of the newspaper *Lacerba* published between January 1, 1913, and May 22, 1915, which contained examples of innovative typography, manifestos, articles, music scores, and photographic reproductions. According to futurist historian Caroline Tisdall, the style influenced a number of other international art reviews, especially *Blast*, founded by Wyndham Lewis in London in June 1914.

57. Ibid., 44, 18, 35.

58. James Joel, *Intellectuals in Politics* (London: Weidenfeld and Nicholson, 1960), 154.

59. Caroline Tisdall and Angelo Bozzolla, *Futurism* (London: Thames & Hudson, 1977), 168.

60. Ibid., 98.

61. Ibid., 102–4.

62. *Lacerba*, Florence, May 11 and 14, June 1913.

63. Ezra Pound, *Literary Essays of Pound*, ed. T. S. Eliot (New York: New Directions, 1968), 49, cited in Materer, *Vortex*. See also Lewis, *Blasting and Bombadeering*.

64. Warde, "Decorative Printing in America," 69–93.

65. Stanley Morison, *Rationalism and the Novelty Appropriate in Display Advertising:* A paper read to the Creative Advertising Circle, London, n.d. [1963], 6, 8, 10, Wing.

66. Ibid.

67. Warde, *Crystal Goblet* (London: Sylvan Press, 1955); John Lee Mahin, *The Commercial Value of Advertising* (Chicago: University of Chicago Press, 1904); "Advertising and Literature," *Fame*, January 1905, 5; Frederick Moxon, "Human Interest," *Fame*, August 1913, 171–72.

CHAPTER 2:
ADVERTISING POETRY AS A VISUAL ART, 1912–1922

1. "Design and Typography," *The Printing Art* 3, 6 (August 1904): 169–71; Wallace Martin and Ian Fletcher, *A Catalogue of the Imagist Poets* (New York: J. H. Woomer, 1966).

2. T. S. Eliot, *The Egoist* 5, 4 (April 1918): 55; Neil Harris, *Cultural Excursions: Marketing Appetites and Cultural Tastes in Modern America* (Chicago: University of Chicago Press, 1990).

3. John Gage, *In the Arresting Eye: The Rhetoric of Imagism* (Baton Rouge: Louisiana State University Press, 1981). See also Kenner, *Ezra Pound*.

4. John Gage, *Arresting Eye*; Frank Luther Mott, *A History of American Magazines 1885–1905* (Cambridge: Harvard University Press, 1957).

5. Harriet Monroe, *Poets and Their Art* (New York: Macmillan, 1926), 248.

6. Susan Otis Thompson. *American Book Design and William Morris* (New York: R. R. Bowker, 1977). See also McGann, *Black Riders*; Warren I. Sussman, "'Personality' and the Making of Twen-

tieth Century Culture," *New Directions in Intellectual History* (Racine, Wisc.: Wingspread, 1977).

7. Ezra Pound, "A Few Don'ts by an Imagiste" *Mosaic*, Winter 1988.

8. Advertisement, specimen for American Type Founders Co., "Notes for the Student of Any Art," *Printing Art* 4 (January 1905): 278.

9. Lloyd Morris, *The Young Idea: An Anthology of Opinion concerning the Spirit and Aims of Contemporary American Literature* (New York: Duffield & Co., 1917), 111.

10. Ezra Pound, *The Selected Letters, 1907–1941*, ed. D. D. Paige (New York: New Directions, 1950), 213–15; Monroe, *A Poet's Life: Seventy Years in a Changing World* (New York: Macmillan, 1938), 38–40. See also Kenner, *Ezra Pound*; Gage, *Arresting Eye*; Daniel Boorstin, *The Image, A Guide to Pseudo-Events in America* (reprint, New York: Atheneum, 1987), 233.

11. Ellen Williams, *Harriet Monroe and the Poetry Renaissance: The First Ten Years of Poetry 1912–1922* (Champagne: University of Illinois Press, 1977), 38–40; *Pound, Selected Letters*, 213–15.

12. Howells, *Hazard*, 213; Christopher P. Wilson, "Markets and Fictions: Howells' Infernal Jungle," *American Literary Realism 1870–1910* 20 (Spring 1988): 2–22. See Howells, "The Man of Letters as a Man of Business" (1893) and other essays cited by Wilson about economic philosophy; Cady, *Realist at War*.

13. Monroe, *A Poet's Life*, 370; *Poetry*, October 1914, 27–29.

14. Monroe, *A Poet's Life*, 370; *Poetry*, October 1914: 27–29; John Rodden, *The Politics of Literary Reputation* (New York: Oxford, 1989); Leo Braudy, *The Frenzy of Renown: Fame and Its History* (New York: Oxford, 1986).

15. Monroe, *A Poet's Life*, 370; *Poetry*, October 1914, 27–29.

16. Monroe, *A Poet's Life*, 370.

17. Monroe, "Poetry Is an Essential Industry," *Poetry*, November 1918, 96. The Monroe editorial is also included in *Poets and Their Arts*.

18. Monroe, "The Free Verse Movement in America," *The En-*

glish Journal 13 (December 1924): 691–706; Harriet Monroe to Frank Crowninshield, *Times Literary Supplement*, 26 May 1920. The *Poetry* and Monroe Papers, Regenstein Library, University of Chicago (hereafter cited as Monroe Papers). William Carlos Williams to Harriet Monroe, 8 May 1915, Monroe Papers.

19. Pound, *Selected Letters*, 213–15; Monroe, *A Poet's Life*, 38–40; Kenner, *Ezra Pound*.

20. Vachel Lindsay, *Letters*, ed. Marc Chenetier, (New York: Burt Franklin, 1979), Vachel Lindsay to Harriet Monroe, 30 November 1915, 125.

21. Ibid.

22. Kenner, *Ezra Pound*.

23. Amy Lowell, *Some Imagist Poets: An Anthology* (Boston: Houghton Mifflin, 1915). Published by the Riverside Press, Cambridge. Additional volumes were published in 1916 and 1917; J. B. Harmer, *Poetry*, October 1912.

24. Pound, *Des Imagistes* (London: The Poetry Bookshop; New York: Albert and Charles Boni, 1914).

25. Lowell, *Tendencies in American Poetry* (Boston: Macmillan, 1917), 252–57.

26. T. S. Eliot, *The Egoist* 5 (April 1918): 55.

27. Harmer, *Poetry*, October 1912, 17; Monroe, *Poets and Their Art*, 248–54.

28. N. W. Ayer, *Directory of Newspapers and Periodicals* (Philadelphia: N. W. Ayer, 1890–1920); Claire Badaracco, "Marketing Language Products 1900–1905: The Case of Agricultural Advertising," *Essays in Economic and Business History* (Fall 1989); Mott, *History of American Magazines*, 4, 24, 36–37; Frank Presbury, *The History and Development of Advertising* (New York: Doubleday, 1929), 360; Richard W. Fox and T. J. Jackson Lears, eds., *The Culture of Consumption: Critical Essays in American History 1880–1920* (New York: Pantheon, 1983); Stephen Fox, *The Mirror Makers* (New York: Vintage, 1985). According to advertising and printing tradesmen, the house organ represented the chief means of self-education for printers. It also served as the primary means for transmitting the philosophical and aesthetic ideals of the arts-and-crafts movement from England to America. The well-known deaf ad-

vertising agent Earnest Elmo Calkins recorded that he profited from such reading while working in the back room of a newspaper. Will Ransom, an impoverished commercial printer who could not afford to buy finely printed books, collected and cataloged publishers' finely printed promotional ephemera over a thirty-year period. In 1929, he published his definitive catalog of private printing in America based on that free publicity information. During the same period, John Johnson, the Oxford University Press printer, also collected ephemeral printing: tickets, matchbooks, and advertisements. All these ephemera—advertisements, political propaganda, business pamphlets, and house organs—proliferated in the United States to the degree that the bibliographer Lawrence Romaine estimated that a catalog of this type of American printing between 1744 and 1900 alone would consist of fifty volumes (and that is prior to the real "boom" period after 1903). Ransom's book-publicity collection filled fifty boxes and his catalogue as many binders, and John Johnson's collection today fills three rooms, floor to ceiling, in the Bodleian library. Commercial fine printing, which fascinated these men, also captured the attention of Harriet Monroe. Earnest Elmo Calkins, *Louder Please* (Boston: Atlantic Monthly Press, 1924); *Advertising* (Chicago: American Library Association, 1929); Will Ransom, *Private Presses and Their Books* (New York: R. R. Bowker, 1929); Lawrence B. Romaine, *A Guide to American Trade Catalogs 1744–1900* (New York: R. R. Bowker, 1960).

29. Richard Pollay, *Information Sources in Advertising History* (Westport, Conn: Greenwood Press, 1979). These advertising trade journals had a decided influence on the imagists, and Monroe's magazine is clearly patterned on such publications. As advertising historian Richard Pollay concluded, advertising journals moved beyond mere trade information, to become part of the movement that differentiated industry segments (advertising from public relations, and printing from publishing) and enhanced the professionalization of the publicity trades. In the midst of intense intrasector competition between advertising agents and allied printers who professionalized publicity literature, the advertising journals tended to cannibalize one another rather than broaden their appeal. The narrow advertising market of the period catered exclusively to the agricul-

tural press. Volatility among the publicity agencies (which merged and changed names and failed with great rapidity) left advertising journals unable to compete effectively with the comparatively well established trade journals and organs of the printing industry. As I point out in chapters 3 and 4, printing corporations developed product lines to accommodate the demands of both advertisers as well as book publishers. While advertising and publicity specialty journals competed for five to eight thousand special-interest readers in the United States, a circulation spread that N. W. Ayer defined around 1910 as the American midmarket; printers already had a long tradition of publishing trade-oriented special-interest journals, and they used that tradition to appeal to mavericks in emerging publicity trades who were anxious to professionalize by establishing advertising agencies.

At the same time, advertising house-organs representing agencies continued to publish for their narrow base of agricultural clients rather than a broader marketplace that included allied tradesmen. They virtually ignored the enormous population of literate printers eagerly looking for useful techniques, new skills, and the market information the journals carried. As advertising house-organs representing agencies proliferated around 1903, their novelty at first raised public interest and then circulation, with some loss to the printers' organs. As printers rapidly integrated advertising interests into their publications, they expanded their circulation, found a new audience, and diversified their product lines permanently as a result. By 1913, printers' journals not only recaptured original market share but also contributed to driving out many of the maverick agencies and their house organs. In 1893, a total of fourteen agent-run periodicals existed in the advertising trades; within ten years, that figure doubled. Even at its peak, circulation remained only about ten thousand. By 1913, the number dropped to twenty-one national publications. Total readership of best-selling printing journals in 1903 reached eighteen thousand, doubling by 1907, with a circulation figure of approximately forty-four thousand for about fourteen leading publications.

30. Chicago Chamber of Commerce, *Printology*, 1929.

31. Badaracco, "Alternatives to Newspaper Advertising, 1890–

1920: Printers' Innovative Product and Message Designs, *Journalism Quarterly* 67 (Winter 1990): 1042–50.

32. Ellen Williams, *Harriet Monroe and the Poetry Renaissance: The First Ten Years of Poetry 1912–1922* (Champagne: University of Illinois Press, 1977), 38–40. The 1893 Columbian Exposition placed Chicago in the forefront of the American commercial literary economy. Vachel Lindsay thought Monroe's *Poetry* magazine "the most permanent child" of the Chicago 1893 World's Fair, transferring the "head-long energies" of architecture, sculpture, and painting into poetry: "I am sure we would not have the poetry of Masters or the poetry of Sandburg without the Chicago World's Fair. . . . On the whole I think the World's Fair of 1893 has flowered in letters rather than in art." Lindsay, *Letters*, Lindsay to Monroe, 30 November 1915, 125.

33. Ibid.

34. *Poetry*, October 1912, 26–30.

35. Dale Kramer, *Chicago Renaissance: The Literary Life in the Midwest 1900–1930* (Chicago: University of Chicago Press, 1965). Badaracco, "The Influence of Publicity Typologies on News Values: Sherwood Anderson's Trade Journalism," *Journalism Quarterly* 66 (Winter 1989): 979–86. *Agricultural Advertising*, Special Collections, Newberry Library.

36. Anderson, *The Modern Writer* (San Francisco: Lantern Press, 1925), 19.

37. Anderson, *Perhaps Women*, 66–74.

38. Anderson, "The Sales Master and the Selling Organization," *Agricultural Advertising* (March–April 1905): 306–8. Anderson Collection, Newberry Library; Gill Papers, Wing Collection, Newberry Library.

39. Ibid.

40. Advertisement, Harriett Monroe, *The Dance of the Seasons*, printed by Ralph Fletcher Seymour and designed by Will Bradley, Wing Foundation Collections, Newberry Library.

41. Ibid.

42. Anderson Collection, Newberry Library; Gill Papers, Wing Foundation Collection, Newberry Library.

43. Harmer, *Poetry*, October 1912, 17.

44. Elkin Mathews to Harriet Monroe, 19 June 1914, Wing Foundation Collection, Newberry Library. Mathews to Monroe, 19 June 1914; Mathews reported that he was unable to dispose of the earlier numbers of *Poetry*. He offered to insert four-page advertisements for his own publications in the issues if Monroe would accept 250 copies of his book and agree to keep them in stock for a year; he would pay shipping costs. Monroe accepted the offer [Monroe to Mathews, 21 July 1914]. See also Henry May, *The End of American Innocence* (New York: Knopf, 1959), 269–78.

45. Amy Lowell to Ferris Greenslet, 19 January 1921, Houghton Mifflin Company Papers, Houghton Library, Harvard University (hereafter referred to as HCo).

46. Lowell to Monroe, 15 September 1914, HCo.

47. Ibid.

48. Lowell to Pound, 7 April 1914, HCo.

49. Ibid.

50. Kenner, *Pound*.

51. Monroe Papers.

52. Monroe, *Poet's Life*; Telegram from the New York *World* to its Chicago office, 24 September 1892, Monroe Papers; Harriet Monroe, "Modern American Poetry," *Poetry Review* 10 (October 1911): 469–72; "Lawsuits as Advertisements," *Fame*, January 1905, 13.

53. Editors of *Colliers* to Harriet Monroe, 22 January 1912, from *Ladies Home Journal*, 22 March 1912; to Monroe from the *Atlantic Monthly*, 11 April 1911; Monroe Papers.

54. Diaries and account books, Monroe Papers.

55. Monroe, *A Poet's Life*, 302–3; Fragments and notes from circuit speeches given at several midwestern universities ca. 1915–20, called "Poetry's First Decade"; Typescript, "American Poetry," published in *Poetry Review* London, October 1912; Frank Adams to Monroe, 7 July 1930. Monroe Papers.

56. "How Will Twenty-First Century Critics Rank Artists of the Present Day," Chicago *Tribune*, 12 July 1912, 11.

57. Advertisement, *Poetry*, Monroe Papers.

58. Ibid.

59. Monroe, *Poets and Their Art*, 248.

60. Between 1909 and 1914, Monroe wrote nearly two hundred columns.

61. Bills and publicity files, Monroe Papers, n.d. Edward Bernays, an important second-generation publicity "father" figure, worked for Ivy Ledbetter Lee on the Creel committee; specialists in war propaganda, they flourished in the late teens and twenties. Monroe's use of a Parisian clipping service in 1914 preceded the work of Lee and Bernays, who claimed to have "originated" concepts of modern publicity management. Several of Lee's monographs, all privately printed and distributed, are in the Newberry Library's collections, including his father's sermon at the funeral of Joel Chandler Harris, edited by Ivy Lee.

62. The magazine's guarantors represented the social and industrial elite of Chicago: more than one hundred people agreed to back the magazine for five years, with a total annual endowment of $5,000. Clarence Darrow, along with McCormick and his wife, Edith Rockefeller, and the families of Charles Deering, George Pullman, F. S. Peabody, F. S. Winston, A. B. Dick, Albert Loeb, Charles Hitchcock, Frederick Sargent, H. C. Chatfield-Taylor, and E. A. Bancroft, were among them.

Each year Monroe issued annual reports to the guarantors. In her first annual report (1913), with receipts from sales and the Guarantors' Fund of $7,344, expenditures of $2,466 for payment to poets, with no prize money given, $2,774 for printing, $771 for rent, she had a positive balance of almost $700 for the first year of business. Keeping the publication in the black, though, was at the expense of the editors, who drew only about $300 a year.

In her 1914 annual report, assets and receipts exceeded those of the previous year by about a thousand dollars, all income from increased circulation. Nearly $3,000 went to pay poets, with about $400 set aside for prize money. With a total budget of $8,567, Monroe ended the year with a $123 surplus, having held editorial salary increases to a minimum, but adding an office assistant. No substantial difference was registered the following year, nor for 1918–19, when salaries rose to $1,603. Monroe again ended the year with a surplus, of $750, reporting a 23 percent increase in paid subscriptions, with book-stand and office sales about 500 per month, and the average monthly number of issues running about 2,800 copies. In her annual report for 1921, Monroe reported a $100 surplus in a $10,000+ budget, with a 50 percent increase in subscription rate. The magazine reported a positive balance, a steady growth in subscribers and circulation, and a healthy economic outlook each year of its existence until the Depression years. See Typed Documents, Annual Reports. Monroe Papers.

63. Chicago *Daily News*, 20 June 1917; Aubrey Cribb, Associated Press correspondent, to Monroe, *Times Literary Supplement*, 27 October 1923, Poetry Magazine Papers; Artemas Ward, "On Municipal Advertising: How Cities Get Reputations," *Fame*, January 1905, 56.

64. Chicago *Daily News*, 8 July 1917; Associated Press, 27 October 1923, Aubrey Cribb to Monroe, Monroe Papers. See also The Chicago Record History at the Newberry Library and columns in *Fame* and *Profitable Advertising*, ca. 1903.

65. Monroe to Howard Elting, Association of Commerce, Monroe Papers, n.d.

66. Typed manuscript, Monroe Papers, n.d.

67. Chicago *Daily News*, 20 June 1917.

68. Publicity fact sheet including testimonials [ca. 1919], Monroe Papers.

69. Monroe to Elting, Monroe Papers, n.d.

70. Advertising circular, 1913, Monroe Papers.

71. *Poetry* 15 (February 1920): 328–30.

72. Ibid.

73. In August of 1917, Alice Henderson wrote an editorial about cowboy poetry, printed selections from John Lomax's *Cowboy Songs* (1910), which included "The Old Chisholm Trail." Monroe Papers.

74. Kenner, *Pound*, 178.

75. Pound, "Contemporania," *Poetry*, April 1913.

76. Ibid.

77. John Fiske, "Sociology and Hero-Worship," *American Mercury*, January 1881 [An evolutionist's reply to Dr. James]; William James, "Great Men Great Thought," *American Mercury*, October 1880 ["Individuals have no initiative in determining social

change"]; Grant Allen, "The Genesis of Genius," *American Mercury*, March 1881, 371–81.

78. *Poetry*, February 1915.

79. Monroe, *A Poet's Life*, 458.

80. "On Being An Editor," autographed manuscript, Monroe Papers, n.d.

81. Publicity file, Monroe Papers.

82. *Poetry*, August 1917, 255–56.

83. Stanford Ackley to Monroe, April 1934, Monroe Papers.

84. R. M. Bartley to Monroe, 4 January 1930, Monroe Papers.

85. Publicity file, Monroe Papers.

86. H. J. Patee to Monroe, St. Louis, 21 August 1913, Monroe Papers.

87. J. Greene to Monroe, Boston, 6 August 1913, Monroe Papers.

88. Anon. [W. Wallowy Swilltub, St. Paul, Minn.] Monroe Papers.

89. C. L. Betts to Monroe, 15 April 1913, Monroe Papers.

90. Anon. to Monroe, 14 June 1913, Monroe Papers.

91. T. Schnarth [?] to Monroe, 12 April 1913, Monroe Papers.

92. Nicholas Joost, *The Dial: Years of Transition 1912–1920* (Barre, Mass.: Barre Publishing Co., 1967), 3–21.

93. Emanuel Carnevali to Monroe, March 1919, Monroe Papers.

94. Ibid.

95. Ibid.

96. Lindsay, *Adventures Rhymes and Designs*, with an essay by Robert F. Sayre (New York: Eakins Press, 1968), 12.

97. Sayre, 13–14.

98. Ibid., 31.

99. Lindsay, *Letters*, 213.

100. Lindsay to Monroe, 15 December 1920, HCo.; Eleanor Ruggles, *The West-Going Heart: A Life of Vachel Lindsay* (New York: W. W. Norton, 1959), 283–86.

101. Amy Lowell to Vachel Lindsay, 20 December 1918, HCo.

102. Lindsay, *The Golden Book of Springfield* (New York: Macmillan, 1920).

103. Lindsay, *Letters*, 125.

104. Vachel Lindsay to Amy Lowell, 3 January 1921, HCo.

105. The "mass of dolts" phrase originated with Pound, but Monroe adopted it as her own and used it frequently. Carnevali uses the phrase also in his 1919 manuscript.

106. Lowell to Lindsay, 9 August 1916 and 20 December 1918, HCo., Lowell to Ferris Greenslet, 10 July 1917, HCo.

107. Kenner, *Pound*, 40.

108. Lowell to Harriet Monroe, 2 November 1914 and 5 November 1914, HCo.

109. Ezra Pound to Lowell, 2 October 1914, HCo.

110. Lowell to Pound, 3 November 1914, HCo.

111. Lowell to Greenslet, 28 January 1915, HCo.

112. Amy Lowell, *Some Imagist Poets*, v.

113. Pound to Lowell, 19 October 1919, HCo.

114. Pound to Lowell, 10 March 1922, HCo.

115. Lowell to Greenslet, 4 August 1916, HCo.

116. Lowell to Greenslet, 28 June 1922, HCo.

117. Lowell to Greenslet, 10 February 1919, HCo.

118. Lowell to Greenslet, 19 October 1921, HCo.

119. Lowell to Greenslet, 28 June 1922, HCo.

120. Greenslet to Lowell, 10 June 1915, HCo.

121. Lowell to Scaife, 9 May 1921, HCo.

122. Lowell to Greenslet, 21 February 1916, HCo.

123. Lowell to Greenslet, 22 April 1915 and 6 August 1915, HCo.

124. Lowell to Greenslet, 21 September 1916, HCo.

125. Lowell to Linscott, 25 May 1921; Lowell to Greenslet, 2 December 1924, HCo.

126. Lowell to Scaife, 10 February 1917, HCo.

127. Lowell to Greenslet, 25 April 1916, HCo.

128. Houghton Mifflin Company to Lowell, 23 January 1925, HCo.

129. Lowell to Greenslet, 1 December 1921, HCo.

130. Houghton Mifflin to Lowell, 14 March 1925, HCo.

131. Lowell to Greenslet, 15 December 1920, HCo.

132. Houghton Mifflin to Lowell, 14 July 1921, HCo.

133. Linscott to Lowell, 11 September 1917, HCo.

Notes to Pages 51–60

134. Greenslet to Lowell, 26 May 1917 and 12 July 1917, HCo.

135. Lowell to Scaife, 20 July 1922, HCo.

136. Houghton Mifflin to Lowell, 16 August 1917, HCo.

137. Houghton Mifflin Company to Lowell, 28 January 1925, HCo.

138. Lowell to Linscott, 5 September 1923, HCo.

139. Frank Bruce to Scaife, internal memoranda, Houghton Mifflin Company, 28 November 1922 and 14 December 1922, HCo.

140. Lowell to Greenslet, 23 June 1921, HCo.; Publicity files, scrapbooks, and notebooks, HCo.

141. Lowell to Greenslet, 6 November 1923, HCo.

142. Lowell to Royal Snow, 18 January 1921, HCo.

143. Lowell to Linscott, 15 October 1921, HCo.

144. Lowell to Greenslet, 25 September 1921, 29 November 1921, HCo.

145. Lowell to Greenslet, 23 February 1923, HCo.

146. Lowell to Greenslet, 26 August 1922 and 8 September 1922, HCo.

147. Lowell to Greenslet, 28 June 1922 and 7 May 1914, HCo.

148. Lowell to Greenslet, 7 May 1914, HCo.

149. Lowell to Greenslet, 17 October 1923, HCo.

150. Greenslet to Lowell, 15 November 1923, HCo.

151. Lowell to Greenslet, 10 October 1922, HCo.

152. Greenslet to Lowell, 28 November 1922 and 11 August 1924, HCo.

153. Lowell to Scaife, 23 June 1922; Lowell to Greenslet, 5 August 1924; Lowell to Greenslet, 28 April 1923, HCo.

CHAPTER 3:

RECUTTING MONOTYPE'S ENGLISH FACES, 1922–1932

1. Warde, *The Monotype Recorder* 19 (September–December 1925): 45–56; Thompson, *American Book Design and William Morris*.

2. A number of other Americans also contributed to building Monotype's empire in its first forty years of business. Among them was the engineer Frank Hinman Pierpont, company works manager, who was dubbed by the company house organ a "genius with an ob-

sessive passion for accuracy and efficiency." *Monotype: A Journal of Composing Room Efficiency*, Philadelphia 1 (June–July 1914): 37–38; 1 (February 1914): 149; 1 (March 1914): 165.

3. Warde, 120; Daniel Berkeley Updike, "The Planning of Printing," *Fleuron Anthology*, ed. Francis Meynell and Herbert Simon (Toronto: University of Toronto Press, 1973), 84.

4. In 1920, the Philadelphia offices of Linotype invited Bruce Rogers, a well-known type designer with an American private press, Rudge, to represent Linotype as its press agent. When he declined, the company hired Frederic Goudy, at the time a Chicago advertising man, who later became an important type designer for Lanston Monotype. See also White, "New Spirit in Advertising," 8; *Monotype* 21, 1–7, 27; Warde, "The Pioneer Days of 'Monotype' Composing Machines," *Monotype Recorder* 39 (Fall 1949): 3–27; Warde, "Twenty Years of Typographic Progress," *The Monotype Recorder* 32 (1942), Wing.

5. Tolbert Lanston, the American who invented the composing machinery using parts from a player piano and typewriter, sold the Linotype mechanical composition typesetter demonstrated at the 1893 Chicago World's Fair to the Earl of Dunraven in 1897 for £222,000 following what the company lore called a "chance shipboard meeting" between the two. Dunraven formed a syndicate and founded the British Monotype Corporation the same year with £555,000 capital. His syndicate built two limited font machines in 1897, one in Philadelphia and one in London, designed for work on newspapers and other uncomplicated printing jobs. Because all art printing traditionally came from hand presses in Britain and machine presses rarely ran anything but newspapers, Dunraven abandoned the limited-font machinery as unworkable, probably as early as 1898. Subsequently, the Linotype company headed by John Sellers Bancroft tried to improve the original limited-font machine, while company art director Frederic W. Goudy designed a number of typefaces drawn exclusively for the company: Garamond, Goudy Light, Kennerley Bold, Italian Old Style, and Forum, among others. Monotype newsletters published by Lanston Monotype in Philadelphia in the Paul Bennett Papers, Special Collections, Columbia University Library.

Notes to Page 68

Today King Black and Associates owns Monotype, now a much smaller graphic arts industry venture-capital company specializing in page layout systems, controllers for laser printers and high-speed laser typesetters, image recorders, and customized graphic-arts systems.

6. Dunraven's improved machine, completed within two years, had a range of 224 characters, including "logotypes" (*th*, *to*, *of*, *at*) designed to speed production. By the time the first ten machines manufactured in Philadelphia reached England in 1901, the British had devised matrices for new typefaces. In 1902, Frank Hinman Pierpont, who had been working for the Typograph Company in Germany, joined Monotype-UK to supervise the construction of a new factory in Salfords, Redhill, where the company would go into business as a printing machine manufacturer. Type specifications differed slightly between the faces cut in England and in Philadelphia, and when American-made machines arrived in England, the Salfords mechanics stripped and reassembled them to accommodate the difference, along with making other improvements. Rather than adjust their machinery to suit the different typeface specifications, the Americans instead tried to develop an exclusive typographical line.

7. Tolbert Lanston's patent application, granted in 1887, described stamping a strip of metal which was then cut into pieces to make type and assembled into justified lines. He filed a second patent application in 1890, granted six years later, for a machine to cast hot metal type. His third patent (1897) secured the idea of a perforation on a paper roll which selected the character to be cast. A combination keyboard and type caster formed the basis of several experimental machines built between 1890 and 1898 in the company's small Washington factory where Lanston perfected the design. This third machine set type in six- eight- ten-, and 12-point sizes only, with a limit of 120 characters in one type size. Over the next twelve years, the number of available characters increased from 120 to 255, accommodating six alphabets, and casting type sizes from four to eighteen points twice as fast.

8. Because keyboards and then type casting had to be manufactured in Philadelphia and shipped to Washington for assembly, he

Notes to Page 68

moved the whole operation to Philadelphia in 1900. The typefaces designed by Goudy included: Pabst Old Style (1911) for the brewer; Goudy Old Style (1910), widely used in Gimbel's advertising; Kennerley Old Style (1923), an attempt to imitate rubbings taken from Trajan's column by Goudy; Goudy Lanston (1926); Goudy Old Style (1927), designed for ATF; Goudy Cursive (1928), an attempt to imitate early Roman cursive writing; Goudy Initials (1916), designed for ATF; Hadrano (1915), based on rubbings of a first-century tablet in the Louvre; Goudy Open (1923–24); Italian Old Style (1924); Goudy Heavy Face (1926), specifically for display work; Deepene (1927), based on Dutch forms; Goudy Text (1933); Lombardic (1929); Sans Serif Bold and Light (1929–30), which Goudy thought a failure because it resembled "dozens of similar" faces; Kaatskill (1929), designed for an edition of Rip Van Winkle in the Limited Editions Club; Remington Typewriter (1927), designed to imitate typewriter spacing; Goudy Village (1932), for the Village Press; Californian (1932), for the University of California Press; Bible (1935), designed for Bruce Rogers's *World Bible*, a recutting of a 1920 face; and Goudy Thrifty (1946). Monotype newsletters published by Lanston Monotype in Philadelphia in the Paul Bennett Papers, Special Collections, Columbia University Library.

9. Disposable type saved labor by eliminating sorting. By recycling plates, melting them down to recast into new printing surfaces, additional labor-saving costs became possible. In 1912, using this method, the company reported costs of only $1 per day for the U.S. Government Printing Office, which produced 116,696 pounds of type, or 57 percent of the total printing done by that office for the year, at a cost of $335.87.

10. This is the opinion of James Wells, a friend and colleague of Beatrice Warde and Stanley Morison.

11. Warde, "A Recent Visit to America and What It Revealed," a talk given at the London Center, *Managing Printer*, November 1953, 17, St. Bride's Library (hereafter referred to as St. Bride's).

12. Warde, "Design and Management," lecture given to The London Centre of the Printers' Managers and Overseers Association, 25 May 1949, London, St. Bride's; "Modern Selling," *The Annals of the American Academy of Political and Social Science*, September

1924, pamphlet no. 204, Wing; Robert S. and Helen M. Lynd, *Middletown: Study in Contemporary American Culture* (New York: Harcourt Brace & Co., 1929); Lippmann, *Public Opinion* and *The Phantom Public*; Edward Bernays, *Propaganda* (New York: Horace Liveright, 1928).

13. Warde, "Design"; John Dreyfus, "Beatrice Warde: First Lady of Typography," Stanley Morison Lecture, 26 November 1985, London, reprinted in special memorial issue; Publicity manuscripts for Warde's United States tour, St. Bride's, *Monotype Recorder* 44 (Autumn 1970).

14. Warde, *Crystal Goblet*, 12–15; Dreyfus, "Beatrice Warde"; Sir Francis Meynell, "The Typography of Advertising," Institute for Practitioners in Advertising, Occasional Paper No. 12, 2 November 1960, 7, Wing. See D. L. LeMahieu, *A Culture for Democracy: Mass Communication and the Cultivated Mind in Britain Between the Wars* (Oxford: Clarendon Press, 1988), 5.

15. Warde, "Design and Management," 20. The ATF company, founded in 1892, by nineteen leading American type foundries, started with $9 million in capital. Later, the firm merged with the Cox Typesetting Machine Company, controlled by the Barnhart Bros. and Spindler type foundry, to form Unitype Company. "Design and Typography," *The Printing Art* 3,6 (August 1904): 169–71; William Morris, "The Art of the People," an address delivered before the Birmingham Society of Arts, 19 February 1879, and printed privately by Ralph Fletcher Seymour, 1902; F. R. Leavis and Denys Thompson, *Culture and Environment* (London: Chatto and Windus, 1933); Lewis Mumford, *American Taste* (San Francisco: The Westgate Press, 1929); Warde, "The Pioneer Days of 'Monotype' Composing Machines," *Monotype Recorder* 39 (Fall 1949): 3–27; Warde, "Twenty Years of Typographic Progress," *The Monotype Recorder* 32 (1942), Wing; Joseph Blumenthal, *Bruce Rogers: A Life In Letters 1870–1957* (Austin: W. Thomas Taylor, 1989).

16. Henry Lewis Bullen, "Observations on Type Design and Type Designers and Their Press Agents," *Inland Printer*, September 1923, 883–37. At Gerard Meynell's suggestion, Monotype recut an eighteenth-century Caslon "Old Face" for *The Imprint* ca. 1912.

17. Ibid.

18. Ibid.

19. Meynell, *My Lives*; Bullen, "Observations," 833–37.

20. Ibid.

21. Dreyfus, "Beatrice Warde," 74. The personal correspondence between Warde and Eric Gill during the period immediately following the breakup of her marriage is in the Meynell papers, Cambridge University. Evidence in these papers and in other business correspondence at St. Bride's contradicts Fiona MacCarthy's view of Warde as a fan of Gill and a disciple of Morison in *Eric Gill: A Lover's Quest for Art and God* (New York: E. P. Dutton, 1989).

22. Dreyfus, "Beatrice Warde," 74.

23. May Lamberton Becker was a well-known children's book review writer for the New York *Herald Tribune*; "Pioneer in a Man's World," London *Times*, 10 February 1964, 13a; Warde's Barnard scrapbook and college juvenilia are in St. Bride's.

24. Bullen, "Observations," 833–37.

25. Joseph P. Thorpe, *Printing for Business* (London: John Hogg, 1919); Beatrice Warde Manuscripts, St. Bride's and Wing.

26. Dreyfus, "Beatrice Warde," 74.

27. Some of the major historical articles that Beatrice Warde wrote up to 1930 include: "Garamond," in the *Fleuron V*, 1926; "Fournier," *Monotype Recorder* 20 (March–June 1926); "On Baskerville," *Monotype Recorder* 21 (September–October 1927); "Charles Nicolas Cochin," *Monotype Recorder* 22 (January–February 1928); "French National Printing Office, Notes on Its Typographic Achievements," *Monotype Recorder* 22 (March–April 1928). In 1930, the *Fleuron VII* published Warde's article on Eric Gill.

28. *Monotype* 21 (August 1927): 1–7.

29. *Monotype: A Journal of Composing Room Efficiency*, Philadelphia, 1 (June–July 1914): 37–38; 1 (February 1914): 149; 1 (March 1914): 165.

30. Stanley Morison, *A Tally of Types: 1922–1934* (Cambridge: privately printed, 1953); Monotype newsletter, Columbia.

31. Meynell, *My Lives*, 144.

32. Morison, *A Tally*; Monotype newsletter, Columbia.

33. "What the Monotype Is," publicity brochure, 1934, Bodleian Library, Oxford, John Johnson Collection. See also James Moran, *Printing in the Twentieth Century* (London: Northwood, 1974); Meynell, *My Lives*, 144; Morison, *A Tally*.

34. Meynell, *My Lives*, 135–49; Warde, "Printers' Marketing Problems," *Monotype Recorder* 31 (November–December 1932): 3.

35. Ibid., 3–5.

36. Ibid.

37. Ibid.

38. Sir Cyril Burt, with W. F. Cooper and J. L. Martin, "A Psychological Study of Typography," *British Journal of Statistical Psychology* 8, 1 (May 1955): 9. Published as a monograph in 1959 by Cambridge University Press, with an introduction by Stanley Morison, and reviewed by Beatrice Warde in the London *Times*. The study points out that Mrs. Warde had recommended to the *British Journal of Statistical Psychology* that its eight-point footnotes be divided into two columns for greater readability. Monotype Corporation supplied the specimen sheets of typeface forms for the study, although I have not found any indications that Burt worked as a consultant for the corporation. Specific titles of typefaces included in the later study are: Bembo, Veronese, Centaur, Garamond, Granjon, Fournier, Plantin, Ehrhardt, Baskerville, Old Style, Imprint, Times New Roman, and Perpetua. He dubbed the Times New Roman the most universally readable.

39. Burt et al., "A Psychological Study," 5–8. Burt reiterated the experiments in the early 1950s, testing the numerous Monotype innovations released prior to the Second World War, comparing mature scientific readers with literary publics, based on their aesthetic responsiveness as well as on his preconceived hypotheses.

40. Ibid., 30.

41. Ibid., 30–43.

42. Tschichold, "New Life," 8, 9, St. Bride's.

43. Ibid., 8, 15.

44. Ibid., 15, 17, 18.

45. McLean, *Jan Tschichold*, 29–30.

46. Ibid.

47. Morison, "First Principles of Typography," *Fleuron VIII* (Cambridge: Doubleday, 1930): 61; James Moran, *Stanley Morison* (London: Lund Humphries, 1971).

48. Morison, "First Principles," 61.

49. Warde, *Crystal Goblet*, 39.

50. Warde, "The Invisible Book," *Times Literary Supplement*, 24 August 1951; *Crystal Goblet*, 1–12.

51. Warde, *Crystal Goblet*, 1–12.

52. Stanley Morison obituary, *Sunday Times*, 15 October 1967, reprinted in *Monotype Recorder* special issue on Warde, 8.

53. Morison, "First Principles of Typography," *Fleuron VIII*, 69.

54. Ibid.

55. Warde, "Twenty Years of Typographic Progress," *Monotype Recorder* 32 (January–February 1933).

56. Warde MSS, "Typographic Renaissance," Lecture, 1947, Edinburgh, St. Bride's.

57. Morison, *A Tally*.

58. Nicolas Barker, *Stanley Morison* (London: Macmillan, 1972).

59. J. M. Dent, 1849–1926, *Memoirs* (London: J. M. Dent & Sons, Ltd., 1928); R. Farquharson Sharp, *The Reader's Guide to Everyman's Library: Being a Catalogue of the First 888 Volumes* (London: J. M. Dent, 1932).

60. Warde, "Fifty Years of Type-Cutting," *Monotype Recorder* 39, 2 (Autumn 1950); "Twenty Years of Typographic Progress."

61. Ibid.

62. Morison, *Politics and Script*; Warde, "The Face of the Printed World," *Monotype Recorder* 36 (March 1937): 25; "A Postscript on the Stylist and the Craftsman," *Monotype Recorder* 39 (Summer 1952).

63. Warde, "Face of the Printed World," 25; "Postscript."

64. Morison, *Politics and Script*; Dreyfus, "Beatrice Warde," 74; Badaracco, "Alternatives to Newspaper Advertising," 1042–50; "The Influence of Public Typologies on Sherwood Anderson's News Values," *Journalism Quarterly* 68, 4 (Winter 1989): 979–86; "The Role of 'Agency' in Language Product Manufacturing, 1910–

1930," *Business and Economic History*, 2d series, 19, 1990: 245–54; "Marketing Language Products 1900–1905: The Case of Agricultural Advertising," *Essays in Economic and Business History* 8 (1991): 131–46.

65. "Typography Is Public Relations," An address by Beatrice Warde to the Institute for Public Relations, 25 October 1955 (London: privately printed), St. Bride's.

66. Dreyfus, on Warde.

67. Title page slogan, *Monotype Recorder*.

68. The sheet is widely reproduced and is the verso front cover of the *Monotype Recorder* memorial issue for Warde, 44 (Autumn 1970).

69. See *Monotype Recorder* memorial issue.

70. Warde, promotional materials, St. Bride's; Morison, *Politics and Script*, 335.

71. Warde, "L.N.E.R. Standardization," *Monotype Recorder* 32 (Winter 1932): 3; "Fifty Years of Type Cutting," *Monotype Recorder* 39 (August 1950): 6; LeMahiue, *Culture for Democracy*, 165; Keith Murgatroyd, "E. McKnight Kauffer, the Artist in the World of Commerce," *Print* 23, 1 (January–February 1969): 30–33.

72. Ibid.; Warde, "Fifty Years of Type Cutting," 6; LeMahieu, *Culture for Democracy*, 165. Kauffer arrived in England in 1914 after having studied architecture in Munich and Paris. He brought a lifelong interest in the international style of the Bauhaus and Russian futurists to England as a result of his early studies and a particular interest in their designs for the poster and use of film in propaganda. Kauffer created 141 posters for Frank Pick's Underground and is credited with having impressed his style on the poster era of the thirties. He quickly became a distinguished and highly respected advertising artist in London, and he received the title of Honorary Fellow of the Society for Industrial Artists. A friend of Sir Francis Meynell, whose first book he illustrated, he joined Crawford's advertising agency in 1929, designing letterhead, cards, wine lists, booklets, timetables, press advertisements, and ballet scenery. Between 1926 and 1933, Kauffer worked with Stephen Tallents of the Empire Marketing Board to promote British products abroad,

advancing his interest in Russian film and German exhibition design.

73. Warde, *Crystal Goblet*, 199.

74. Ibid.

75. James Mosley, *British Type Specimens Before 1831* (Oxford: Oxford Bibliographical Society, Bodleian Library and University of Reading, 1984); *History of Letterforms and Typography: A Bibliography*, pamphlet, October 1988, St. Bride's.

76. Ibid.; Advertising booklet, reprint of a 1925 Roger Fry article in the *Nation*, the John Johnson Collection, Bodleian Library, Oxford; *Crystal Goblet*, 198.

77. Morison, *Politics and Script*; Francis Meynell and Herbert Simon, eds., *Fleuron Anthology*; Nicolas Barker, *Stanley Morison* (London: Macmillan, 1972).

78. Morison, *Politics and Script*.

79. Ibid.

80. Ibid.; Grant Shipcott, *Typographical Periodicals Between the Wars: A Critique of the Fleuron, Signature and Typography* (Oxford: Polytechnic Press, 1980); Meynell, "The Typography of Advertising," 7, 115.

81. Morison, *Politics and Script*, 335, 336–39.

82. Paul Beaujon, "Eric Gill," *Fleuron VII* (Cambridge: Doubleday, 1930): 27–59.

83. Morison, *Politics and Script*, 336.

84. Ibid., 339.

85. Ibid., 330.

86. *Monotype Recorder* 21 (May–June 1927), 8; White, "New Spirit in Advertising."

87. Warde, *Crystal Goblet*; Meynell, "Typography of Advertising," 115–16.

88. Warde, MSS typescript, "The Meaning of Modern," ca. 1935, St. Bride's; Warde, MSS 1933, typescript, "100% More Uses for Printing," possibly a draft for a printing trade journal article in December 1932; MSS, "Two Kinds of Effectiveness," St. Bride's.

89. Warde, "Meaning of Modern"; ca. "A Recent Visit to America," *Managing Printer* (November 1953): 17, St. Bride's.

90. British Federation of Master Printers Members circular (June 1918): 183, St. Bride's.

91. Federation of Master Printers Members circular (June 1918): 183, St. Bride's.

92. Warde, *Crystal Goblet*, 198. The suggestion that she designed the piece comes from James Mosley; MSS, "Two Kinds of Effectiveness," St. Bride's.

93. British Federation of Master Printers, Members circular (June 1918): 182–87, St. Bride's. Subsequent page references will be cited parenthetically in the text.

94. Warde, MSS, "Two Kinds of Effectiveness," St. Bride's.

95. Warde, "L.N.E.R. Standardization," *Monotype Recorder* 32 (Winter 1932): Mosley, *Type Specimens*; *History*.

96. Warde, "L.N.E.R."

97. Ibid.

98. Ibid. Second to that, the Old Style, the company's first face introduced in 1901, sold close to 25,000 sets; third the Baskerville introduced in 1923, which sold 20,000; fourth, the Modern Extended, another of the company's innovations in 1902, sold close to 20,000; fifth, the Gill Sans, selling 18,330. Monotype corporate sales records.

99. Warde, Eric Gill issue, *Monotype Recorder* (October 1958): 18.

100. Warde, "L.N.E.R."

101. Ibid. and Gill issues.

102. Ibid.

103. Gill to Warde, 4 April 1932; Gill issue, *Monotype Recorder*, 18.

104. Gill issue, *Monotype Recorder*, 18.

105. Gill to Warde, 4 April 1932, Cambridge University Library.

106. Warde to Gill, 21–22 March 1932, Cambridge University Library.

107. Ibid.

108. Ibid.

109. Ibid.

110. Stanley Morison, *Memorandum on a Proposal to Revise the Typography of the Times, 1930*, printed in the Office of the *Times*, 21

November 1930; Warde, "The Times and Its New Roman Type," *Monotype Recorder* 31 (1932).

111. Ibid.

112. Daniel Berkeley Updike, *Printing Types: Their History, Forms, and Use, A Study in Survivals*, 2d ed.; 3 vols. (Cambridge, Mass.: 1969); Meynell, "Typography of Advertising," IPA Occasional Paper; David McKitterick, *Stanley Morison and D. B. Updike: Selected Correspondence* (New York: Moretus Press, 1979).

113. McKitterick, *Morison and Updike*. See also Moran, *Printing in the Twentieth Century*, 123.

114. Barker, *Stanley Morison*.

115. Moran, *Printing in the Twentieth Century*, 123–33.

116. Morison, *Memorandum*; Warde, "The Times and Its New Roman Type," *Monotype Recorder* 31 (1932) and "Modern Newspaper Typography," *Monotype Recorder* 35 (Spring 1936).

117. Moran, *Printing in the Twentieth Century*, 123; David McKitterick, *Works of Stanley Morison*, 2 vols. (Cambridge: Cambridge University Press), 296.

118. Morison, *Memorandum*, 296.

119. Ibid.

120. Ibid., 295–329.

121. Warde, "The Times."

122. Morison, *Memorandum*, 295–329; Warde, "The Times."

123. Warde, "The Times."

124. Robert Darnton, *The Literary Underground of the Old Regime* (Cambridge: Harvard University Press, 1982); Philip M. Taylor, *The Projection of Britain: British Overseas Publicity and Propaganda 1919–1939* (Cambridge: Cambridge University Press, 1981).

125. Harold Keeble, "The Typography of Psychological Warfare," *Alphabet and Image* 4 (April 1947): 49–60.

126. Ibid.

127. Morison, "Picture-Printing and Word-Printing," pamphlet ca. 1948, James Wells Papers, Newberry Library.

128. Morison, "Politics and Script."

129. Henry May, *The End of American Innocence* (New York: Knopf, 1959), 269–78.

CHAPTER 4:
DEFINING DONNELLEY'S AMERICAN CULTURE, 1926–1935

1. Today R. R. Donnelley & Sons Company is estimated to be the largest printing company in North America. With its $570-million acquisition in 1990 of Meredith/Burda Companies, which is owned jointly with the Meredith Corporation, a leading American publishing company, and Franz and Frieder Burda of West Germany, Donnelley is a major competitor in a global printing market.

2. James Weber Linn's letter about R. R. Donnelley to the Chicago *Daily Times*, 30 November 1931, was distributed as a publicity reprint, "A Printing Shop: Work and Beauty, Shrine of Labor," Ransom/Wing.

3. John Tebbel, *A History of Book Publishing in the United States*, vol. 3, *1920–1940* (New York: Bowker, 1978), 48–67.

4. "Too Many Books," "Advertising and the Book Trade," and "The Concentration of Advertising," *Publishers Weekly* 117 (4 January 1930): 39–51.

5. See "The Lakeside Press, Chicago: A Brief Note on Its History, Aims, Purposes, and Resources," "The Lakeside Press, 1929." See also "Donnelley History," *Donnelley Printer* (Spring 1965): 38–44; (Summer 1965): 30–33; (Fall 1965): 34–37; (Winter 1965): 28–32; (Spring 1966): 32–35; (Summer 1966): 33–36; (Fall 1966): 39–41; (Winter 1966): 12–15; (Spring 1967): 16–19; (Summer 1967): 16–19; (Fall 1967): 35–37.

6. "Printing Engineers: A Small Book of Facts Regarding the Organization of R. R. Donnelley & Sons Co., Chicago" (1923), William A. Kittredge Papers, Wing Foundation Collection, Newberry Library (hereafter cited as Kitt/Wing). See also "Giving Distinction to Small Printing Orders" (Lakeside, n.d.), Kitt/Wing. See also *Kelmscott, Doves, and Ashendene: The Private Press Credos*, with an introduction by Will Ransom (New York: New York University Press: The Typophiles, 1952).

7. "Training Craftsmen at the Lakeside Press 1908–1927," 13, Ransom/Wing; Carl Dewitt Davis, *A Study of the School for Apprentices of the Lakeside Press* (Chicago: R. R. Donnelley, 1922).

8. *Fine Printing and Large Printers* (Chicago: Lakeside Press,

n.d.), Ransom/Wing. To meet the legal requirements of child labor laws, boys fourteen to sixteen years old could not work more than eight hours per day, and not on any power-driven machinery. These boys were placed in school three and a half hours a day and in the factory or offices running errands or doing other light work for four and a half hours daily. This was called "preapprenticeship." They studied English, drawing, and design, including typefaces, as well as economics, the history of printing, and other subjects. The Apprenticeship School also had a track for university graduates and another cooperative arrangement with the Universities of Chicago and Cincinnati, where undergraduate students could take a five-year program of training leading to a university degree. The students worked in pairs, alternating each twelve weeks or by term. By 1927, there were 165 apprentices who had graduated to journeymen, of which 130 stayed with the press. Of the 130 who stayed, 19 became foremen, 3 became salesmen, and 14 became executives.

9. "Training Craftsmen"; Davis, *Study of the School for Apprentices*.

10. "1931 Catalogue: Illustrated Books," Ransom/Wing. Among the exhibits were paintings from the "Business Men's Art Club of Chicago" (1935); a display entitled "Title Pages" (1947), and exhibits of bindings, the work of type designers and illustrators, and examples of other aspects of printing. Apparently there were as many as four exhibits a year.

11. Linn, "A Printing Shop"; "Training Craftsmen at the Lakeside Press 1908–1927," 13, Ransom/Wing; Davis, *Study of the School for Apprentices*.

12. Advertising brochure, "Jacob Wrestling with an Angel," 1954, Ransom/Wing. *Publishers Weekly* 115 (4 May 1929) carried the trade announcement. Binder file labeled "RRD History," Donnelley corporate archives, R. R. Donnelley & Sons Co., Chicago.

13. Binder file, Donnelley archives.

14. "Memorial Tribute to William A. Kittredge, 1891–1945," designed by Rudolph Ruzicka, Ransom/Wing.

15. Binder file, Donnelley archives.

16. "Authoritative Design in Typography and Printing," Ransom/Wing; Four American Books prospectus, 1930, Ransom/Wing.

17. Herbert Zimmermann's typed notes on company history, binder file labeled "RRD History," Donnelley corporate archives. See the Parke-Bernet auction gallery catalog *The Distinguished Collection of Americana*, February 5–6, 1945, for a list of C. G. Littell's collection.

18. Internal memorandum, Littell to Kittredge, 3 April 1930, Kitt/Wing; Binder file, "Company History," written by Herbert Zimmermann, Donnelley corporate archives; *Fine Printing and Large Printers*; Kitt/Wing.

19. *Fine Printing and Large Printers*.

20. Ibid.

21. Thomas Tanselle, *A Checklist of Editions of Moby-Dick, 1851–1976*, exhibition catalog (Chicago: Newberry Library, 1976), 17. Tanselle calls Rockwell Kent's *Moby Dick* "one of the finest examples of bookmaking to be found among all the [126] editions of his works."

22. Kittredge to Dwiggins, 4 January 1927, Kitt/Wing; internal memorandum, Littell to Kittredge, 3 April 1930, Kitt/Wing.

23. Kittredge to Kent, 24 June 1927, Kitt/Wing.

24. For example, their success especially impressed George Macy, who came to be known as a father of direct-mail publicity. Macy's subscription scheme for The Limited Edition Club flourished during the Depression, even though it was launched the day after the stock market crashed. See also Carl Purington Rollins, "A Survey of the Making of Books in Recent Years," *Dolphin* 1 (1933): 288–301. See also Paul Standard, "The Limited Editions Club: A New Influence in American Printing," *Penrose's Annual* 37 (1935): 44–49. Volume 3 of the *Dolphin* was devoted to a history of the printed book, well received in its day, which continues to be regarded as the journal's major achievement. Also among prospective titles first considered were: Mark Twain, *Tom Sawyer*; George Cable, *Creole Days*; Henry James, *The Portrait of a Lady* and *Daisy Miller*; Nathaniel Hawthorne, *The House of the Seven Gables*; Bret Harte's *Tales*; Frank Norris, *Lady Letty*; Stephen Crane, *The Red Badge of Courage*; O. Henry, *The Four Million*; Washington Irving, *The Sketch Book*; Willa Cather, *My Antonia*; George Ade, *Fables in Slang*; James Fenimore Cooper, *The Last of the Mohicans*; and Herman Melville, *Typee*.

25. Littell to Kittredge, 17 January 1930, Kitt/Wing.

26. Internal memorandum; Littell to Kittredge, 3 April 1930, Kitt/Wing.

27. Ibid.

28. Ruzicka to Kittredge, 3 February 1929, Kitt/Wing. Badaracco, "Inventing Book News, 1930–35: The *Colophon*," *Book Research Quarterly* (Winter 1990): 17–30.

29. Exhibition Catalog, 1931, RRD Wing.

30. Littell to Kittredge, 17 January 1930, Kitt/Wing. Wilson's illustration of Robinson Crusoe for the Grabhorn Press (1930), widely distributed as an advertisement for the *Colophon* magazine.

31. Dwiggins to Kittredge, 29 September 1925, Kitt/Wing.

32. "Rex Ellingwood Beach, Coral Gables, Florida," 1926 advertising brochure with eight illustrations, Kitt/Wing.

33. Wilson to Kittredge, 19 December 1927, Kitt/Wing.

34. Kittredge to Kent, 6 November 1928; Kittredge to Kent, 28 September 1927; Kittredge to Dwiggins, 10 May 1928, Kitt/Wing: *MSS by WAD* (New York: The Typophiles, 1947), Kitt/Wing.

35. Memo from Herbert Zimmermann to Gaylord Donnelley, 25 September 1951, Donnelley corporate archives.

36. Kent to Kittredge, n.d., 1928; Kittredge to Kent, 8 November 1928, Kitt/Wing.

37. Kittredge to Kent, 8 November 1928, Kitt/Wing.

38. R. R. Donnelley sales records, Donnelley corporate archives.

39. Dwiggins to Kittredge, 23 July 1928, Kitt/Wing; Kittredge to Dwiggins, 5 October 1928, Kitt/Wing.

40. Ibid.

41. Dwiggins to Kittredge, September 20, 1926, Kitt/Wing; Kittredge to Dwiggins, 10 October 1928, Kitt/Wing; See also Frederic Melcher, "The Fifty Books Idea," *Gutenberg-Jarhbuch*, 1936 (Mainz, American Institute of Graphic Arts): 218–21.

42. Ibid.

43. Kittredge to Ruzicka, 23 March 1929, Kitt/Wing.

44. Kittredge to Dwiggins, 5 October 1928, Kitt/Wing.

45. Paul Beaujon [pseudonym for Beatrice L. Warde], "On Decorative Printing in America," *Fleuron I* (1928): 69–94.

46. Interview with Rockwell Kent by Paul Cummings, 26 February 1969, in Dan Burne Jones, *The Prints of Rockwell Kent: A Catalogue Raisonné* (Chicago: University of Chicago Press, 1975).

47. Thomas Dreiser, *The Power of Print and Men* (Brooklyn: Mergenthaler Linotype Co., 1936), illustrated by Dwiggins, celebrates the fifty-year anniversary of the Linotype.

48. Beaujon, "On Decorative Printing," 73–76.

49. R. R. Donnelley sales records, Donnelley corporate archives.

50. Internal memorandum, Littell to Kittredge, 29 March 1927, Kitt/Wing.

51. Adams to Kittredge, 23 February 1930, Kitt/Wing.

52. Adams to Kittredge, 23 February, 1930, where he replied, "Use the first edition absolutely."

53. Kittredge to Kent, 14 December 1928, Kitt/Wing; Kent to Kittredge, 11 November 1927, Kitt/Wing; Kent to Kittredge, 26 May 1927, Kitt/Wing.

54. Ibid. Four Books Prospectus; and "Give Us Small Books," Lakeside pamphlet, Ransom/Wing. The aluminum slipcase makes the current auction value greater but has caused preservation difficulties: the fit of the three volumes into the aluminum case is too tight, often damaging the bindings.

55. Beaujon, "On Decorative Printing," 73–76.

56. Kittredge to Dwiggins, 5 October 1928, Kitt/Wing.

57. Kittredge to Ruzicka, 15 June 1929 and Ruzicka to Kittredge, 3 February 1929.

58. Kittredge to Ruzicka, 15 June 1929, Kitt/Wing.

59. Kittredge to Ruzicka, 23 March 1929, Kitt/Wing; Kittredge to Kent, 9 April 1930, Kitt/Wing; Kittredge to Ruzicka, 23 March 1929, Kitt/Wing.

60. Internal memorandum, Littell to Kittredge, 17 January 1930, Kitt/Wing.

61. Ibid.

62. Kittredge to Kent, 7 May 1930, Kitt/Wing.

63. Kent to Kittredge, 31 January 1930, Kitt/Wing.

64. Kittredge uses this phrase in his correspondence with each of the illustrators.

65. In 1936 Merrymount Press published an edition of *Walden*, illustrated by the photography of Edward Steichen, for George Maas.

66. Wilson to Kittredge, 18 September 1930, Kitt/Wing.

67. Kittredge to Wilson, 5 January 1930, Kitt/Wing.

68. Littell to Wilson, 5 January 1930, Kitt/Wing.

69. Memo from Herbert Zimmermann to Gaylord Donnelley, 25 September 1951, Donnelley corporate archives. All subsequent sales figures are taken from the handwritten sales records in the company history binder file compiled by Zimmermann and Donnelley.

70. Production costs relative to sales value in 1930 showed the greatest profit for *Moby Dick*, which cost $39,464 to produce and yielded $51,844 sales value. With *Walden* and with Poe's *Tales*, the company broke even. The *Walden* edition cost $10,631 to produce, with a sales value of $10,740, and the Poe cost $10,706 to produce with a sales value of $10,695. Only Edward Wilson's book presented a loss: the production cost was $19,740 and the approximate sales value $15,460. Sales records, Donnelley corporate archives; *American Book Prices Current*, 1933–87; sales records, Donnelley corporate archives.

71. Binder file labeled "History, R.R.D., R. R. Donnelley corporate archives; memo from Herbert Zimmermann to Gaylord Donnelley, 25 September 1951, Donnelley corporate archives.

72. Sales records, Donnelley corporate archives.

73. Kittredge to Kent, 9 April and 7 May 1930, Kitt/Wing.

74. Ibid.

75. Kittredge uses these phrases repeatedly throughout all his correspondence with the illustrators,

CHAPTER 5:
LIMITING EDITIONS AND ILLUSTRATING BOOKS,
1929–1939

1. *The Books of WAD* [William Addison Dwiggins], compiled by Dwight Agner (Baton Rouge: Press of the Nightowl, 1974), Wing; Tebbel, *History of Book Publishing*; Lewis Coser, Charles Kadushin, Walter Powell, *Books: The Culture and Commerce of Publishing* (Chicago: University of Chicago Press, 1982).

2. Warde, "The American Book: Recent Trends of Interest to British Booklovers," *Monotype Recorder* 26 (1937): 11–18 and "Modern Fine Book Printing—A Review," *Monotype Recorder* 18 (January–February 1929): 34–39.

3. Advertisement, Ransom/Wing; Warde, "The American Book," 11–18; "Modern Fine Book Priting," 34–39.

4. Warde, "The American Book."

5. Standard, "Limited Editions Club."

6. Warde, "The American Book."

7. Philip Brooks, "The Colophon Enters Its Third Year," *New York Times Book Review*, 20 March 1932, 2.

8. Standard, "Limited Editions Club"; *An Index to Printing Trade Periodicals for the Year 1931*, Printing Industry Research Association, September 1932, St. Bride's Foundation; National Association of Book Publishers, Economic Survey of the Book Industry, 1930–31 (New York: R. R. Bowker, 1931).

9. Maurice Robert and Frederic Warde, "A Code for the Collector of Beautiful Books," trans. Jacques LeClerq (New York: LEC, 1936), 7; *New York Times Book Review* advertisement quoted in the *New York Times*, 27 September 1936; *New York Times* advertisement for LEC, 8 November 1931, Wing; Warde, "American Book." Experiments in subscription publishing occurred during the 1920s along with a number of others such as the *Reader's Digest* (founded in 1922), *Time* (founded in 1923), the *New Yorker* (founded in 1925); George Macy, *Quarto-Millenary* (New York: The Limited Editions Club, 1959), 3.

10. Warde, "American Book," 11–18 and "Modern Fine Book Printing," 34–39.

11. Advertisement, *New York Times*, 8 November 1931, Wing.

12. Macy's promotional literature, Ransom Papers; *Limited Editions Club Newsletter* (hereafter referred to as *LECN*) 34 (March 1932) and *LECN* 2 (July 1929), Wing.

13. *LECN* 14, Wing.

14. *LECN* 44 (January 1933).

15. Macy, *Quarto-Millenary*, 3–5; *LECN* 2 (July 1929), Wing.

16. Warde, "George Macy," 36.

17. Ibid.

18. James Moran, "Printing in the Twentieth Century"; "Penguins and Pelicans," *Penrose Anthology* (London: Northwood Pub. Ltd., 1974), 159–62; Beatrice Warde, "The Background of Penguin Typography," in "Exhibition of the Typography and Production of Penguin Books," 40–47; Warde's "The Penguin Look and 'Monotype' Faces," St. Bride's; "Tradition and Progress in Printing," *Times Literary Supplement, Book Production Section*, 5 February 1950, i–ii; typed draft, introduction to King Penguin editions, with cover memo to Stanley Morison, St. Bride's; J. E. Morpungo, *Allen Lane King Penguin* (London: Hutchinson, 1979); W. E. Williams, *Allen Lane: A Personal Portrait* (London: The Bodley Head, 1973); J. W. Lambert, *Michael Ratcliffe, The Bodley Head 1887–1987* (London: The Bodley Head, 1989).

19. Dwiggins to Kittredge, 1929, Kittredge Papers, Wing.

20. *LECN* 23 (April 1931); LEC advertisements, Wing.

21. Annual Reports, LEC, Columbia; Lakeside Press File, Ransom Papers; Kitt/Wing.

22. *LECN* 2 (July 1929), Wing.

23. Macy's promotional literature, Ransom Papers, Wing; Rubin, *Middlebrow*, 116, 133, 175, 182, 248, 265.

24. Robert and Warde, "Code," xii–xiii; Claire Badaracco, "Value Issues"; Ruth Shephard Graniss, "Modern Fine Printing," in *A History of the Printed Book* (New York: Limited Editions Club, 1928).

25. "Code," 16; Macy, Heritage Club Advertisement, 1936, Wing. LECN 3.

26. Macy, *Quarto-Millenary*.

27. Morpungo, *Allen Lane*; A. J. A. Symons, Desmond Flower, Francis Meynell, *The Nonesuch Century: An Appraisal, a Personal Note and a Bibliography of the First Hundred Books Issued by the Press, 1923–1924* (London: The Nonesuch Press, 1936).

28. Warde, "George Macy," 36.

29. Random House Papers, Columbia University. Boise-Cascade bought the Limited Editions Club and its four principal subsidiaries in 1970 from Macy's wife, who had managed the firm after his death in 1956 until 1979, when Sidney Shiff purchased it and in-

creased the cost of a subscription in 1985 to $2,000 for six books. Competitors failed while Macy flourished.

30. *Kelmscott, Doves and Ashendene: The Private Press Credos*, introduction by Will Ransom (The Typophiles, 1952); Thompson, "Kelmscott Influence on American Book Design" (Ph.D. diss., Columbia University, 1972); John Feather, *A History of British Publishing* (London: Routledge, 1988).

31. Macy, *Quarto-Millenary*, 3. Macy asked "Paul Beaujon" to contribute an essay to his anniversary publication celebrating twenty-five years of the Limited Editions Club; Warde, "George Macy"; Terry Treachout, "Seven Hundred Pretty Good Books," *New Criterion*, October 1987, 38; J. M. Dent, *Memoirs 1849–1926* (London: J. M. Dent & Sons, 1928); R. F. Sharp, *Everyman's Library: The Reader's Guide . . . Catalogue of the First 888 Volumes* (London: Dent, 1932); Charles Lee, *The Hidden Public: The Story of the Book-of-the-Month Club* (New York: Doubleday, 1958); Richard W. Fox and T. J. Jackson Lears, *The Culture of Consumption* (New York: Pantheon, 1983); Tebbel, *History of Book Publishing*.

32. Donald Klopfer to Robert Gibbings, 27 February 1927, Golden Cockerel file, Columbia University; Tebbel, *History of Book Publishing*. Random House also offered a number of limited editions printed in the United States, among them *Songs of George Gershwin* (a print run of 300 copies, listed at $25 each), the *Complete Poems of Robert Frost* (1,000 copies, listed at $15 each), a Walt Whitman's *Leaves of Grass* based on the 1892 "Death-bed Edition" (400 copies sold at $100 each), and Ralph Waldo Emerson's *Essay on Nature* (250 copies at $25 each). Random House also represented the deluxe editions that exemplified the elite traditions of British printing to the American trade. In 1928, at that year's prices, a *Candide* by Rockwell Kent sold for $75 (discounted from $125), a *Scarlet Letter* sold for $15 (discounted from $25), but *Leaves of Grass* held its initial price of $100, according to the sales catalog. At the same time, Random House joined with fine presses to issue trade editions of once-limited deluxe books. They were "reasonably priced" for both the "exacting scholar" and the "discriminating collector" from $3.50 to $7, according to the company's catalogs. In addition

to Kent's *Moby Dick* and *Candide*, Random House offered trade editions of English classics, with seldom the same emphasis on American works, except for well-known works by Melville, Whitman, and Hawthorne.

33. Donald Klopfer to Oliver Simon, 22 April 1929; 18 April 1928; Bennett Cerf to Robert Gibbings, 6 June 1927; 1929 sales catalog; 1931 sales catalog, Random House Papers, Columbia University Library; *LECN* 23 (April 1931); LEC advertisements, Wing.

34. *Publishers Weekly*, 4 January 1930, 42–44.

35. Warde, "American Book"; Stanley Morison, *Modern Fine Printing* (London: Ernest Benn, Ltd., 1925), xi.

36. Macy, *Quarto-Millenary*, 286.

37. *LECN* 44 (January 1933), Wing.

38. Jeanne Somers, *Index* (Westport, Conn.: Greenwood Press, 1986); Macy, *Quarto-Millenary*, 286; *LECN* 44 (January 1933); *LECN* 14 (July 1930), Wing.

39. Annual Reports, LEC, Columbia; Lakeside Press File, Ransom Papers; Kitt/Wing.

40. Standard, "Limited Editions Club."

41. Advertisement, Ransom/Wing.

42. Standard, "Limited Editions Club"; *An Index to Printing Trade Periodicals for the Year 1931*, Printing Industry Research Association, September 1932, St. Bride's; Beatrice Warde, "The 50 Best Books of 1930: An Account of the Exhibition of the First Edition Club," *Monotype Recorder* 29 (August 1930): 5–11; National Association of Book Publishers, *Economic Survey of the Book Industry, 1930–1931* (New York: R. R. Bowker, 1931).

43. Somers, *Index*.

44. Cerf to Macy, 11 July 1929; LEC annual reports, 1929–35, Random House Papers, Columbia University Library.

45. *LECN* 14 (July 1930), Wing; Cerf to Macy, 11 July 1929; Annual Reports, LEC, 1929–35, Random House Papers, Columbia University Library.

46. Standard, "Limited Editions Club"; Advertisement, *New York Times*, 8 November 1931, Wing.

47. Standard, "Limited Editions Club."

48. *LECN* 2 (July 1929) and 26 (July 1931), Wing.

49. Annual Reports, LEC, 1929–35, Random House Papers, Columbia University Library.

50. Heaton & Co. report, Columbia University Library.

51. Annual Reports, LEC, 1929–35, Random House Papers, Columbia University Library.

52. Dwiggins to Kittredge, 1929, Kitt/Wing.

53. Maurice Robert and Frederic Warde, "A Code for the Collector of Beautiful Books," trans. Jacques Le Clerq (New York: LEC, 1936), xii–xiii.

54. Heaton & Co. report, Columbia University Library.

55. *LECN* (March 1933), Wing; *LECN* 32 (January 1932), Wing. The two essays on the ideal book were jointly awarded. The prize went to Francis P. Dill and Porter Garnett. LEC published the forty-two-page pamphlet in hardcover. Garnett taught printing at Carnegie Tech and Dill studied with him. According to Macy, they won the contest over 200 other entries.

56. 1936 advertisement; advertisement, *New York Times*, 8 November 1931, Ransom/Wing.

57. LEC prospectus, 1929, Wing.

58. Annual Reports, LEC, 1929–35, Random House Papers, Columbia University Library.

59. Macy, *Quarto-Millenary*.

60. Warde, "American Book."

61. Dwiggins, *Reform of Paper Currency*, LEC, 1932.

62. Claire Badaracco, "Value Issues in Modern Propaganda and Book Printing: Their Impact on Printers' Publicity Circa 1920–1940," *Essays in Business and Economic History* 9 (Winter 1990): 170–82.

63. *LECN* 3.

64. Warde, "American Book."

65. LEC edition of Munchausen, i–iv.

66. Macy, *Quarto-Millenary*.

67. Rene Clarke later became president of his own advertising firm, Calkins and Holden.

68. Advertisement in *Saturday Review of Literature*, 12 October 1929, Wing.

69. *LECN* 25 (June 1931), Wing.

70. *LECN* 34 (March 1932), Wing.

71. Macy, *Quarto-Millenary* 242.

72. The discrepancy between production cost and sales must have alarmed Macy. All illustrators received the same fee; each was paid approximately $1,500 per book. James Fenimore Cooper's *The Last of the Mohicans*, designed by Will Ransom and illustrated by Edward Wilson, cost $10,496 to produce but recorded sales of only $4,007. Similarly, *South Wind*, by Norman Douglas, designed and printed by Elmer Adler's Pynson Printers in New York, and *Batoula*, by Rene Maran, designed by Peter Beilenson and printed by Walpole Printing in New Rochelle, New York, cost nearly $11,000 to produce, with sales barely reaching $4,000. These works abandon the masculine cliché of the adventure novel altogether for a feminized version of the same superficial equivalent. The illustrations are full of sentiment from the bland emotional world of greeting cards and wrapping paper. In two books that Macy admired particularly—Jorrocks' *Jaunts and Jollities*, designed by Daniel B. Updike, and a three-volume edition of Balzac's *Droll Stories*, designed by W. A. Dwiggins—the discrepancy between production costs and profits reached more than $6,000 per book. Macy designed *Tom Jones* and *The Cloister and the Hearth*. His *Jones* represented the most expensive production of the year, a reported $4,348, second only to *Kwaidan*, printed by Shimbi Shoin, in Tokyo, at a cost of $4,968. Annual Reports, LEC, Columbia University Library.

73. *LECN* 34 (March 1932), Wing.

74. Note on production of the *Bible*, Ransom/Wing.

75. Ibid. In 1933, Helen Macy hand-set a New Year's gift book, *The Philosophy of Limited Editions*. Hart Benton illustrated both a $15 edition of *The Grapes of Wrath* and a $16.50 *Tom Sawyer*. In the club's eleventh year, Macy published a thirty-seven-volume edition of Shakespeare's works; in a promotional pamphlet concerning the value of first editions, Macy reprinted an essay by Richard Le Gallienne first published by G. P. Putnam in 1894, ten pages on hand-laid paper with rubricated pagination from the LEC Connecticut press. The typeface and an initial capital at the beginning of the essay, designed by Frederic Goudy, reiterated the style of the arts-and-crafts era.

76. Macy, *Quarto-Millenary*, 246.

77. Note on production of the *Bible*, Ransom/Wing.

78. Catalog, *Eleven Years of the LEC 1929–1940*, Duschnes, 1940, Wing.

79. Macy, *Quarto-Millenary*, 252.

80. Ibid., 337.

81. Ibid., 250.

82. Ibid., 252. Macy also published Sir Thomas Browne's *Religio Medici*, edited by Geoffrey Keynes; and Chaucer's *Troilus and Cressida*, priced at $8; a five-volume edition of Hugo's *Les Misérables*, with a preface by André Maurois, for $17.50; Edith Wharton's *Ethan Frome*, with an introduction by Clifton Fadiman ($12.50); and Theodore Dreiser's *Sister Carrie*, which sold for $13.50. In Macy's next scheme, he enlisted leading American painters to illustrate books: William Kittredge designed Sinclair Lewis's *Main Street*, and Grant Wood supplied the illustrations for this Macy publication, which sold for $16.50.

83. Catalogue, *Eleven Years of the LEC*.

84. *LECN* 14 (July 1930); advertisement, 13 September 1931, Wing.

85. Philip Brooks, "The Colophon Enters Its Third Year," *New York Times Book Review*, 20 March 1932, 2; "Three Years and This Year: A Record of the Colophon Adventure and an Invitation to Partake of Its Future"; "Burton Emmett 1871–1935," reprint from *PM Magazine*, March 1937; *LECN* 33 (February 1932), Wing.

86. Elmer Adler, "Apostle of Good Taste, An Address delivered January 21, 1941, on the Occasion of an Exhibition of the Work of the Pynson Printers" (Princeton: Typophiles); catalog, "An Exhibition: A Selection from Work of the Pynson Printers 1922–1932," Wing.

87. Brooks, "Colophon Enters."

88. *American Book Prices Current, 1929–1940*, 1987.

89. Adler, "Apostle."

90. Brooks, "Colophon Enters."

91. Adler, "Apostle."

92. John Winterich, *Colophon Index . . . Original Series 1930–1935*, 24, Wing.

93. Ibid.

94. George Sargent, "Firsts, Issues and Points," *Colophon* 1, 1930. The small pool of subscribers included other fine presses: The Lakeside, Grabhorn, Merrymount, University of Chicago, Harvard and Yale, Rudge, Bruce Rogers, Abbey, Aldus, Village, Franklin Printers, Canfield & Tack, and Leo Hart Presses.

95. "Emmett," *PM Magazine*.

96. Adler, "Apostle."

97. "Emmett," *PM Magazine*; Sargent, "Firsts."

98. Adler, "Apostle."

99. Ibid.

100. Ibid.

101. Colophon File, Ransom Papers, Wing.

102. Ibid.

103. Adler, "Apostle."

104. Colophon File, Ransom Papers, Wing.

105. Winterich, *Colophon Index*.

106. Ibid.

107. Standard, "Limited Editions Club."

108. Colophon advertisement, *Book Collector's Quarterly*, 1932, Ransom Papers, Wing.

109. Adler to Ransom, 18 January 1932, Ransom Papers, Wing.

110. "Selections from the Renowned Libraries of Alphonse Caphony," 26 April 1932, Detterer File, Wing.

111. Colophon File, Ransom Papers; Winterich, *Colophon Index*; Adler, "Apostle."

112. Ibid.

CONCLUSION:
READING AND COMMERCIAL MODERNISM

1. See Ivan Illich, *In the Vineyard of the Text: A Commentary on Hugh's Didascalicon* (Chicago: University of Chicago Press, 1993) and Armando Petrucci, *Public Lettering: Script, Power, and Culture* (Chicago: University of Chicago Press, 1993).

2. Among others who make this point, see Tedlow, *New and Improved*; Boorstin, *Image*; Levine, *Highbrow*; Rubin, *Middlebrow*; Rodden, *Politics of Literary Reputation*.

3. Warde, "The Meaning of Modern," n.p., n.d., typescript fragment, and "The Typographic Renaissance," typescript of lecture given at the Printing Conference convened by the Council of Industrial Design, Edinburgh, Scotland, 18 April 1947, both St. Bride's.

4. Jesus Martin-Barbero, *Communication, Culture, Hegemony: From the Media to Mediations* (London: Sage, 1993); Boorstin, *Image*; Tedlow, *New and Improved*.

5. Edwin Cady, *The Realist at War*; Kenneth S. Lynn, *William Dean Howells: An American Life* (New York: Harcourt, Brace, 1970).

6. J. Baudrillard, *For a Critique of the Political Economy of the Sign* (St. Louis: Telos, 1981).

7. Warde, "Meaning of Modern."

8. William Addison Dwiggins, *Towards a Reform of the Paper Currency: Particularly in Point of Its Design* (New York: Limited Editions Club, 1932).

9. Warde, "Typographic Renaissance."

10. Hugh Kenner, "The Politics of the Plain Style," in *Literary Journalism in the Twentieth Century*, ed. Norman Sims (New York: Oxford University Press, 1990), 185; David Easton, "New Journalism and the Image-World," in *Literary Journalism in the Twentieth Century*.

11. Kenner, "Politics of the Plain Style."

12. Walter Benjamin, "The Work of Art in the Age of Mechanical Reproduction," in *Illuminations* (New York: Harcourt, Brace, 1968), 217–52; Martin-Barbero, *Communication*, 55; Richard Perloff, "Third-Person Effect Research 1983–1992: A Review and Synthesis," *International Journal of Public Opinion Research* 5 (1994): 2, 179.

13. Warde, "Meaning of Modern."

14. The phrase "democracy of goods" belongs to Daniel Boorstin's classic study of the pseudo-event, *The Image*.

A
·
NOTE
·
ON
·
SOURCES

Several collections of archival documents, manuscripts, and rare books have been important in writing this study. In the United States, the Newberry Library, the University of Chicago, and the Houghton Library of Harvard, and in Great Britain the Bodleian at Oxford University and the St. Bride's Printing Library have been the primary repositories contributing to this research. Other collections have been important in building connoisseurship, in clarifying corporate history and other particular points. This note describes these resources.

AMERICAN COLLECTIONS

Houghton Mifflin Papers

The Manuscripts Division of the Houghton Library at Harvard University contains an extensive collection concerning nineteenth- and twentieth-century literary publishing in America, among other topics. The Houghton Papers (designated in the Notes by HCo.) are described in a bound finding-guide occupying several shelves behind the reference desk; this provides a comprehensive overview of the collection, with general subject headings. For more specific access to letters, first editions, and articles about each author, though, consult the card catalog under each author's name. The collection contains 242 letters from Amy Lowell to Houghton Mifflin between 1914 and 1927, and a comparably extensive correspondence from the publisher to Lowell during the same period. The collection also contains correspondence among Ezra Pound, Harriet Monroe, and Lowell, and between Lowell and the Riverside publishing company, as well as a complete set of important imagist anthologies published between 1912 and 1917, and first editions of books by Amy Lowell, Pound, and other writers during the "Imagist" years including H.D., F. S. Flint, William Carlos Williams, Ford Maddox Hueffer, and Richard Aldington. The collection of literary journals of this period is also representative and includes issues of the *Egoist*, *Blast*, *Smart Set*, the *New Republic* and *Little Review*, as well as *Poetry*, *Poetry Journal*, and the *Poetry Review* where literary groups published and responded to manifestos. Houghton Mifflin's Publicity Clip Book 1919–1922 contains ephemera, publishers' lists, dust jacket covers for such best-sellers as *Stella Dallas* and *Babbitt*, and transcripts of promotional talks given to the trade by company executives discussing the house list.

The John M. Wing Foundation Collection

The Newberry Library has a comprehensive collection on the History of Printing spanning centuries and continents. Among the general collections are publications by and about the American Institute of Graphic Artists and their Fifty Books of the Year annual competitions, a full run of the printing, publishing, and advertising trade weeklies between 1890 and 1940, including the *Monotype Recorder*. These provided sources of information about the new technologies introduced in the early modern period, the dissemination of skills, techniques, print styles and faces, and ideas that contributed to professionalization, including the formation of editorial, advertising, and printers' associations. The extensive collection of trade magazines between 1890 and 1930 includes sources originally noted in Richard Pollay's census and in Frank Luther Mott's bibliography. In addition to data about the trade, these journals include tipped-in specimen sheets from the leading ink manufacturers, paper suppliers, and allied publishing industries, and so provide a range of physical evidence about style that demonstrates what producers aspired to imitate. In addition to the *Monotype Recorder*, *Publishers Weekly*, *Inland Printer*, and *Penrose Annual*, the publicity trade magazines consulted for this research include: *Brains*, *Profitable Advertising*, *Advertising Experience*, *Ad Sense*, *American Printer*, *Art in Advertising*, *Fame*, the *Printer and Bookmaker*, *Judicious Advertising*, *Mahin's*, and *Graphic Arts*. N. W. Ayer's statistics about circulation and the longevity and distribution of these journals, although unreliable, are also in the collection. Additionally, nineteenth-century trade cards, posters, and other commercial ephemera provided a visual survey of the use of technology at the turn of the century. Bylined articles in these magazines provided additional biographical information about the life of a job printer, and some contain a "who's who" of the printing industry during the early modern era in the U.S. and Great Britain.

The Midwest Manuscripts in special collections at the Newberry contain copies of Sherwood Anderson's columns printed in *Agricultural Advertising* between 1903 and 1912. Additionally, the work of Chicago presses and publishers is represented between 1880 and 1920, when the city's printing industry flourished, along with examples of fine and rare printing in first editions by Chicago presses including W. Irving Way and Chauncey Williams, A. C. McClurg & Co., and Covinci-McGee. Among first editions about the publicity trades produced by Chicago printers are several important volumes: Herbert Stone & Ingalls Kimball's *Chap Book* and Kimball's tenth-year anniversary annual report for his New York Cheltenham advertising agency; and a 900-page, one-volume encyclopedia for publicity published in 1897 by one Nath'l C. Fowler titled *Publicity*. The general collection also includes other important turn-of-the-century books on the history of advertising, printing, publishing, and bookmaking, including works by McKnight Kauffer on the art of the poster and William Addison Dwiggins on layout in advertising.

Among the books in the Wing collection at the Newberry are examples of rare and fine printing in limited editions, as well as typographic specimen sheets, broadsides, handbills, and other ephemera executed by Will Bradley, Eric Gill, Frederic Goudy, Stanley Morison, Rockwell Kent, and others prominent in the early modern printing renaissance. The multivolume catalogue for the Wing collection is available on the reference floor as well as in the special collections area; published in three editions over several decades, the volumes are not cumulative. Additional handlists of ephemera and binder files of modern manuscripts can be found in the special collections area on the fourth floor.

The Will Ransom Papers

Ransom's bibliography of the American private-press movement, for which this collection was to serve as a resource, was published in 1929; the primary focus of the collection is between 1905 and 1935. Materials are contained in approximately fifty archival boxes arranged by press title or individual printer's name. With the aid of his wife and his daughter, Will Ransom also kept complete records of the private-press movement in about fifty binder notebooks with meticulous handlists, precisely written in fountain pen on lined three-hole paper, with press clips from trade weeklies about important publications pasted in. Among the most important private presses and contemporary fine printers represented among Ransom's papers are: Merrymount, Cuala, Cranbrook, Dove, Golden Cockerel, Grabhorn, Lakeside, Limited Editions Club, Officina Bodoni, Nonesuch, Pynson, and Rudge presses, as well as information about Daniel Updike, Elmer Adler, Eric Gill, Bruce Rogers, Rudolph Ruzicka, William Addison Dwiggins, Frederic Warde, and others. Finely printed broadsides, booklets, posters, and a number of handsome prospectus-style invitations to subscribers, specimen plates, and advertisements, including a full run of the newsletters issued by George Macy during the initial years of his Limited Edi-

A Note on Sources

tions Club (noted as *LECN*) are part of the collection. The Wing collection also has a complete set of the Limited Edition Club books published by Macy between 1929 and 1950.

The Kittredge Papers

This collection contains correspondence between William Kittredge and prominent graphic designers, typographers, and printers during the twenties and thirties, internal corporate memoranda between Kittredge and the executives of the R. R. Donnelley & Sons company concerning the Four American Books Campaign of 1926–1930, sales figures and other financial data (designated Kitt/ Wing). Finely printed mailing labels and a letterhead for the Department of Design and Typography designed by Kittredge are also in the collection. Personal correspondence between Frederic Warde and Kittredge in 1927 concerns the relationship between Beatrice and her husband prior to their divorce.

The Harriet Monroe and Poetry Magazine Papers

The Regenstein Library of the University of Chicago possesses two related collections: the Harriet Monroe collection and the Poetry Magazine collection. The Monroe collection pertains to the poet's life and her family between 1860 and 1936. In addition, the library houses a variety of archival and documentary materials, including personal correspondence relevant to the early years of *Poetry* magazine. The collection also contains material relevant to Monroe's girlhood, including a copy of her "Ode" and the Western Union telegram to the New York *World* charging them with violation of her copyright to the "Ode," a lawsuit won by Monroe's father. The university's modern poetry collection also includes published works by twentieth-century writers, including the imagists, found on the open shelves. Among the Poetry collection papers that I consulted are correspondence pertinent to its guarantors, miscellaneous business correspondence including financial reports 1913–1933, institutional correspondence, crank letters directed to Monroe, and publicity circulars used between 1912 and 1914 printed by Ralph Fletcher Seymour, whose private press operated

A Note on Sources

out of the Fine Arts Building near Printer's Row in downtown Chicago.

Some of the most valuable materials in the Poetry Magazine collection describe what Monroe confronted in the form of public opinion; these are contained in a file labeled "boosts and slams," which also contains newspaper clippings both favorable and critical between 1912 and 1916. A separate clippings folder covers the years between 1912 and 1936: a part-time journalist and art critic, Monroe tracked the press response as avidly in the Midwest, in the Far West, or in Paris, where she hired a clipping service, whose bills are included. Among Monroe's personal papers are royalty contracts, bank statements from the family estate, photographs, and an index to the poet's newspaper articles that appeared in the *Chicago Tribune* between 1909 and 1914, essays and short stories that she drafted but did not publish, rejection letters from mass-market magazines turning down her poems as too long, and correspondence with readers, poets, writers, and friends between 1888 and 1899, as well as correspondence between Monroe and Sara Teasdale between 1913 and 1933. Monroe's many literary friendships with Vachel Lindsay, Sherwood Anderson, Richard Aldington, and her rivalries with Ezra Pound, Amy Lowell, and others, as well as her wit and tenacity in launching a literary magazine are completely documented by this collection. Among the ephemera in the Monroe-Poetry papers are the poet's lecture notes on a string, which she tied onto her finger as she spoke promoting the Art of Poetry to the American Public.

BRITISH SOURCES

Beatrice Warde and Monotype Corporation Papers

St. Bride's Printing Library, Fleet Street, in the old printing district, even today the site of many newspapers and publishers, houses a provocative and stimulating collection pertaining to modern printing, including printing presses and a far-reaching collection of works by scholars of modern printing in several countries, including the 1927 International Book Exhibition at Leipzig. The general collections provided the means to draw connections between the artistic revolutionaries of the 1900–25 period in Russia, Germany, and Italy and the Anglo-American tradesmen. Among the works by British printing historians housed in the St. Bride's collection, I drew upon the work of Brooke Crutchley, Stanley Morison, John Dreyfus, Nicholas Barker, Oliver Simon, Douglas Cleverdon, Francis Meynell, James Moran, and Ruari McLean.

The Warde and Monotype collections at St. Bride's, which came there from Warde's estate, contain a representative sample of the business correspondence, manuscripts, and promotional lectures by Warde between 1922 and 1969 during her long career as publicity manager for the Monotype Corporation. Virtually nothing is left at the corporation at Redhill, where the company archivist recounted how some in the company can still recall the day when the letters carved by Eric Gill in the Sans style had been taken down from the top of the building and burned in a bonfire in the yard during a corporate takeover; a few photographs of the period remain of workers at the Redhill plant. The sales records from the plant for the 1922–39 period contributed to this research in estimating the effectiveness of Warde's publicity campaigns and the reach of Monotype during the 1929–32 years. Among the Warde papers at St. Bride's are her juvenilia from Barnard; news clipping files, including critical reviews of her speeches and publications, especially *Crystal Goblet*; the obituary of Henry Lewis Bullen from the *British Printer* of July 1938; the history of the Monotype machine; an incomplete run of *Monotype Recorder* magazines; a consecutive set of Monotype newsletters; a number of important specimen sheets for new typefaces being introduced by Warde; the controversial broadside from the 1929 Blackpool British Federation of Printers' meeting, which introduced the Gill Sans typeface to a near riot; and several boxes of business correspondence demonstrating her work as a publicist for the company, including examples of her calligraphy being used to write internal memoranda to Stanley Morison. The range of Warde's international interests in the printing business and her devotion over several decades to the cause of improving educational conditions for printers are reflected in the speeches, reviews, clips, and ephemera related to her career with Monotype.

A Note on Sources

The John Johnson Collection

In three rooms of the Bodleian Library at Oxford University, in floor-to-ceiling archival boxes arranged alphabetically, is the extensive printing ephemera file of the Oxford University printer, John Johnson, who is reported to have lived in the rooms housing the university's press during the interwar years. Matchbook covers, railroad and theater tickets, napkins, posters, handbills, flyers, all printed by unknown jobbers, are boxed along with rarities such as a baker's label engraved by Eric Gill and a mailing envelope that once contained "America's most beautiful magazine," the *Colophon*. This collection is probably the best in the world for any study examining popular printing in the twentieth century.

The Morison and Meynell Papers

The special collections of the Cambridge University Library house the personal correspondence between Beatrice Warde and Eric Gill, and between Warde and Stanley Morison, along with etchings of Warde by Gill, photographs, and other important ephemera relevant to her relationships with Gill and Morison, and her interest in Catholicism.

The Random House and George Macy Papers

The manuscript division of the Columbia University Library has among its collections the annual reports for 1929 through 1933 for the Limited Editions Club and relevant publicity materials, correspondence, and publications by and about Bennett Cerf and the early work by Random House as an agent for private-press British printers.

OTHER REPOSITORIES CONSULTED

The British Library, London: the collections contain newspaper articles written by Beatrice Warde during her work for Monotype and five letters that she wrote to Sir Sydney Cockerell late in her career.

The Chicago Historical Society: possesses hard-to-find copies of *Class Advertising*, an advertising trade magazine published in Chicago. Its collection of published materials about the 1893 World's Fair is good, containing more news reports than books or ephemera.

R. R. Donnelley & Sons Company corporate archives: when the memorial Library at the Lakeshore Drive plant was closed, the rare materials were divided between the University of Chicago and the Newberry Library. A good resource for photographs and some first editions of the Lakeside Classics.

English Speaking Union, London and New York: an excellent collection of photographs and books documenting interwar propaganda and the books-across-the-sea campaign begun by Beatrice Warde and her mother May Lamberton Becker, and headed by T. S. Eliot.

Library of Congress, Washington, D.C., general collections: has a good collection of early-twentieth-century trade magazines, in very fragile condition; representative rather than comprehensive.

London School of Economics Library: has a complete set of King Penguin editions given by Hans Schmoller, who designed them. The general collections also contain significant economic studies about the history of publishing and printing in Britain.

Royal Institute of British Architecture; Royal Society for Arts and Industry, London; Royal Archive of Art and Design, London, general collections: house government materials, especially speeches and commissioned publications designed to promote and improve public taste in the industrial and commercial arts.

The Victoria and Albert National Library Design Archives: houses a small collection of advertising designs relevant to the period, including the work of McKnight Kauffer.

A Note on Sources

INDEX

Adler, Elmer, 5, 12, 150–53, 155, 157–58, 186–87, 190
advertisements, 14, 30–31, 52, 57–59, 66, 76, 101, 108
advertising, 118, 123, 150, 152–53, 161; agency, 120, 122, 186; agents, 7, 71, 99; artists, 122, 149, 175; brochures, 25, 60; illustrators, 130, 132, 134–36, 173, 180, 194; and industrial signs, 14, 25, 56, 71, 86, 95; prospectus, 25
aesthetic(s), 12, 15, 16, 21, 27, 29, 31, 33, 40, 43, 75, 78, 81, 90, 92, 96, 110, 113, 127, 151,

164, 169, 193; principles of, 11, 16, 21, 53, 55, 129; and revolutionary movements, 7, 9, 10–11, 15, 27–29, 192
Aldington, Richard, 33–34, 52, 57
American Institute of Graphic Artists (AIGA), 145–46, 155, 186
American Monotype, 139
American Type Founders Company, 31, 71, 73–74
Anderson, Sherwood, 4, 7, 30, 36–37, 41, 186
Arts and Crafts movement, 17,

Index

LIBRARY OF CONGRESS CATALOGING-IN-PUBLICATION DATA

Badaracco, Claire.
    Trading words : poetry, typography, and illustrated books in the modern
literary economy / Claire Hoertz Badaracco.
        p.   cm.
    Includes bibliographical references (p.   ) and index.
    ISBN 0-8018-4859-8 (acid-free paper)
        1. English poetry—20th century—History and criticism.
    2. Poetry—Publishing—Great Britain—History—20th century.
    3. Poetry—Publishing—United States—History—20th century.
    4. American poetry—20th century—History and criticism.
    5. Illustrated books—Publishing—History—20th century.
    6. Printing—Great Britain—History—20th century.
    7. Printing—United States—History—20th century.   8. Literature
publishing—Economic aspects.   9. Poetry—Illustrations.   I. Title.
PR601.B33   1995
302.2'244'097309041—dc20   94-45323
                                                                    CIP

DATE DUE
